JAMAICA...

Jamaican Thesaurus & English-to-Patois Dictionary
Common Spellings Version
2022 edition

Compiled and Edited by
ERIC ROSENFELD

Contributing Editors and Consultants:

JOSEPH FARQUHARSON
BYRON JONES
ANTON WILSON-SHIM
JULIE MALCOLM
LARRY CHANG

Copyright 2016 - Jamaicasaurus Digital Publishing

Sources Consulted:

Asprey, G. F. and Phyllis Thornton. <u>Medicinal Plants Of Jamaica</u>. West Indian Medical Journal. Vol. 2 No. 4. Vol. 3 No. 1

Cassidy, Frederic Gomes. <u>Jamaica Talk: Three Hundred Years of the English Language in Jamaica</u>. University of the West Indies Press, 1982. ISBN 9766401705 & 9789766401702

Cassidy, F.G. and R.B. Le Page. <u>The Dictionary of Jamaican English, Second Edition</u>. University of the West Indies Press, 2002. ISBN 976-640-127-6

Chang, Larry. <u>Biesik Jumiekan: Introduction to Jamaican Language</u>. Washington D.C., USA: Gnosophia Publishers, 2014. ISBN 978-0-9773391-8-1

Reynolds, Ras Dennis Jabari. <u>Jabari Authentic Dictionary of the Jamic Language</u>. Waterbury, CT: Around the Way Books, 2006. ISBN 13 978-0-9755342-5-0

Williams, Joan. <u>Original Dancehall Dictionary, Sixth Edition</u>. Yard Publications. ISBN 978-976-610-771-0

www.jamaicanpatwah.com

www.jumieka.com

www.real-jamaica-vacations.com/jamaican-slang.html

Acknowledgements:

Writing a dictionary or any reference book for the Jamaican Creole dialect has to be a labour of love, by necessity. I take off my hat to those who have written the few other dictionaries and reference books published for the language so far, particularly Frederic Cassidy, Robert LePage, Ras Dennis Jabari Reynolds, and Larry Chang. Their books (cited above) are quite extensive, and I can imagine how much time and effort went into writing and editing them. Along with Joan Williams's Original Dancehall Dictionary, these have been important resources. I also wish to thank Joseph Farquharson (University of the West Indies) for his help and encouragement, and the various members of his Jamaican National Dictionary group page on Facebook who have offered their opinions and input over the past several years. I also honour and respect Hubert Devonish and Carolyn Cooper (both of University of the West Indies) and all others working to increase the recognition of Jamaican Creole.

This 2022 edition features many entries added since the first edition and numerous corrections to errors and typos that we discovered. Surely there are more we didn't catch, and if you come across any, we welcome you to inform us by email: blueparrotlanguage@gmail.com

- Eric Rosenfeld

THINGS TO KNOW BEFORE USING THIS BOOK

1. Generally:
The Jamaicasaurus functions as both a translation dictionary and thesaurus. To use it as a thesaurus, simply look up the closest English equivalent of the Jamaican word or phrase you have in mind, and you will see the various Jamaican synonyms listed there.

In addition to words and phrases, you can look up slang expressions, idioms, and common statements or questions such as *How old are you?* or *I'm on my way*. Importantly, you will also find some exclamations such as *Awesome!* and *Exactly!* listed as separate entries of their own.

Don't miss the lists in the end of the book. You'll find expletives, exclamations, curious malapropisms (such as using the word *extinguish* for *distinguish*), metatheses (such as *aks* for *ask*), portmanteau (e.g. *appreciate + love = apriishalov*), Jamaican place names pronunciations, and a long list of plants and trees of use in Jamaica.

The Jamaicasaurus can also be used as a grammar guide. Just look up the name of a verb tense (e.g. *Past Perfect Tense*) and you should find the grammatical structures displayed and explained there.

This 2022 edition features 33 pages of new entries added since the first edition, and numerous corrections to errors and typos that we discovered. Surely there are more we didn't catch, so if you come across any, we welcome you to inform us by email: blueparrotlanguage@gmail.com

Section 3 below explains why a second spelling system is sometimes used in this book, and section 7 explains how to read these Jamiekan spellings.

2. Entries that are missing:
If an entry cannot be found, think of a synonym for that entry. For example, if you can't find *Entirely*, look up *Completely*.

In order for an entry to be included in this book, it must have at least one possible translation that is uniquely Jamaican in form or usage. If you don't find an entry for an English word (or any of its synonyms), that could mean that there is no uniquely Jamaican translation for it. Of course, it could also mean that it simply slipped thru the cracks and won't appear until a later edition of this book.

3. How the Jamaican words are spelled:
This version of the Jamaicasaurus has Jamaican words spelled more or less the way most people write them today, which is based on English. Jamaican linguists, however, have developed another system that's more consistent and accurate to how Jamaican words really sound. A modified version of this 'Cassidy-JLU' or 'Jamiekan' system is also used in this version of the Jamaicasaurus, but only for sample sentences, pronunciations, and in part of the Appendix. We recommend that you familiarize yourself with this system as explained in section 7 below. It is quite easy to master if you're willing to try.

One of the goals of this book is to bridge the gap between English-based and Jamiekan spellings, not only by presenting them side by side, but also by altering them slightly in order to make them resemble one another just a little more. For example, most Jamaicans today write *yuh* (you) and *nuh* (no). But we have them here as *yu* and *no*, which is how the Cassidy-JLU system has them too. This is easy, because any Jamaican or foreigner can still read and understand them either way.

4. Jamaican translations that are NOT presented in this book:
English words that are commonly used in Jamaican speech for the same meaning are generally not included in this book, neither as entries nor as translations. This is a tough choice to make, because Jamaicans sometimes use an English word for a given meaning more often than any of the uniquely Jamaican words for it. But listing such an English word doesn't serve the purpose of this book.

5. Some additional things that should be known:
When several different Jamaican translations are given, effort has been made to list either the newest or most common first, at least where this is easy enough to determine.

Wherever a Jamaican phrase requires a possessive, we can't use the generalized English word *one's* because it doesn't exist in Jamaican Creole, so we use the Jamaican second-person possessive *yu* for the same function. The same holds for *yuself* as a replacement for *oneself*

Past participles are not usually included in this book. It just needs to be known that the past participle of any Jamaican verb is typically the same as the simple present form. For example, clothes are not *worn*; dem *wier* (wear). And the story was not *written* by the author; *it rait* (*write*). Some of the few exceptions to this rule are included as entries in the book.

Jamaican speech has a tendency to substitute the letter B for V, especially in basilectal speech. This book lists mostly the V forms of words, because a choice had to be made, and the V form is more common nowadays. But readers should know that almost any V in any Jamaican word can be switched to B, and often is.

Likewise, the S can be eliminated from Jamaican words beginning with SK, SP, SQ, or ST. It would cause confusion for this book to include all variants of such words, so it has been decided to keep the S, but you should know it can be dropped in these cases.

Now for something quite technical: For Jamaican words ending with the following combination of letters: {vowel + N or M}; it needs to be known that some such words have that ending nasalized, particularly when the vowel is A, E, or I. This is mostly the case with very common short words such as *an*, *dem*, *him*, and *kyan*. The Cassidy-JLU system has traditionally indicated this nasalization with HN, and writer Larry Chang has even shortened this simply to H in his publications. One problem with doing so is that Jamaican nasalization often doesn't occur where such a word is followed by a next word beginning with a vowel. Another problem is that this practice further widens the gap mentioned above in section 3, despite its noble intention to portray real pronunciation. Therefore, in this book's modified version of Cassidy-JLU, the N or M is usually retained for these words, and readers simply have to know that nasalization exists there, even if it isn't spelled out for them. The written forms of other languages don't account for every single nuance of pronunciation, so why should Jamaican Creole be expected to?

Additionally, a decision also had to be made about which past tense indicator to use for entries that require past tense. There are several such past tense indicator words in Jamaican Creole (*did*, *di*, *id*, *wen*, *en*, *ben*, *den*, and *min*) and it would be quite inefficient to present them all. Furthermore, there is an argument to be made for reduction to a standard. Therefore, only *did* and *en* are used here, in most cases.

6. Abbreviations used in this book:

n = noun
v = verb
vt = transitive verb (an action that has a receiver: *She felt the soft silk*)
vi = intransitive verb (an action having no receiver: *She felt happy*)
adj = adjective (can occur before or after the noun it describes)
pred adj = predicate adjective (only occurs after the noun its describing)
adv = adverb
pred adv = predicate adverb
prep = preposition
ppl = past participle
pr: = prounounced:
~ = repetition of the entry's head word/s
X or Y = place-holders for any noun, adjective, or verb as explained

7. How to read the Cassidy/Jamiekan spellings in this book:

To begin, take a look at this example:

free = frii

In other words, "free" becomes "frii". It looks different, but it's the same word. Only the spelling has changed. Now look at some more examples:

free = frii	nice = nais	low = luo	face = fies
leave = liiv	white = wait	know = nuo	late = liet
piece = piis	high = ai	bone = buon	chair = chier

As you can see, /ii/ corresponds to the so-called 'long E' of English.

/ai/ is simply a combination of two vowel sounds. It is the short /a/ sound 'ah', immediately followed by the short /i/ in words like *if* and *in*.

/uo/ is the Jamaican version of the English 'long O' in words like *grow*. But in Jamaican speech, this really does sound like /u/ followed by /o/

/ie/ corresponds to the English 'long A'. In Jamaican speech, this really does sound like the /i/ in *win* or *wing*, directly followed by /e/ in *bet*.

Other phonemes as spelled in the Cassidy/Jamiekan system:

a ………. as in *hat*	ow ……. as in *throw*
aa ……. as in *tall*	ou …….. same as *ow*
o …….. as in *love*	h …….. usually silent
u …….. as in *put*	i ………. as in *sit*
uu …… as in *flu*	ng …….. as in *singer*
ur …….. as in *curl*	ngg …… as in *single*
or ……. same as *ur*	s ………. only as in *soft*

Here are some more examples for practice:

box = bax	girl = gurl	food = fuud	feel = fiil
song = sang	herb = urb	true = chuu	easy > iizi
wall = waal	world = worl	thru = chruu	hair = ier
start = staat	push = push	light = lait	place = plies
some = som	foot = fut	hype = aip	singer = singa
funny = foni	look = luk	icey = aisi	linger > lingga

feel new = fiil nyuu	fakeness = fieknis
ease up = iiz op	stranger = strienja
release = riliis	age = iej
singer = singa	care = kier
linger = lingga	guess = ges
bongo = bonggo	fire = faya

A LITTLE 1 (n) a piece, a smalls, a skimps, a kimps 2 (adj) a likkle, a piece a

A LOT 1 (n) wholeap, nuff, bans, nuff nuff 2 (adv) wholeap, nuff, kulu kulu 3 (*a lot of X*) wholeap a X, nuff X, nuff nuff X, bans a X, X like rice, X like wow, X like wah, X like dirt, X like sand, X fi stone dog

ABANDON 1 (*vacate*) leggo 2 (*walk out on*) gwaan leff, cut leff, run leff, cyaad, splurt pan, dish X dirt (X=person)

ABLE 1 (adj) fit 2 (v. *be able*) cyan, able fi, able fi cyan - *You should be able to get through*: Yu shuda kyan get chruu

ABORTION pr: abaashan (v. *to have an abortion*) dash weh belly

ABOUT 1 (*regarding*) bou 2 (*approximately*) bou, sittin laka, supm laka

ABOUT TO out fi, bou fi, go fi, a set up fi, a mek out fi - *It's about to rain*: It go fi rien, It a set op fi rien, etc.

ABOVE 1 (for airborne objects) ova 2 (for fixed objects) topside 3 (adv) topside - *There is a restaurant above the shop*: Dem hav a restarant tapsaid di shap

ABRUPTLY juss so, baps, foops, bragadaps

ABSCESS (n) yaw

ABSENT-MINDED (adj) stray-minded, stray-mind

ABSOLUTE 1 (when followed by adj) full - *my absolute best*: mi ful bes 2 (*utter*) peer, bare, bey, pure, suoso, lone - *It's absolute mayhem out there*: A bier mixop out deh; A suoso mixop out deh; etc

ABSOLUTELY 1 (*utterly*) strait, bline, ded, full, to X (X=expletive) - *You're absolutely crazy*: Yu ded mad, Yu mad tu blurtnaat 2 (pred adv) tu di fullness, cyaa done, so till, full stop, gaan to bed, to X (X=expletive) 3 Also see *ABSOLUTELY!*

ABSOLUTELY! Straight!, Yu done know!, No muss!, How yu mean!, Tank yu very much!, Chuss mi!, Chat bout!, To di worl!, A mi fi tell yu!, Fi real!, A it dat!, A it mi a seh!, A dat mi a seh!, Desso mi a seh!, Every time!, Sed speed!, Sed way so!, Fullness!, No chu?, No so?, See it deh!, Yu tink a joke?

ABUNDANCE wholeap, nuffness, plenty, x amount, kulu kulu

ABUNDANT see *PLENTIFUL*

ABUSE 1 (n) hacklinz, beatinz 2 (v. *take advantage of*) tek step a, tek step wid, tek liberty wid, advantage 3 (v. *verbally abuse*) violate, coas up, cole up, rax up 4 (v. *physically abuse*) hackle up, manackle, bad up, ruff up, lick up, batta up

ACCENT 1 (jokingly) accident 2 (*American accent*) twang 3 (v. *to speak with an American accent*) twang, yank

ACCEPT 1 (*agree to*) gree tu, low 2 (*allow*) low 3 (*take on*) tek up 3 Also see *PUT UP WITH*

ACCORDING TO az caadin tu

ACCOST (v) rush, flip up pan, fly dung pan, draw dung pan, run een pan, harbourshark - Also see *BERATE* or *CUSS OUT*

ACCOUNTED FOR (pred adj. of things only) lock, set, cool, strap up, deh pan ice, chock an belay, fit an frock, cook an curry

ACCUSE cuse, cyaad, pick out, cry pan, rang

ACCUSTOMED (*accustomed to*) custom fi

ACHE (v. *to ache*) bun, hot, (of stomach) gripe, (of teeth) deh pan edge - *My head is aching*: Mi hed a bon mi - *My tooth is aching*: Mi teet deh pan ej

ACHIEVE (v) ketch, hol, reach, touch

ACID (adj. of fruit) scratchy, scratch, sibble, sowa

ACID REFLUX bad stomach, bun stomach, mauli gripe an fluxy complaint

ACKNOWLEDGE (v. *credit*) mention

ACKNOWLEDGEMENT (n) mention

ACNE 1 (n) bump, love bump, bumpy face, grater face 2 (*covered in acne; full of pimples*) wormy, bumpy, bumpy bumpy, grater face

ACQUIRE (*take possession of*) paan up, tek up, captcha

ACT 1 (*behave*) gwaan, galang, ack, flex, move 2 (*pretend to be*) form, pattan, shape 3 (*act right*) move right, balance

ACT LIKE 1 (*behave as if*) gwaan like, flex like, move like, galang like 2 (*pretend to be*) shape, form, pattan, du like

ACTUALLY (when positioned at the head of the sentence): A chu seh, A chu, Mattarafak

ADAPT (*improvise; make do*) try a ting, try a way, tun han mek fashion, fadge, run wid it, hustle, run road, nyam a food

ADMIRE 1 (*respect; look up to*) rate 2 (*admire romantically*) pree, penny, check fi, like off - *She admires me*: Shi a peni mi, Shi laik mi aaf, etc.

ADOLESCENT jubie, (male only): youtman, yout, (female only): dawta, filly

ADULT 1 (n) big smaddy, big people 2 (n. *adult man*) big man, hard back man 3 (n. *adult woman*) big ooman, hard back ooman 4 (adj. of topic or thing) big man, big people 5 Alse see *MATURE*

ADVANCE 1 (n. *cash advance*) truss, borrows 2 (v. *move forward*) step up, faawud

ADVANTAGE 1 (v. of situation: *take advantage of*) advantage 2 (of person: *take advantage of*) tax, advantage, tek step a, live pan, nyam a food off a, boops out, nyam out

ADVENTUROUS out an bad, bentasome (from *venturesome*)

ADVERTISEMENT advatizment, avatizmen

AFFAIR 1 (n. *issue*) matta, subjeck, parangle 2 (n. *romantic or sexual fling*) go-rung 3 (v. *have an affair with*) av a ting wid, deal wid, talk wid, dance wid, av a go-rung wid 4 Also see *AFFAIRS*

AFFAIRS 1 (n. *daily affairs*) runninz 2 (n. *complicated affairs*) parangles, fandangles

AFFECT (v) reach, touch

AFFORD (*I can't afford that; That's not affordable*) Dat naa kip

AFICIONADO tetes

AFRAID 1 (adj) fraid, frightn 2 (v. *become afraid*) ketch yu fraid

AFRICAN 1 (n. *a culturally conscious or mystical black man from Africa or of African ancestry*) bongo man, congo man 2 (n. *a woman from Africa or of black African ancestry*) African queen 3 Alse see *COMPLEXION*

AFTER afta, afa, ata, afta wen

AGAIN back - *Do it again*: Du it bak

AGAINST gainst - Also see *OPPOSED*

AGE 1 (n) size 2 see *HOW OLD ARE YOU?*

AGGRESSIVE 1 (*belligerent*) ignarant, ig, warify, talawa, brawlin, crabbit, ruffa, tuffa, trong physic, rhygin 2 (n. *aggressive person*) talawa, tegereg, chucky, war monger, war boat, (female only): virago, ratchet, champong nanny 3 (*Be aggressive!*) run it red!, Gi dem!, Go deh! 4 Also see *ASSERTIVE*

AGITATED bummy, jumpy, kra kra

AGO 1 (adv) a back 2 (*a little while ago*) no too lang, likkle while 3 (*a while ago*) back a while, some time a back

AGREE 1 (v) gree 2 (*not agree; not get along*): no plant peas, no tek tea 3 (*I agree!*) see *TOTALLY!*

AIR (n) breeze

AIR OUT (v) breeze out

ALBINO 1 (n) doondoos, quaw, mudu 2 (adj) doondoos, quawy, mudu

ALCOHOL (n. *liquor*) alkuwol, wataz (from *waters*), waters, juice, babylon wata

ALCOHOLIC (n. *person addicted to liquor*) rum head

ALL 1 (n) all an all 2 (*all of*) di whole a 3 (*all the*) di heap

ALL ACROSS clear cross

ALL AROUND /ALL OVER all bout

ALL DAY whole day

ALL GONE 1 (*finished*) done, (of food) nyam off, (of weed) smoke off, (of drinks) drink off 2 (*sold out*) sell off

ALL GOOD see *IT'S ALL GOOD*

ALL NIGHT 1 (adv) whole night 2 (v. *stay out all night*) bleach

ALL RIGHT 1 arite, cool, balance, level, set, irie, deh ya, deh deh 2 Also see *GOT IT; ACCOUNTED FOR; SO SO*

ALL SET (pred adj. of things only) lock, set, cool, strap up, deh pan ice, chock an belay, fit an frock, cook an curry

ALL THE MORE 1 (when appearing at the end of a sentence) fi di beta, fii beta 2 (when appearing at the beginning of a clause) wors, wos - *It was wrong, all the more because you lied about it*: A did rang, wos ka yu tel lai bout i

ALL THE TIME all di while, every time

ALL THE WAY 1 (*until it stops*) til ih buck, clear, full stop 2 (*without holding anything back*) full hundred, full stop 3 (of location: *all the way to X*) clear up a X, slap up a X, quite up a X

ALLOW 1 (v) low 2 (*let*) mek, lek

ALLSPICE pimento

ALMOST nearlymost, likklemost - *I almost fell out of my chair*: Mi liklmuos drap out a mi chier, Liklmuos mi drap out a mi chier

ALOE sinkle bible, bittaz

ALREADY 1 (when appearing at the end of the clause or sentence) areddy 2 (when appearing between the subject and verb) done - *I already did it*: Mi du it aredi - *You already know*: Yu don nuo

ALSO (pred adv only) same way, as well

ALTERCATION 1 (n. *verbal altercation*) kass kass, mix up, blenda, mix up an blenda, confusion, cobell, hell an powda house 2 (n. *physical altercation*) scuffle, blenda, cobell, plam plam, palam pam, pam pam, bam bam, palangarang

ALWAYS 1 (*from now on*) evah, allsway 2 (of behavior: *habitually*) every time, all di while, allsway - *I will always remember you*: Mi wi eva rememba yu - *She always says that*: Shi seh dat evri taim; Shi seh dat aal di wail

AM see *I AM* or *I AM NOT*

AMAZING 1 (of thing or event) wow, mad, terrible, superble, wikid, crucial, craab up, shot, sell off, pop off, slap weh, a seh one, tun up, tun ova 2 (of person) mad, bad, wikid, terrible, superble, artical, craab up, well skill, shot, sell off, pop off, slap weh, tuff, turnt, tun up, tun ova

AMBARELLA (*Spondius dulcis*) june plum, jew plum

AMBIENCE (n) vibes, medz

AMBITION 1 gumption 2 Also see *SELF-ESTEEM*

AMBITIOUS ambitionable, trong eye, crabbit, no easy

AMBIVALENT (adj) two-minded, two-mind

AMBLYOPIA 1 (n) cyaas eye 2 (adj. *having amblyopia*) cyaas eye, look a bush

AMERICA pr: Murika (*The United States*) Farin (from *foreign*), Big Farin

AMERICAN pr: Murikan (n. *American person*) yankee, farinah (foreigner)

AMMUNITION see *BULLETS*

AMONG mongx

AMPUTATED 1 (adj) chop off, lass off, bobbit 2 (*missing the end; having the end chopped off*) tumpy, tumpa

AMUSEMENT pleasuration, funjoy

ANAL SEX bugarism, batty-ism, funny man ting, fishy bizniz

ANATOMY structa

AND SO FORTH an ting, an so, an ray ray, an ray tay tay, an one bag a supm, an x-y-zed, an all a dem ting deh, an all a dem sittin deh, an all a dem supm deh, an teeri (from *theory*), an blar blar blar, an labba labba, an tarra warra, an warra warra, an wat nat, an rat nat

ANEMIC bilyas (from *billious*)

ANEMONE sea flowaz

ANGER 1 (n) bexation, bextation, ignorancy, hot skull 2 (vt) bex, mek bex, mek bringle, mek ignarant, mek ig, (where X=person): get X bex, hot up X head, hot up X skull, get X ignarant, get X ig, mek X bringle, mek X ben - *They anger me*: Dem a get mi ig; Dem a hat op mi hed; Dem a mek mi bringgl; etc.

ANGRY 1 (adj) bex, ben, cross, red, daak, ignarant, ig, puff up 2 (*outraged*) rhygin, raatid, red, ignarant, ig 3 (v. *feel angry*) bex, bringle, rue, chaw fyah, screw 3 Also *GET ANGRY*

ANI BIRD (*Crotophaga ani*) blackbud, tick eater

ANKLE pr: henkl

ANNOY see *PESTER*

ANNOYING 1 (of person) disgustin, ninghy ninghy 2 (of situation) disgustin, bodderashous

ANOLE green lizard, green guana

ANOTHER 1 (adj) a nex, one nex, anadda, anedda, waanedda 2 (n. *another person*) a nex one, a nex man, wan nex man, one nex one

ANT (n) ants - *an ant*: wan ans

ANTAGONIZE 1 (v) hype pan, rail up pan, wile up, hackle wid, sheg wid, bait, draw cyaad pan, chuck it pan, chuck pan, cold up, coarse up 2 Also see *PROVOKE*

ANUS battyhole, bumbo hole, rass hole

ANXIETY fretty fretty, nerve prablem

ANXIOUS 1 (of personality) fretty fretty 2 (of current state or mood) fretful, kra kra 3 (v. *to feel anxious*) fret, belly bottom a bun yu - *I'm feeling anxious*: Mi beli batam a bon mi 4 Also see *AGITATED*

ANY 1 (adj) no - *I don't have any bread*: Mi no av no bred 2 (n) none - *I don't have any*: Mi no av non

ANY BETTER none betta, no betta

ANY TIME (*any time that...*) weneva time, wen time - *Any time you need it let me know*: Weneva taim yu niid i mek mi nuo; Wen taim yu niid i mek mi nuo

ANYBODY nobaddy

ANY MORE again, no more, no longa - *I don't live there any more*: Mi no liv deh agen

ANYTHING (after negative verbs or *if*) nuttin, nuttn

ANYTHING ELSE nuttn more

ANYWAY same way, still - *I'll give you the money anyway*: Mi wi gi yu di moni stil

ANYWHERE any which paat

APART FROM (*other than*) sep fi, paat from, save fi, puttin weh

APARTMENT flat 2 Also see *HOME*

APOCALYPSE attaclaps, revelations

APOLOGIZE 1 (v) beg sorry 2 (*apologize for what one said*) tek back yu chat

APPEAR 1 (v. *emerge*) brok out, buss out 2 (v. *seem*) look, come een - *That appears wrong to me*: Dat luk rang tu mi - *It appears that she doesn't love you*: Kom iin laka shi no lov yu.

APPEASE pet an pampa, powda, skin up yu teet wid, hush, hug up

APPLAUD 1 (vi. *clap hands and cheer*) hype 2 (vt. *clap for*) clap 3 (*commend*) rate up, big up, large up, sallute, count

APPLAUSE hype

APPRECIATE 1 (*feel grateful for*) apprecialove, glad fi 2 (*understand the value of*) rate, count

APPRECIATION appricialove

APPRECIATIVE gladfah

APPRENTICE prento

APPROACH 1 (n. *technique*) style, flex 2 (*walk up to*) move to, flex to, shape up to 3 Also see *ACCOST*

APPROPRIATE 1 (adj) riteful, fit 2 (v. *be appropriate for the situation*) mek it 3 (v. *to be appropriate for*) fit - *That's not appropriate for children*: Dat no fit fi pikni 4 (v. *seize*) pawn up, pawn, capture, pra pra

APPROVAL see *PRAISE*

APPROXIMATELY bou, sittn laka, supm laka

APRIL FOOL'S DAY Tom Fool Day

ARE 1 (when followed by a noun) a - *They are friends*: Dem a fren 2 (when followed by an adj) Ø - *You are crazy*: Yu mad 3 (+ verb) a, deh - *We are talking*: Wi a chat; Wi deh chat 4 (+ location) deh - *We are here*: Wi deh ya 5 (when terminating a phrase that contains *how*) stay, tan - *That's how we are*: A so wi stie 6 (when terminating a phrase containing *what* or *who*) be - *I don't care who they are*: Mi no bizniz huu dem bi 7 Also see *AREN'T*

ARE YOU CRAZY? (*What's wrong with you?*) Yu mad?, Wah wrong wid yu?, Wappn tu yu?, Wah <u>du</u> yu?, Yu lick yu head?, Wah tek yu?, Weh yu a defen?, Yu a jrink mad puss piss?, Yu a nyam mad puss brain?

ARE YOU KIDDING? Wappn tu yu?, Wah du yu?, Weh yu a deal wid?, Weh yu a defen?

ARE YOU SERIOUS? see *ARE YOU KIDDING?* or *SERIOUSLY?*

AREA 1 (n. *vicinity*) districk, side 2 (*this area*) dis side

AREN'T 1 (when followed by a noun) a no - *They aren't friends*: Dem a no fren 2 (when followed by an adj) no, doan - *We aren't crazy*: Wi no mad; Wi duon mad 3 (+ verb) naa - *We aren't joking*: Wi naa ramp 4 (+ location) no deh - *They aren't here*: Dem no deh ya

ARGUE 1 (vi. *argue respectfully on a topic; argue on behalf of an idea*) reason, hol chapta 2 (v. *bicker*) trow wud, fling wud, war out, wile up, cuss cuss, trace

ARGUMENT 1 (n. *line of reasoning*) medz 2 (n. *quarrel*) cass cass, cuss cuss, confusion, passa passa, parangles, fandangles (for more see *QUARREL*)

ARGUMENTATIVE warify, cuss cuss, trong mout

ARM han

ARMPIT arm hol, arm

AROUND 1 (*surrounding; throughout*) bout, bou, rung 2 (adv. *approximately*) bou, sittn laka, sinting like, supm laka 3 (*around here*) bou ya, rung ya, dis side

AROUSE (*arouse sexually*) hot up, staat up, stir up - (female to male only) tease up di lion, wake up di lion

AROUSED (*sexually aroused*) hot up, staat up, ready fi wine, stir up

ARRANGE 1 (*coordinate; plan*) set up 2 (*put in order*) dechakalize

ARRANGEMENT dealinz

ARREST 1 (*take into custody*) tek up, bring up 2 (*put handcuffs on*) bite 3 (*get arrested*) get bite, get hol 4 (*to have someone arrested*) bring up

ARRIVE 1 (v) reach, touch, ketch 2 (*arrive at*) reach, touch pan, ketch a

ARROGANCE boassy boassy, stushness, high chest, nyanga

ARROGANT see *STUCK UP; CONCEITED; PRETENTIOUS*

ARTHRITIS afritis

AS 1 (*while*) as, same time 2 (*as X as Y*) *He's as tall as his brother*: Im lang siem wie laka im breda - *She's as pretty as money*: Shi priti laka moni 3 Also see: *AS FAR AS; AS MUCH AS; AS LONG AS; AS SOON AS*

AS A MATTER OF FACT (when positioned as the head of the sentence) A chu, Mattarafak

AS FAR AS 1 (*inasmuch as*) far as, to how 2 (*regarding*) far as, wen it come on tu, bou 3 (*all the way to*) slap up a, clear up a, quite up a, way up a

AS FOR (*regarding*) far as, wen it come on tu, bou

AS LONG AS long as, solanks, from, while

AS MUCH AS 1 *You can take as much as you want*: Yu kyan tek umoch yu waan 2 *I earn as much as a thousand dollars sometimes*: Mi get aal touzn dala somtaim

AS SOON AS same time, so X so Y - *He ran away as soon as the dog barked*: Him ron weh siem taim di dag baak; So di dag baak so him ron weh

ASHAMED 1 (adj) shame 2 (v. *feel ashamed*) feel shame, feel a way, lap yu tail

ASIDE 1 (adv) one side 2 (*aside from*) sep fi, save fi, paat from, puttn weh

ASIDE FROM 1 (adv) one side 2 (*aside from*) sep fi, save fi, paat from, puttn weh

ASK 1 (v) aks 2 (*ask for*) beg, aks fi 3 (*ask person X to do Y*) beg X fi Y - *She asked me to tell her*: Shi did beg mi fi tel har 4 Also see *SUMMON*

ASKEW (*off center*) cyaas, offish

ASLEEP 1 (adj) deh sleep 2 (*fall asleep*) jrap asleep

ASPHALT nylon, babagreen, tar

ASS 1 (n) batty, backside, bumpa, bumbo, fenda, raas 2 (n. *ass crack*) batty crease 3 (*ass cheek*) batty jaw, batty peg 4 Also see *FOOL or DONKEY*

ASSAULT 1 (*physically assault*) bad up, chuck pan 2 (*verbally assault*) trace, flip up pan, wild up, throw wud pan, rax up

ASSERTIVE no easy, trong mind, trong mout, mannish

ASSHOLE 1 (n. *obnoxious despicable male*) fassy, fassyhole, pussyhole, bomboclaat, bombohole, crowbait, cacafawt, pussyfawt, pussymout, bait, crow bait, curr, dutty johncrow, crab inna barrel, harbour shark, heathen, pagan, chapunko 2 (*despicable and disreputable female*) dutty stinkin gyal, nassy gyal, streggeh, sketel, credell, screbbeh, jezibel, pancoot, pazart, parasite, kinarky, crebbeh crebbeh 3 (n. *anus*) battyhole, bumbohole, rass hole

ASSOCIATE WITH 1 (*mingle with*) mix wid, move wid, flex wid, par wid, roll wid 2 (*hang out with regularly*) move wid, flex wid, par wid, roll wid

ASSUME 1 (*suppose*) check seh, figga seh 2 (*assume X to be Y*) tek X fi Y - *They assume that I'm a tourist*: Dem tek mi fi tuoris 3 (*take on*) tek up

ASTHMA shaatnis (from *shortness*), pressin

ASTONISH (v) frightn lick X fi ten

AT 1 (of location) a 2 (of clock time) Ø 3 (with unkind intentions: e.g. *laugh at; throw rocks at*) afta 4 (*look at*) look pan, coo pan 5 (*point at*) point pan 6 (*smile at*) smile wid

AT ALL (following negative phrases) nonatall, nontall

AT FIRST at fuss

AT ONCE juss so, same time, baps, foops

AT THAT TIME inna dat deh time deh, inna dat time deh, dat time deh

AT THE SAME TME one time

ATHLETE'S FOOT grunge

ATTACK 1 (*physically attack*) bad up, chuck pan 2 Also see *DENOUNCE*

ATTEND 1 (v. as a lecture or concert) tek een, penetrate 2 (*attend to*) look afta, hangle, govaan

ATTITUDE 1 (n. *frame of mind*) medz 2 (n. *personal way of looking at things and expressing self*) style, medz, flex, movement

ATTRACT trac, track

ATTRACTED see *ADMIRE; INTERESTED*

ATTRACTIVE see *PRETTY; HANDSOME; SEXY*

AUDACIOUS 1 (adj) dry yeye, facety, bright, eggs up, bumptious, pomptious 2 (v. *be audacious*) fly paas yu nest, pass yu place, tek liberty, tek step, eggs up yuself

AUDACITY dry yeye, facetyness, brightness, bumptiousness

AUDIENCE massive, crowd a people

AUTHENTIC see *GENUINE*

AUTHORITY pr: ataariti (n. *authority figure*) bigga head

AVERAGE 1 (n) miggle, migglin 2 (adj. *common*) migglin, common fowl, white fowl

AVOCADO pear, abacado pear

AVOID 1 (*dodge; evade*) site 2 (of person: *avoid speaking to*) go roun 3 (*abstain from*) keep weh fram, stay wide a

AWARE 1 (*generally aware of how things go*) deh pan top 2 (v. *be aware; know what's up*) know bout, know wa clock a strike, know wat o'clock 3 (*become aware of; notice*) pick up pan, sight 4 (*perceive at a deeper level*) penetrate, sight 5 (*become aware that*) see *REALIZE*

AWARENESS (*general awareness and understanding of things*) ovastandin, consciousness, full yeye, sense, sabi-so

AWAY weh

AWESOME 1 (of situation or event: *fantastic*) wow, mad, terrible, superble, wikid, craab up, turnt, tun up, tun ova, shot, splendacious, splendifarous, fabilocious, boonoonoonoos 2 (of person: *impressive*) mad, bad, wikid, terrible, superble, crabbit, tuff, turnt, well skill, craab up, shot 3 (v. *to be awesome*) see *RULE*

AWESOME! Mad ting!, Mad!, Wikid!, A it dat!, Ray!, Up!, Up mi seh!, Way up!, Up! Up! Up!, Brap! Brap!, Det! Det! Det!

AWFUL 1 (*dreadful*) bad bad, bad bad bad, hoodias, turbl 2 (*lacking talent or quality*) see *LOUSY*

AWKWARD 1 (of situation) funny 2 (of person: *socially awkward*) dunce, poppy show 3 (n. *guy who is awkward around women*) gyal clown, board man 4 Also see *CLUMSY*

BABBLE 1 (n) labba labba, ray ray, blar, chat chat, labrish, warra warra 2 (v) labba labba, run yu mout, fly yu mout, labrish, su su

BABY 1 (n. *infant*) pickney 2 Also see *SWEETHEART*

BABYSIT mine (from *mind*), look afta

BABYSITTER sitta, nana

BACHELOR (n) batchie

BACK 1 (v. *support*) carry, defend 2 See various phrases containing *BACK*

BACK AND FORTH faawud an back, dilly an dally

BACK AWAY 1 (*move back a bit*) back back, jess back 2 (*retreat*) back weh

BACK COUNTRY see *BACKWOODS*

BACK OFF 1 (*retreat*) back weh 2 (*ease up*) tek time, easy, cool, sekkle

BACK OUT 1 (*renege*) tun back, dis di program, sheriff 2 (as a car: *reverse*) reverse back

BACK OUT ON (*reneg on*) tun yu back pan, backslide pan

BACK TALK backchat, back ansa

BACK UP 1 (*move back a bit*) back back, jess back 2 (*drive in reverse*) go backways, reverse back

BACKGROUND pr: bakrong - Also see *UPBRINGING*

BACKPACK napsack

BACKWARD (adj. *regressive*) backways, dark, butu, bugu bugu, boogooyaga, backawall, moko

BACKWARDS (adv. of direction) backways, backway - *You're going backwards*: Yu a go bakwiez

BACKWATER 1 (n) bush, backabush, outlaw districk, moko 2 (adj) back a bush, back a moko, boogooyaga, behind God back, back a God back, backa beyond

BACKWOODS 1 (n) bush, backabush, outlaw districk, moko 2 (adj) back a bush, back a moko, boogooyaga, behind God back, back a God back, backa beyond 3 (*in the backwoods*) back a bush, back a moko, behind God back, back a God back

BACON hog back

BAD see *LOW QUALITY; LOUSY; DEPRAVED; EVIL*

BAD ASS 1 (*a daring and respected male*) bad man, gorgon, don, notch, general, shotta, knockis, kwenga, gyangsta, steppa, baddaz, tuggz, bantan, aatikal, duppy conqueror 2 (*a tough and dangerous woman*) big ooman, champong nani, bad gyal, ratchet 3 (adj of person: *impressive; fearless*) bad, wikid, terrible, crabbit, superble, out an bad, notchilous, talawah, tuffa 4 Also see *TALENTED*

BAD BEHAVIOUR outa orderness, badness, sketelness, luu, fuckry, sheggry, dragupsy, renkness, renkity, ugliness, ugly, muckry, neckry

BAD BREATH sowa mout

BAD GUY see *BAD MAN; TROUBLEMAKER; THUG*

BAD LUCK 1 (n) crosses, buzu 2 (v. *to have bad luck*) see *OUT OF LUCK; UNLUCKY*

BAD MAN 1 (*a daring and respected male*) bad man, gorgon, don, notch, general, shotta, knockis, kwenga, gyangsta, steppa, baddaz, tuggz, bantan, aatikal, duppy conqueror 2 (*troublemaker; thug*) tuggz, hot skull, rudebwoy, starbwoy, guineagog, screwface, ruffneck, ruffian, russian, war monga, sluggard, hooligan, scufflah, baddaz, chucky, radge, tuff, bullbucka, badlaw, baddy boo

BAD MINDED badmind, pagan, ceitful, grudgeful, red yeye, cubbitch, cramoojin, cov̲eechous, misareble, crampify, payaka, harbour sharkin, harbour shark, crab inna barrel

BADGER see *NAG* or *HASSLE*

BADLY bad, (*really badly*) bad bad, bad bad bad

BADMIND 1 (n. *spite; envy*) badmind, grudgeful, red yeye, payaka-ism, crab inna barrel 2 (vt. *to begrudge*) badmind, grudge, harbourshark, bun bad cyangle fi, bun bad light fi

BADMOUTH 1 (vi. *say negative things*) chat fuckry, badmout, dis, hype 2 (vt) chat fuckry bout, hype pan, badmout, dis, violate, tek liberty wid, walk up an dong pan X name (X=person) 3 Also see *GOSSIP*

BAG 1 (n. *supermarket style plastic bag*) scandal bag, scandal 2 (*luggae bag; suitcase*) grip 3 (*burlap sack*) krokos bag

BAGGAGE (*luggage*) bag dem, grip dem, bag an ting, (potentially insulting when used in reference to another person's luggage): bag an pan, karowchiz

BALANCE (vi. *as on a tightrope*) cotch

BALD 1 clean head, peel head 2 (*balding; having scanty hair*) dry head, picky picky 3 (n. derogatory: *bald person*) peel-head johncrow

BALDING dry head

BALLS see *TESTICLES; COURAGE*

BANISH (v) run, tun out, put out, drive weh, dish X dirt (X=person)

BANTER 1 (n) bantan, jostle 2 (v) run jostle, bantan

BANTU KNOTS chiney bump

BARGAIN (v. *haggle*) bawl dung di price, talk dung di price, higgle

BARK (n. of a tree) wood skin

BARRACUDA barracouta

BARREL pr: baril 1 (n. *metal barrel*) pan 2 (n. *oil barrel*) drum pan, joe pan

BASTARD 1 (n. *despicable male*) fassy, fassyhole, pussyhole, cacafawt, pussyfawt, pussymout, bait, crow bait, curr, dutty johncrow, crab inna barrel, harbour shark, Judas, heathen, pagan, chapunko 2 (*bastard child*) outside pickney, out chile, (if father doesn't know it's not his): jacket 3 Also see *TRAITOR*

BAT 1 (n. *flying mammal*) rat bat 2 (n. *billy club*) baton stick, junka

BATH 1 (n. *bath tub*) tub 2 (n. *a soak*) fresh, washoff, (*quick bath*) chooks

BATHE bade, hol a fresh, wash off 2 (*bathe quickly*) chooks

BATHING SUIT baat suit

BATTERY pr: bachri

BATTLE 1 (n. *battle of egos and reputations between two people*) war 2 (n. *competition between two sound systems*) clash 3 (v. *to battle*) war

BE (The infinitive form of the verb *BE* is avoided where possible in Jamaican speech. Here are some examples of how English phrases using the word can be tranlsated into Jamaican Creole) *Be wise*: Yu fi wise - *Don't be like that*: No galang so - *Let it be*: Mek i tan - *That could be*: Coulda so i go - *It must be*: A mussi so - *I want to be a fireman*: Mi waan fi bi a fayaman - Also see *I AM; ARE; AREN'T; IS; ISN'T; WAS; WASN'T; WERE; WEREN'T*

BE CAREFUL 1 (v. *to be careful*) tek time, tekyah, mind sharp, mine sharp, stay wide, tek sleep mark death 2 (*to be careful of*) watch, mind, mine, tekyah, stay wide a, tek time wid 3 (*Be careful not to X*) Mind yu X (X must be an affirmative verb) - *Be careful not to drop the glass*: Main yu jrap di glas

BE CAREFUL! Mind sharp!, Tek time!, Ave Caution!, Tekyah!, Stay wide!

BEANS peas

BEAR (v. *suffer; endure*) suffah, go chu, deal wid, cross ova, pass chu, liv out, get chu, angle, clear

BEARDED beard up, bush up

BEAT 1 (n. of music) drum an bass, patta 2 (*backing track of a particular song*) riddim 3 (v. *hit violently*) lick, lick up, batta batta, pung 4 (v. *beat in a competition; defeat*) shell dung, slap weh, lick, lick fi six, kill, slew, slawta, wya, tump, clawt, duss, vank, trample

BEAT AROUND THE BUSH bob an weave, buckshuffle

BEAT UP 1 (adj. of thing: *shabby; worn out*) macheted, mash up, ben up, rev out, batta batta, nyaka nyaka 2 (adj. of person: *battered*) mash up, lick up, batta batta, nyaka nyaka 3 (v. *physically beat up*) lick up, sheg up, beat tu X (X=expletive)

BEATING (n. *a beating*) a beat'n, one piece a lick, a kuffin, a tumpinz, a lickinz, a floggin, a fum fum

BEAUTIFUL 1 (of thing or place) pretty like wow, pretty laka X (X=anything of value), pretty no Y (Y = expletive), boonoo<u>noo</u>noos, splendacious, splendifarous 2 (of woman) kris, nice, pretty pretty, pretty like wow, pretty laka X (X=anything of value), pretty no Y (Y = expletive), boonoo<u>noo</u>noos 3 (n. *beautiful woman*) goodaz, goodie, glama gyal, hot gyal, block-traffic, daphne walkin

BECAUSE 1 (adv) caw, chu, as 2 (*just because*) no becaw 3 (*because of*) sake a, chu, cause a, count a 4 (*It's because XY that Z*) *It's because Jimmy ran that he's tired*: A ron Jimi ron mek him tayad

BECOME 1 (v) come, tun, bikomps, X up - *It's becoming dark*: It a daak op 2 (*become X again*) tun back X - *We have become friends again*: Wi ton bak fren

BEDBUG chink

BEE 1 (n) beez 2 (n. *bumble bee*) bongo beez

BEETLE (n. *water beetle*) titty biter

BEFORE LONG see *IN A LITTLE WHILE; LATER ON*

BEFRIEND fren up

BEG 1 (v. *panhandle*) tretch out yu han 2 (*wait around for a handout*) henka

BEGGAR begga man, come aroun, budger

BEGRUDGE see *ENVY* or *RESENT*

BEHAVE 1 (*act*) gwaan, galang, ack, flex, move 2 (*behave well; behave oneself*) balance, move right 3 Also see *ACT LIKE; MISBEHAVE*

BEHAVIOUR 1 (n) style, flex, movement 2 (*good behaviour*) balance, uprightness, broughtupsy 3 (*bad behaviour*) outa orderness, badness, sketelness, luu, fuckry, sheggry, dragupsy, renkness, renkity, ugliness, ugly, muckry, neckry

BEHIND 1 (prep) back a 2 (*behind schedule*) deh aback 3 (*behind the building*) rounaback

BELCH (v. *burp*) buss gyas

BELIEVE 1 (*believe in; support*) defen 2 Also see *MAKE BELIEVE; I DON'T BELIEVE YOU*

BELITTLE (v) class, violate, tek step wid, reduce, style, hype pan, pop style pan, low count

BELLIGERENT 1 cuss cuss, ignarant, ig, warify, crabbit, brawlin, trong physic, rowasome, rhygin 2 (n. *a belligerent person*) tegereg, chucky, war monger, war boat, (female only): virago, ratchet, champong nanny

BELLY 1 (n) belly, gut, bem bem 2 (n. *pot belly; paunch*) bang belly, big belly, pawnz belly, wanga gut, ten penny 3 (n. *pot-bellied man*) pawnzo, big belly man 4 Also see *BELLY ACHE*

BELLY ACHE 1 (n) bad belly, colic, gripe, low stomach, belly hot 2 (v) gripe - *My belly is aching*: Mi beli a graip mi

BELLY BUTTON belly cork, nabel

BELOW unda, bottomside - *the apartment below mine*: di flat batamsaid fimi own

BEND DOWN ben dung, tip dung, (in a flirtatious way) bessy dung

BENT ben up, twiss

BEQUEATH ded leff gi - *My grandfather bequeathed the house to me (handed the house down to me when he died)*: Mi granfaada ded lef gi mi di ous

BEQUEST (n. *goods or money passed on to an inheritor*) dedleff

BERATE trace, wild up, rax up, run up yu mout pan, throw wud pan

BESIDE 1 (*next to*) side a, gainst, begainst 2 (*aside from*) sep fi, paat from, save fi, puttn weh

BESIDES (adv. *apart from; aside from*) sep fi, paat from, save fi, puttin weh

BEST 1 (adj) bess, numba one, toppa top, bessis 2 (*It's Y'est X*) No X no Y so - *It's the tastiest coffee*: No kafi no swiit so 3 (v. *be the best*) a seh <u>one</u> - (for more see *KICK ASS*) 4 Also see *BEST FRIEND*

BEST FRIEND key, key spar, shadow, goodie goodie, (for male only): brogad

BETRAY (v) bait up, draw cyaad pan, cyaad, bandulu, samfai, lamps, craff, maringle, bamboozl, mash X sore toe, brok X foot (X=person)

BETRAYER frenemy, switcha, culprit, back-an-belly rat, white belly rat, twincoat, bag-o-wyah

BETTER 1 (adj) betta 2 (v. *improve*) step up, sort out

BIASED parshal

BICKER (v. *quarrel verbally*) trace, war, war out, wile up, cuss cuss, throw wud, fling wud

BIG see *HUGE; POPULAR*

BIG SHOT 1 (n. *governmental authority figure*) bigga head, backra 2 (n. *leader of a gang*) don, gorgon, general, notch

BILIMBI blim blim

BILLY CLUB (n) baton stick, junka

BINOCULARS binnickle

BIRD 1 bud 2 (*little bird*) chi chi bud 3 Also see specific types of birds

BIRTH 1 (n) bot 2 (v. *give birth*) birt, baa

BIRTH CERTIFICATE age paper, birt paper

BIRTHDAY (Rasta) earthstrong, earthday

BISEXUAL 1 (n) twin cam, AC-DC man 2 (adj) twin cam

BIT BY BIT bit bit, piece piece, peessa peessa, likkle likkle, one one

BITCH 1 (n. *spiteful woman*) miserable ooman, teggereg, virago, warboat, kinarky, pancoot 2 (n. *subservient male*) press-button, remote, figaree, prekeh, mantu 3 (n. *irritating male; little bitch*) bait, fassy, fassyhole 4 (v. *whine*) run up yu mout, ningy ningy 5 Also see PROSTITUTE

BITCHY 1 (*nagging; whiny*) ningy ningy 2 (*mean and spiteful*) misareble, disgustin, badmind, waasy, mampala 3 (of male: *moody*) funny, mampala

BITE 1 (v. *aggressively, as a wild animal*) lash 2 (v. *chomp down*) lash yu mout, lash yu teet

BITTER 1 (*bitter tasting*) sowa, bitterish 2 (*resentful*) sowa, bitta 3 (v. *feel bitter; feel resentful*) carry feelings, carry belly, keep malice

BITTERNESS 1 (*bitter taste*) sowaness 2 (*resentment*) feelinz, sowa belly

BLABBER 1 (n. *idle talk*) labba labba, ray ray, ray tay tay, su su, seh seh, passa passa, blar, labrish, yabba yabba, warra warra, tarra warra, carry-go-bring-come, come-come-seh, lippy lippy 2 (v. *to blabber*) run up yu mout, fly yu mout, labba, labrish, labba up yu mout, labba labba, yabba yabba

BLABBERMOUTH labbamout, baggamout, fullamout, chatty chatty mout, yabba mout, mout-a-massy, long tounge, labrisher, lippy lippy, nuttn-fi-du

BLACK see COMPLEXION or AFRICAN

BLACKOUT (n. *power outage*) powa cut

BLAH BLAH BLAH ray ray ray, ray tay tay, blar blar blar, labba labba labba, warra warra, tarra warra

BLAME 1 (v) rang (from *wrong*) - *I don't blame him*: Mi no rang im 2 Also see ACCUSE

BLAND fresh, insipid, so so

BLATANT bayface, dry yeye

BLEND 1 (n) blem, mesh, mashup, meshup 2 (v) blem, mesh

BLENDED (adj) blem, blem up

BLESSED pr: blesid (adj) bless

BLINK quint

BLISS niceness, medz, ites

BLOATED 1 (of belly) bang, swell 2 (of any object) buff out, bufu bufu 3 (v. *eat until bloated*) ketch yu lent, nyam til yu buss

BLOCK (v) hinda, hol dung

BLOW 1 (n. *a hit from a fist or weapon*) tump, kuff, lick, clap, clot, bulla, baff, boof 2 (n. *a heavy blow from a fist or weapon*) clot, bitch lick, beast lick, kuff, bulla, gaza bax, gully bax

BLOWJOB see *FELLATIO*

BLUFF 1 (n. *empty threat; trick*) olo, olo gyow, gyow 2 (vi) sell gyow, blar, draw cyaad 3 (vt) gyow, draw cyaad pan

BLUNDER (n. *careless mistake*) eedyat ting, flop, bum prime

BLUNT 1 (n. *large weed cigarette*) spliff 2 (*straightforward*) strait, no easy, coas, dry yeye, widout folly 3 (v. *be blunt*) talk di tingz, no skin teet, no skin up, no lotion, no pet nor powda

BLURRY mud up

BOA CONSTRITOR (*Jamaican boa constrictor; yellow bo*a) nanka

BOARD (v. *live at a site for a limited time*) cotch, stop, black

BOAST boas off, braff, hype up yuself, talk up yuself, nuff up yuself, puff up yu chest, palaav

BOASTFUL braggadocious, boasify, boasy

BODY 1 (n) badi, structa, soul case 2 (n. *physique*) badi, bizeek, status

BODY ODOR (ODOUR) 1 (n) green arm 2 (v. *reek of body odor*) smell green, smell ripe, smell frowzy

BOIL 1 (n. *pustule; abscess*) Yaw 2 (v) bwile

BOK CHOY pop chow

BOLD 1 (*daring*) bad, out an bad, no easy, trong mind, bentasome (from *venturesome*), mannish 2 (*assertive*) facety, no easy, dry yeye, trong mind, crabbit 3 Also see *BRAZEN*

BONAFIDE see *GENUINE*

BONG chalice, chalwah, chillum

BONY see *EMACIATED* or *LANKY*

BONUS (*a little something extra*) brawta, mek-up

BOOGER booboo, boogoo, buggaboo

BOOGEYMAN blackheart man

BOONDOCKS see *BACKWOODS; REMOTE*

BOONIES see *BACKWOODS*

BOOR butu, cruff, streggeh, screbbeh, screbz, crebbeh, creb, dutty bungle, boogooyaga, zutupeng, zutupek, nyamps, (male only): guineagog, cuffy, kwaco, (female only): sketel, pancoot, virago, war boat

BOORISH butu, brawlin, raw chaw, unmannersable, cruff, crebbeh, screbbeh, streggeh, hoggish, pancoot, renk, outa aada, slack, slacka, zutupeck, zutupeng, boogooyaga, boogoo boogoo, nyamps

BORING 1 (of place) ded, deadstock 2 (of person) so so, deadstock 3 (n. *boring person*) ded stock

BOSS (n. *supervisor*) boss man, bossy, Missa T, busha

BOTCH (v) mash up, sheg up, mud up, nassy up, kaba kaba, sawka sawka, soak

BOTHER 1 (v) see *PESTER; HASSLE* 2 (*not bother with*) no bizniz wid, no deal wid, no pay no mind tu, no feneh pan - *I don't bother with that stuff*: Mi no bizniz wid dat; etc

BOTTLE bokkle

BOTTLE OPENER pulla

BOTTOM 1 (n) battam 2 (v. *get to the bottom of*) suss out

BOUNCE 1 (v) bunks, jump up 2 Also see *LEAVE*

BOURGEOIS 1 (adj) uptong, stoosh, itey titey, chest high, risto, top rankin 2 (n. *a bourgeois person*) topanaris, top rankin, ristocrat, risto, money man, saaf han

BOURGEOISIE (n) di society, di bigga heads dem, di risto dem, di top rankin dem, di saaf han dem, di tapanaris dem

BOWLEGGED 1 (adj) bandy leg 2 (*walk bowlegged*) walk pan a roll

BOX FISH 1 (*horned box fish*) cow fish, horn head, buck buck 2 (n. *trunk fish; hornless box fish*) sheep head

BOY bwoy, yout, likkle man

BOYFRIEND 1 (n) spoogy, spoogz, speego, kingman 2 Also see *SWEETHEART*

BRA brazinette, blouse cup

BRACELET 1 (n) bangle 2 (n. *chain bracelet*) chapareyta

BRAG see *BOAST*

BRAGGART fullamout, baggamout

BRAID plat

BRAIDED 1 (adj) plat 2 (n. *braided hair*) plat hair, plat head

BRAIN head piece, head cup, head part, marrow

BRAKE 1 (n. jokingly) brok 2 (v) draw brakes, draw yu brakes

BRANDISH (v. as a weapon or gun) pop off, ease off, rise, flash

BRAVE see *COURAGEOUS*

BRAVERY see *COURAGE*

BRAWL 1 (n) scuffle, frakas, blenda, cobell, plam plam, pam pam, bam bam 2 (v) scuffle, brok fight, ketch fight, palm buckle

BRAZEN 1 (adj) dry yeye, facety, bright, eggs up, bumptious, pomptious 2 (v. *to be brazen*) fly paas yu nest, pass yu place, tek liberty, tek step, eggs up yuself

BREADFRUIT (n) breshi, buju

BREAK 1 (n. *temporary rest*) breeze-off, breeze 2 (n. *rupture*) pop, buss 3 (n. *second chance; opportunity*) bly, ease 4 (*to break*) brok, buss, pop 5 Also see various phrases with *BREAK*

BREAK A PROMISE brok promise, sheriff

BREAK DOWN 1 (*stop working*) pop dung 2 (*break down emotionally*) pop dung 3 (vt. *demolish*) buss dung, brok dung, mash dung, lick dung, kick dung

BREAK EVEN squits

BREAK IN (v. *trespass*) brok di door, brok dung di door, go een

BREAK IN HALF pop

BREAK INTO brok, come een pan, go een pan

BREAK OPEN buss, pop out, tear out

BREAK OUT 1 (*break free*) brok out, get weh 3 (*break out laughing*) buss out a laaf

BREAK OUT buss out, brok out

BREAK THROUGH 1 (*break thru a barrier*) buss chu, brok chu 2 (vi. become famous) buss, name gaan abroad

BREAK UP 1 (*break up a relationship*) brok up, dash weh 2. (*break up into pieces*) buss up, pop up, brok up

BREAKFAST brekfass, brekfuss

BREASTS (n. of a woman) titties, bress, booby, girlz

BREATH 1 (n) bret 2 (n. *bad breath*) sowa mout, stinkin mout 3 (*hold your breath*) cork yu bret 4 (*take a breath*) draw bret 5 (*shortness of breath; difficulty breathing*) shaatnis, pressin

BREATHE (v) draw bret

BRIBE (v. *bribe person X*) peel off X, squeeze X han

BRILLIANT see *INTELLIGENT* or *EXCELLENT*

BRING 1 (*bring person or thing X*) carry X come, bring X come - *Bring them*: kyari dem kom; bring dem kom 2 (*bring back*) carry back

BRITTLE frocky, brickle

BROKE (*out of money*) brok pocket, pocket dry, dry, salt, bawlin

BROKEN 1 (*shattered*) buss, buss up, mash up, brok up 2 (of machine: *not functioning*) buss, pop dung, pop

BROKEN DOWN 1 (*not working*) pop dung 2 (*old and rickety*) ole brok, rookoondung, macheted, buss up, waan fix up

BROKEN OFF 1 (adj) pop off, brok off 2 (*missing the end*) tumpy, tumpa

BROTHEL fuck shop

BROTHER bredda, breds

BROWN see *COMPLEXION*

BRUSH AGAINST groundz, groundz pan

BRUTAL 1 (of weather or punishment or situation) dread, turble   2 (of person or ruler) cowl, evilous, misareble, daak, cruwel, rhygin, turble

BS see *BULLSHIT*

BUFFOON see *FOOL*

BUILD bill

BULGE 1 (n) swell   2 (v) push out, buff out, pulp

BULGING buff out, pulp, pum pum

BULL 1 (n) bull, man cow, bull cow   2 Also see *BULLSHIT*

BULLETS coppa shot, coppa, teeth, corn, grains, lead, teflon, blue steel

BULLSHIT 1 (n. *false claims*) gyow, blar, bag a mout, fullamout, chattinz, lie an story, liad story, mek up story   2 (n. *nonsensical mischief*) mixup, mixup mixup, passa passa, ray ray, fuckry, sheggry, muckry, alms house bizniz, alms house, chupidness, folly grong, poppy show, foolooloops, foolinish, choopity, eedyat bizniz, carry go bring come, parangles, fandangles, runkus, nyamps   3 (v. *to talk bullshit*) run yu mout, sell gyow, gyow, blar, tell lie, mek up story   4 Also see *DRAMA*

BULLSHITTER baggamout, fullamout, gyowah, so so mout, nyamps

BULLY 1 (n) tegereg, chucky, screwface, bull bucka, war monger, sluggard, (female only): virago, war boat, ratchet, champong nanny   2 (v) bad up, hackle up, tek set pan, chuck ih pan, cold up, coas up

BUM (n. *one who begs for a living*) cruff, begga man, come aroun, henkabout, budger, dutty bungle, boogooyaga

BUMP 1 (*a swollen bump on one's head*) coco, cocabola   2 Also see *PIMPLE*

BUMP INTO 1 (*ram*) buck, bunks, run inna   2 (*unexpectedly encounter*) buck up pan, buck up, buck

BUMPKIN 1 (n. *simple country person*) country, country man, country bwoy, country gyal, (derogatory and for male only): kwashi, kwaco, kwao, kwamin, bongo

BUMPY (adj. *as a road*) karra karra

BUNCH 1 (n) bungle   2 (*bunch of*) bag a, set a, bungle a

BUNDLE (n) bungle   2 (v. *tie together in a bundle*) bungle up

BUNDLED 1 (adj) bungle up   2 (*sold together as a package*) married

BURDEN 1 (n. *a burden*) a stress, a bodderation, a crosses, a tax 2 (vt. *to burden*) tax, cost 3 (v. *be a burden to do something*) cost, tax - *It's a burden for him to take care of me*: It a kaas him fi luk aafa mi

BURGLAR tief, puss

BURN 1 (n) bun 2 (vi. *be on fire*) bun, blaze 3 (vt. *destroy by fire*) bun dung, blaze dung

BURNED OUT (n. *exhausted and sick of it all*) pop dung, rev out

BURP (v) buss gyas

BURROW (n. *animal lair*) bung

BUSINESS bizniz, biniz

BURST buss, pop

BUST A MOVE mek a flex

BUST DOWN 1 (v) buss dung, brok dung 2 (v. of door specifically) kick off, brok

BUST OPEN (v) buss, brok, kick off

BUST OUT (v. *break out*) buss out, brok out 2 (v. *take out, as a weapon from a pocket*) pop off, draw 3 (v. *show your skills*) brok out, crack out

BUST THROUGH (v) buss chu, brok chu, cut an go chu, (for door specifically) kick off, brok

BUSY see *CROWDED*

BUTCH 1 (n. *masculine woman*) man royal 2 (adj. of woman: *masculine*) mannish, man royal

BUTT 1 (n. *cigarette butt*) end 2 (n. *buttocks*) batty, backside, bumpa, bumbo, fenda 2 (n. *butt crack*) batty crease 3 (*butt cheek*) batty jaw

BUTTER UP see *FLATTER*

BUTTOCKS batty, backside, bumpa, bumbo, fenda

BUTTON pr: botn

BUY SOMETHING ON CREDIT truss

BUZZED (*slightly drunk*) tipsy, sweet

BY THE TIME by time, betime

BYE see *GOODBYE*

CACKLE 1 (n) keke 2 (v) keke

CAFE (n. *small restaurant*) cookshop, funda

CALAMITY 1 (n) hottaclaps, prekeh, puru, crosses, tribulation, bangarang, bam bam, palangarang, parangles, fandangles, kete, buzu, dog cornpiece 2 (*What a calamity!*) Wat a joke!, Wat a raas!, Wat a liv an bambayeh!, Wat a rocks of ages!, Wat a X! (X=any of the terms listed above or any expletive (See list of expletives in Appendix))

CALENDAR almanac

CALF 1 (n. *back of lower leg*) footback 2 (n. *baby cow*) cow cyaaf

CALICO FLOWER Duppy fly trap, Duppy basket

CALL 1 (n. *phone call*) link 2 (v. *to call by phone*) link, knock 3 (*Call me*) Link mi, Knock mi, Shout mi 4 (v. *call someone something*) cuss smaddy X - *He called my brother a fool*: Him kos mi breda fuul

CALL ATTENTION TO (v. of misdeed or controversy) loud up, rinse, show up, talk up

CALL FOR see *SUMMON*

CALLOUS cowl, dry yeye, donkya, dog heart, daak, ugly, cruwel, evilous, misareble, pagan, cramoojin

CALM DOWN 1 (v. of people: *to stop quarreling*) sekkle, cool, balance, bill, level, quat, eazy yuself, eazy, eaze up, cool out, breeze out, satta, simma dung, cool yu foot, res yu spirit 2 (v. as wind or noise: *level off*) ease up, sekkle dung, sekkle, simma dung, level 3 Also see *CALM DOWN!*

CALM DOWN! Juss cool!, Easy Yuself!, Bill!, Balance!, Level!, Seckle!, Quat!, Cool noh!, Ease up!, Easy noh!, Breathe easy!, Satta!, Simma dung!, Go simma!, Cool yu foot!, Res yu spirit!

CAN 1 (n. of soup or drink) tin 2 (n. for garbage or paint or oil) pan 3 (v. *be able to*) cyan, able fi, able fi cyan, cyan able fi

CAN OPENER cutta

CAN YOU BELIEVE? *Can you believe he went to the beach in a suit and tie?* Im no go a biich ina ful suut an tai?, Yu biliiv mi seh him gaan a biich ina ful suut an tai?

CANCELLED nah kip, kyansl

CAN'T cyaa

CANDLE cyangle

CANDY sweetie

CANNABIS 1 (n) ganja, herb, collie weed, collie, sensi, Ishence, lambsbread, sleng teng, kushumpeng, kush, peng, kaya, iley, oily, macka, sess 2 (n. *highest quality cannabis*) high grade, grades 3 (n. *low quality cannabis*) bush weed 4 Also see SMOKE CANNABIS

CANNED 1 (adj) tin - *Canned mackerel*: tin makril, dutty gyal, wutliss, flash out

CANOE (n) cyano, kunu

CANTANKEROUS 1 cramoojin, ignarant, ig, warify, crabbit, brawlin, trong physic, rowasome, rhygin 2 (n. *a cantankerous person*) cramoojin, tegereg, chucky, war monger, war boat, (female only): virago, ratchet, champong nanny

CANYON gully

CAP 1 (n. *hat*) cyap, snapback, fitted 2 (n. *bottle cap that screws off*) cork, cova, screwcork, bokkle cork 3 (n. *bottle cap that needs to be pulled with an opener*) bokkle stoppa

CAPABLE able fi cyan, fit, pass, qualify

CAPITULATE 1 (vi) bow dung, lap yu tail 2 (vt. *capitulate to*) bow dung tu

CAPSIZE captize, kin ova, pitch ova

CAR cyar

CARAMBOLA (*star fruit*) chiney jimbilin

CARBOHYDRATES see STARCH

CARBONATED WATER aerated wata

CARE ABOUT 1 (v) matta bout, bizniz bout, cya bout, count 2 (*not care about*) no bizniz bout, no matta bout, no cya bout, no check fi, no watch 3 Also see I DON'T CARE

CARE FOR mine, look afta, govern - Also see CARE ABOUT

CAREFREE 1 (of person) gyalantin 2 (of situation) easy, sweet, irie, vibesy

CAREFUL see CAUTIOUS; CONSCIENTIOUS; BE CAREFUL

CARELESS (*negligent*) donkya, nigretful

CARELESSNESS donkya, negret

CARESS (v) brush

CARIBBEAN (n. *the other islands of the Caribbean*) Likkle Foreign

CARPENTER pr: k‍yapinta

CARRY 1 (*transport*) kyari, kya, tangalang 2 (*contain*) hol 3 (*carry X to Y*) kyari X go a Y - *Carry the books to school*: kyari di buk dem go a skuul

CARRY A GRUDGE carry feelinz, carry belly, keep malice, av up

CARRY-ON LUGGAGE han luggage

CART 1 (n. *shopping cart*) trolley 2 (n. *cart for selling wares*) handcart

CASHEW FRUIT cashew apple, kushu apple

CASSAVA (sometimes pr): casaada

CAST EYE (adj. *having a cast eye or amblyopia*) cyaas eye, look a bush

CAT 1 (n) puss, cyat 2 (n. *tom cat*) ram puss

CATARACT yeye daak

CATASTROPHE 1 (n) hottaclaps, prekeh, puru, crosses, tribulation, bangarang, bam bam, palangarang, parangles, fandangles, kete, buzu, dog cornpiece 2 (*What a calamity!*) Wat a joke!, Wat a raas!, Wat a liv an bambayeh!, Wat a rocks of ages!, Wat a X! (X=any of the terms listed above or any expletive (See list of expletives in Appendix))

CATCH ON (v. *catch on to a trick*) sight, sight di rake

CATEGORIZE class - *They categorize me as a poor person*: Dem klaas mi az sofara

CATEGORY cyatigery, set

CATERPILLAR bugaboo

CAUCASIAN see *WHITE PERSON*

CAUGHT 1 (ppl.) ketch 2 (adj. *tangled up*) ketch up 3 (*caught up in*) ketch up inna, mix up inna, blen up inna

CAUGHT UP see *CAUGHT*

CAUSE A STIR mek alarm, hype up, rail up, wild up, bring dong excitement, call crowd, draw dong scandal

CAUTION 1 (n. *attention; restraint*) caution, sense 2 (v. *admonish*) warn 3 Also see *BE CAREFUL!*

CAUTIOUS 1 (adj. *hesitant due to fear or inexperience*) bummy 2 Also see *BE CAUTIOUS*

CAUTIOUSLY 1 (adv) one one, likkle likkle, bit bit 2 (v. *move cautiously*) pinch an bite, tek time

CAVE (n) stonehole, bung

CELEBRATE 1 (vt. *toast; honour*) big up, sallute 2 (vi. *have fun; party*) fulljoy yuself, sree, lively up yuself, go haad

CELEBRATION 1 (n. *cheer*) jollification 2 (n. *festival; event*) jamminz, spree, jollification

CELEBRITY 1 (n. *famous person*) supa dupa, big supa, big supe 2 (n. *small-time celebrity; locally popular person*) star bwoy, star gyal

CEMETERY simichri, bone yaad, buringgrung, burying grung

CENTIPEDE fortyleg

CEREAL Corn flakes (applies to any brand of dry cereal)

CEREMONY 1 (n. derogatory: *pomp and ceremony*) poppy show - *I don't want to go thru the whole damn ceremony*: Mi no waan go chruu di wol dyam papi shuo 2 Also see *WAKE*

CERTAIN 1 (*specific*) suttn, direck 2 (of person: *sure*) suttn, shuor 3 (of information: *definitely true*) suttn, shuor 4 (of plan: *confirmed*) set, lock, suttn

CERTIFICATE pr: surfitikit - see *BIRTH CERTIFICATE*

CHALLENGE 1 (n. *hardshis*) crosses, trials 2 (v. *confront; take someone on*) tess 3 Also see *DARE*

CHALLENGING 1 ruff, hard 2 Also see *HARSH*

CHAMBER POT chimmy, chim chim, kimbo lady

CHANCE 1 (n. *opportunity*) bly 2 (v. *take a chance on*) tek chance pan

CHANGE 1 (n. *loose change; coins*) loosaz, coppa, duss, silva 2 (v) change up

CHANNEL (v. *channel a spirit*) call dung

CHANNELING (n. *spirit mediumship*) myal

CHAOS see *MAYHEM*

CHARCOAL (n) coal (*live burning coal*) fya coal

CHARGE 1 (n. *fee*) chaaj, tax 2 (v. *demand payment*) tax 3 (*accuse*) cuse 4 (*rush at*) rush, run dung, run een pan, fly dung pan

CHARM 1 (n. *lucky charm; talisman*) gyaad 2 (v. *flirt; entice*) lyrics, sweetmout

CHARRED 1 (of food) bun-bun 2 (n. *charred part of meat or food*) bun bun

CHASE (v) run dung, mek afta

CHASE OFF run, jive weh - *Chase them off!* Ron dem!; Jraiv dem weh! - *Chase off the enemy*: Jraiv weh di enemi, Ron di enemi

CHATTER 1 (n. *idle talk*) chattinz, labba labba, ray ray, ray tay tay, su su, seh seh, passa passa, blar, labrish, yabba yabba, warra warra, tarra warra, carry-go-bring-come, come-come-seh 2 (v. *to chatter*) run up yu mout, fly yu mout, labba labba, labrish, chat chat, labba up yu mout, yabba yabba

CHATTERBOX labbamout, chatty chatty mout, baggamout, yabba mout

CHATTY 1 (*talkative in a friendly way*) vibesy, jolly 2 (*too chatty*) chatty chatty, labba labba, labbamout, long tongue, yabbamout

CHAYOTE (*Sechium edule*) cho cho

CHEAP 1 (*cheap in price and lacking quality*) crebbeh crebbeh, tufenkeh, fenkeh fenkeh, fluxy, dibby dibby, wutlis, wuklis, batta foot, batta ears, sketel, streggeh, screbbeh screbbeh, kaba kaba, chamba chamba, boogooyaga, butu, common, half inch, half staff, knockoff, riff raff, casco, tikki tikki, jingbang, pyaa pyaa, no wut, no use, pop dung, ol bruck, nyamps 2 (*penny pinching*) chinky

CHEAT 1 (v. *deceive; swindle*) jinnal, bait up, fool up, cyaad, bandulu, lamps, craff, samfai, maringle, pop 2 (*cheat on sexually*) gi bun - *Lucy cheated on her man*: Lusi gi har man bon

CHEATER (n) jinnal, Jim Screechy, radge

CHEATING 1 (n. in business or sports or gambling) chicaney, jimscreechy, jinnalship, draw cyaad, cramoojin, samfai ting, almshouse business, almshouse, camaroun, come-aroun 2 (n. of relationships: *infidelity*) bun

CHECK MARK ticky

CHECK OUT 1 (v. *take a look at*) pree, check, tek a stock a 2 (v. *observe*) penny, watch an pree 3 (v. *pay at register; process purchase*) cyash, cyash out 4 (*Check it out; Look into it*) Pree it, Check it, Penitrate it, Tek a stock, Look bout it

CHECK OVER pree, tek a stock a

CHECK THIS OUT! see *LISTEN UP!* or *LOOK AT THIS*

CHECKERED /CHEQUERED checky checky

CHEEK jaw

CHEEKY facety, bright

CHEER 1 (n. *positive energy; merriment*) vibes, gladness, niceness, jollification, upliffment, upfulness 2 (vi. *whistle and shout*) rail up 3 (vt. *encourage with whistles and applause*) hype, gi X a hype (X=person), salute 4 (with gunshots) lick shot fi, buss shot fi, blaze gun fi 5 Also see *ROOT FOR*

CHEERFUL 1 (of person) irie, upful, jolly 2 (of music or art or place) irie, upful, positive, jolly

CHEERFULNESS vibes, gladness, jollification, niceness, upfulness

CHEST (n. *metal storage container*) tin case, chunk

CHEW chaw

CHEWING GUM wriggleys, ching gum

CHEWY chowy

CHICK (*baby chicken*) fowl

CHICKEN fowl

CHICKEN POX Fowl Pox, Yaws

CHICO FRUIT (*Sapota achras*) neesberry

CHIEF 1 (n. *ruler; leader*) gorgon, ginigog, guineagog, big supe, don 2 (adj) toppa top

CHILD 1 (n) pickney, pitney 2 (*illegitimate child*) outside pickney, out chile, (if father doesn't know it's not his own) jacket 3 (*last and final child; youngest child*) wash belly, lassy 4 (*naughty child*) leggo beast, jingbang

CHILDISH picknify

CHILDLIKE picknify

CHILL see *HANG OUT* or *RELAX*

CHILL OUT see *HANG OUT* or *RELAX* or *CALM DOWN*

CHILL OUT! see *SETTLE DOWN!*

CHILL OUT WITH 1 (v) endz out wid, bill back wid, bill wid, medz out wid, medz wid, flex wid, hol a vibes wid, wibes wid, jooks wid, cool out wid, cool wid, lime wid, satta wid, cotch wid 2 Also see *ASSOCIATE WITH*

CHILL WITH 1 (*relax with*) endz out wid, bill back wid, bill wid, medz out wid, medz wid, flex wid, hol a vibes wid, wibes wid, jooks wid, cool out wid, cool wid, lime wid, satta wid, cotch wid 2 (*associate with*) move wid, flex wid, par wid, roll wid

CHINESE 1 (adj) chiney 2 (n. *Chinese person*) chiney, squeez eye, Missa Chin, (derogatory): nyam-dog

CHOCOLATE (sometimes pr): chaaklik

CHOMP (v. *eat loudly and sloppily*) chamba chamba

CHOP OFF (*sever*) wap, lass off, bobbit

CHOPPED UP (*hacked up*) lass up, macheted, nyaka nyaka up, saaka saaka up, malahack, mammick

CHRISTMAS pr: krismos (n. *Christmas Eve*) Grandmarket Night

CHRISTOPHENE (*Sechium edule*) cho cho

CHUBBY see *FAT*

CIGARETTE fronta, cat, blindz

CINEMA (n. *movie theater*) pichaz, pictures

CISTERN cestan, sestant

CLASSY 1 (of person) stoosh, society, risto, topanaris, top rankin 2 (of place) stoosh, quality, kris

CLAW han

CLEAN 1 (adj. *fresh; spotless*) criss 2 (*tidy*) criss, primps 3 (v. *to tidy up*) primps up, pran up (*to clean hastily and incompletely*) give a lick an a promise, gyow out, gyow, palla palla

CLEAN UP 1 (v. of person's appearance) sort out, dechakalize, primps up 2 (v. of place: *spruce up*) dechakalize, primps up, pran up 3 (*clean up hastily*) gi a lick an a promise, gyow out, gyow, palla palla up

CLEAN UP YOUR ACT fix up, sort out yuself, dechakalize yuself, balance, liff up yuself, raise up yuself, set up yuself

CLEAN-SHAVEN 1 (adj) clean-face 2 Also see *BALD or BUZZ-CUT*

CLEANING LADY helpa

CLEANSE 1 (n. of intestines: *a flushing out*) operation, washout 2 (v. *clear the intestines*) operate, wash out 3 Also see *CLEAN*

CLENCH/ CLENCHED toonch up, toonk up

CLEVER 1 sumaat, skill, no easy, soonah, cunny 2 Also see *ELUSIVE*

CLIFF gullyside

CLIMAX 1 (n. *climax of a story*) bump 2 (n. *orgasm*) extasy, agony 3 (v. of story: *reach a climax*) come up to bump 4 (*achieve orgasm*) reach climax

CLITORIS (n) punny tongue, pum pum tongue

CLOSE 1 (v. of door) shet, lock, push up 2 (v. of mouth or lid) shet, lock, kibba 3 (v. of business or building) lock 4 (adj. as friends) tick, laka batty an bench, a points, groundz 5 Also see *NEAR; APPROXIMATELY*

CLOSED 1 (of door) lock, shet 2 (of building or business) lock up

CLOSET hanga, press

CLOT (v. *coagulate*) sleep up, set

CLOTHES 1 (n) clothes 2 (*nice clothes*) crissaz 3 (*everyday clothes*) judgin 4 (*old tattered clothes*) reg jegz, jeng jeng, yagga yagga, yeg yeg, rullucks, lurrucks

CLOUDY 1 (*overcast*) bleaky, dark up 2 (*unclear, smudged up*) mud up

CLOWN 1 (n) bubu 2 (*social clown; class clown*) mascot 3 (*social idiot; a joke*) claffy, cartoon, mascot, menkeh, iddyboo, sample, prekeh, poppy show, acrobat

CLOYING 1 (adj) cliding 2 Also see *STICKY* or *SYRUPY*

CLUB (*billy club; truncheon*) baton stick, jonka

CLUE 1 (n) prips 2 (v. *give a helpful clue*) prips off, pinch

CLUELESS 1 (adj) dark, simple, no know bout, no know di time, no know wah clock a strike, no know what o'clock, no know di Schweppes, born back a cow, born when yu big, grow wid yu granny, juss fall out a di truck 2 (n. *clueless person*) prekeh, simpleton, salad, kunumunu, menkeh, goose, cuffy, kwashi, kwaco, bongo, moko

CLUMSY (*lacking physical coordination*) baff han, waggaty, bufutu

CLUSTER 1 (n) bungle 2 (vi) bungle up, hitch up tugedda

CLUTTER 1 (n) chaka chaka 2 (v) chaka chaka up, chuck up

CLUTTERED chaka chaka, chuck up chuck up, nyaka nyaka

CLUTZ /CLUTZY baf han

COAGULATE sleep up, set

COAX inveegle

COBRA pr: kabra

COCK 1 (n. *rooster*) cock chicken 2 see *PENIS*

COCKROACH roach, (*large cockroach*): drumma, night janga

COCONUT 1 (n) cocanat, coke nut, dread nut 2 (n. *fresh green coconut*) jelly, waata cocanat 3 (*coconut water*) jelly waata

COD salt fish

COERCE inveegle, trongmout

COINCIDENCE joke

COINS loosaz, coppa, duss, silva

COLD 1 (n. *low temperatures*) kowl 2 (n. *respiratory infection; head cold*) mole cole, cole inna di mole 3 (adj) cole 4 (*very cold*) kowl 5 Also see *CRUEL*

COLD FEET (v. *get cold feet*) tun back

COLD BLOODED see *CALLOUS; RUTHLESS*

COLLECT 1 (vt) callek, gyadda up, ketch up, prah prah 2 (vi) kom tugedda, calleck, gyadda, rope een, fall een

COLLIDE 1 (vi) buck, bunks 2 (*collide with*) buck, bunks

COLLIDE WITH buck, bunks, boof, baff

COMBATIVE warify, cuss cuss, ignarant, ig, cross, hot skull, brawlin, trong physic, rhygin

COME 1 (v) faawud 2 (of female: *reach orgasm*) reach climax 3 (of male: *ejaculate*) buss a juice, pop

COME ACROSS 1 (*encounter*) buck up pan, buck 2 (*seem*) come een, tan

COME BACK faawud back, rally back, return back

COME CLOSE 1 (v) draw near 2 (v. *almost hit the target*) juss miss, likklemost lick

COME HERE! Come!, Come ya man!, Faawud!

COME TO A HEAD (*reach a climax or tipping point*) come up to bump

COMEDIAN brinjah

COMFORT (n. *bliss*) niceness 2 (v. *to comfort; soothe*) hush

COMMEND rate up, big up, large up, sallute, liff up, count

COMMENT pr: koment (v) jrap two wud

COMMENTARY pr: ko̱menchri

COMMITMENT (n. *dedication*) gumption, trong eye

COMMITTED 1 (adj. *focused and ambitious*) ambitionable, trong mind, trong eye, purpose, no easy 2 (adj. *obligated*) muss an boun, lock, een deh, deep inna it

COMMON 1 (*ubiquitous*) common as salt, like rice, like dut, like san 2 (n. *simple; ordinary*) common fowl, white fowl

COMMOTION 1 (n) kanfusion, piece a noise, bag a noise, galangin, bangarang, palangarang, palam pam, bam bam, jingbang, hell an powda house, ruption, ruption, rig jig 2 (v. *cause commotion*) mek alarm, hype up, rail up, wild up, bring dong excitement, call crowd, draw dong scandal

COMMUNE (n) cyamp

COMMUNITY pr: ko̱miniti - Also see *COMMUNE*

COMPACT (adj. *dense*) tight, pack up

COMPANION 1 (n) kombolo, quabs 2 Also see *FRIEND*

COMPARABLE (*comparable in age or status*) size

COMPARE pree tugeda, comparison

COMPASSION (*feel compassion for*) feel a way fi, sorry fi

COMPATIBLE 1 (as people) irie, skinteet, goundz 2 (*very compatible; inseparable*) a points, laka batty an bench

COMPETE (*compete aggressively*) war

COMPETENT see *SKILLED*

COMPETITION 1 (n. *battle of egos and reputations between two people*) war, clash 2 (n. *competition between two sound systems*) clash

COMPETITIVE 1 (*competitive in a spiteful and greedy way*) crabbit, warify, badmind 2 (*motivated and determined*) no easy, skill, trong eye, trong mind, purpose

COMPLAIN 1 (v) cry, grumble, raise a kite 2 (*complain against; whine about*) cry pan 3 (vi. *whine*) run up yu mout, ningy ningy

COMPLETE 1 (*finished*) done, box off 2 (*comprehensive*) full 3 (*utter*) peer, bare, bey, pure, so so, lone - *It's complete mayhem out there*: A bier mixop out deh 4 (v. *finish*) done, box off

COMPLETELY 1 (*utterly*) strait, bline, dead, full - *You're completely insane*: Yu schriet mad; Yu blain mad; etc. 2 (pred adv. *thoroughly*) done, full, full stop, clear, clean clean

COMPLEX 1 (n. *housing complex*) scheme, housin scheme 2 (*complicated*) technical, sipple, too haad

COMPLEXION 1 (*very light brown complexion*) high color, clear skin 2 (n. *female of lighter-toned-brown part-African complexion*) brownin, reds 3 (n. *male of lighter-toned-brown part-African complexion*) brown man, reds 4 (n. *person of very dark African complexion*) blacks, blacka, burn corn, bun caan, blacky tutus, nega, bongo 5 (*of light mixed-African complexion*) yellow, clear, red 6 Also see *ALBINO*

COMPLICATED 1 (*not simple*) technical 2 (*difficult to control; hard to grasp*) sipple

COMPLICATIONS parangles

COMPLIMENT 1 (n) big up - *Pay her a compliment*: Gi har a bigop 2 (v. *pay a complment to*) rate, rate up, big up, large up 3 (*go well with; balance out*) help - *The wine compliments the fish*: Di wain a elp di fish

COMPLIMENTARY pr: komplimenchri

COMPREHEND penetrate, annastan, ovastan, ovahs, sabi

CON see *SWINDLE*

CON MAN samfai man, bandulu, scyamma, alias man, radge

CONCEITED 1 (*full of oneself*) nuff, too hype, bumptious, pomptious, swell head, puff up, extra, consequential 2 Also see *PRETENTIOUS; BOASTFUL*

CONCERN 1 (n. *issue*) matta 2 (v. *pertain to*) haffi du wid 3 Also see *CONCERNED; WORRIES*

CONCERNED 1 (adj) bizniz, response 2 (v. *be concerned about*) bizniz bout, response bout, matta bout, check fi, watch 3 Also see *I'M NOT CONCERNED*

CONDEMN 1 (*strongly oppose*) bun, fight gainst, lick out gainst, bun out, bun faya pan, fling faya pan, dash faya pan, chant dung 2 (*condemn to*) sen go a

CONDENSED MILK sweet milk, tin milk

CONDESCENDING see *STUCK UP*

CONDITIONAL TENSE (The Jamaican conditionals follow the same pattern as the conditionals in Standard English: The future conditional (type 1) uses the present tense. The present irreal conditional (Type 2) uses the simple past tense. And the past conditional (Type 3) uses the past perfect tense. Note that the Jamaican past perfect tense is the same as the Jamaican simple past tense when the phrase or question is affirmative) - *If you are wise you will go*: If yu waiz yu wi go - *If you were wise you would go*: If yu did waiz yu wuda go - *If you had been wise you would have gone*: If yu did waiz yu wuda did go - *If you hadn't been late you would have passed*: If yu neva did liet yu wuda did paas.

CONDOM boot, jacket, rubbahs, bullet-proof vest, vest

CONFIDENT (adj) confidence - *I am very confident*: Mi wel kanfidens

CONFINE TO /CONFINED TO huol tu

CONFIRMED (adj. *certain*) set, lock, suttn

CONFLICT see *DISAGREEMENT or FIGHT*

CONFRONT 1 (*aggressively or assertively confront*) shape up to, draw dung pan, push up pan, flip up pan 2 (*deal with; face*) shape up tu, deal wid

CONFRONTATIONAL warify, cuss cuss, ignarant, ig, crabbit, cantankarous, rowasome, trong physic, virago

CONFUSE confuse up, mix up, mud up

CONFUSED 1 (adj) canfuse, head mix up, head craab up 2 (*get confused*) tun fool

CONFUSING 1 (adj. *unclear*) mud up 2 (*daunting; hard to grasp*) sipple, technical

CONFUSION see *COMMOTION; DRAMA; MISCOMMUNICATION*

CONGRATULATE big up, large up, salute, wowatu

CONGRATULATIONS 1 (n) big up, large up, hype, ratings, salute 2 Also see *CONGRATULATIONS!*

CONGRATULATIONS! Big up!, Big up yuself!, Large up yuself!, Bare ratings!, Ray!, Up!, Up! Up Up!, Wowatu!

CONNECTIONS 1 (for social or business purposes) links 2 (*support from people in power*) backative

CONQUER see *DEFEAT*

CONSCIENTIOUS conscious, positive, upful, ites, goody goody

CONSCIOUS see *AWARE or CONSCIENTIOUS*

CONSCIOUSNESS see *AWARENESS*

CONSENT TO gree tu

CONSIDERING THAT chu, afta, as, since as how

CONSTIPATE bine, bine up

CONSTIPATED haad boun, bine up, bung up, block up, brice

CONSTIPATION bine, brice

CONSUME 1 (v) nyam 2 (*use up*) nyam up - *Big cars consume a lot of gas*: Big kyaar nyam op wol iip a gyas

CONTEMPLATE 1 (vt) tink pan, medz, medz ova, penny, penetrate 2 (vi. *reflect*) hol a medz, medz, hol a medi, penetrate, study yu head, consida yu head

CONTEMPTUOUS see *CONCEITED*

CONTENT (adj. *pleased*) cool, good, irie, inna yu ackee, inna yu gungo

CONTENTMENT gladness

CONTINUE 1 (*carry on*) push on, press on, galang galang 2 (*continue + -ing*) keep on a X (X=verb) - *continue working*: kipaan a wok

CONTRARIAN trong mout, facety, argumentable

CONTROL 1 (v) canchol, mantrol, manchol 2 (*dominate*) mantrol, canchol up 3 (*restrict*) clap dung, clap dung pan 3 Also see *MANAGE*

CONTROVERSY pr: kan<u>tra</u>vasi 1 (n. *controversy in general*) ray ray, passa passa, bag a argument, bag a chat, mix up, ism-schism 2 (n. *a specific controversy*) mix up, cass cass, passa passa, bangarang, parangles, fandangles

CONVERSATION 1 (n. *a conversation*) a reason, a reasonin 2 (v. *have a conversation*) chat, reason, hol a reason, hol a vibes

COOK 1 (vi) run a pot, bubble pot 2 (vt) run - *Let's cook some curry chicken*: Mek wi ron a kori chikin 3 (*cook with others to make a communal meal*) run a boat

COOKIE (n) biskit

COOKING POT 1 (*very large pot*) bellagut, big daddy pot 2 (*with handles on both sides*) dutchy 3 (*black iron pot with one long handle*) bun pan 4 (*covered pot with straight handle*) jestah 5 (*earthenware pot*) yabba

COOL 1 (of person: *socially in tune and respected*) hype, shot, bad, a lead, a hapm, name brand, artical, bonafide, bashy, cris, ites 2 (adj. of thing or vehicle) hype, mad, craab up, bad, shot, a lead, a happen, name brand, criss 3 (of place: *stylish; happening*) hype, mad, craab up, shot, a lead, a happen 4 (of clothes: *stylish; admired*) sell off, hype, mad, bad, craab up, tun up, name brand, shot, a lead, a happen, bashy - Also see *FRIENDLY; COOL OFF; EVERYTHING'S COOL*

COOL OFF 1 (*cool off physically*) breeze off 2 (*cool off emotionally*) cool out, cool, breeze out, bill, sekkle, balance, level, quat, satta, res yu spirit

COP see *POLICE*

COPE 1 (*make do*) get on, run wid it, tun yu han mek fashion 2 (vi. *cope emotionally*) manage, run wid it

COPY see *IMITATE*

COPYCAT (n. *one who imitates*) carbon, knockoff, follow-fashion monkey

CORD pr: kaad

CORK pr: kaak (n. of wine bottle) stoppa

CORKSCREW (n) pullcork

CORNROWS (hairstyle) cane row

CORNED BEEF bully beef, caan beef, tin beef

CORRECT 1 (adj. *right*) carrek   2 (*proper; appropriate*) proppa, riteful   3 (vt. *to correct person X; bring X into line*) draw X up, gi X a sticky, gi X a hook-stick   4 Also see *THAT'S RIGHT*

CORRUPT /CORRUPTED 1 (adj. *corrupt*) dutty, mud up   2 (vt. *to corrupt*) mud up   3 (adj. *corrupted*) mud up

COUCH (n) setty

COULD 1 (v) coulda   2 (*could have* + verb X) coulda en X, couldan X, coulda did X   3 (*That could be*) Coulda so ih go

COULDN'T 1 (v) couldn   2 (*That couldn't be*) Cyaa go so

COUNT (v) check

COUNTRY see *RURAL* or *COUNTRYSIDE* or *BACKWOODS*

COUNTRY PERSON country, country man, country bwoy, country gyal, (derogatory and for male only): kwashi, kwaco, kwao, kwamin, bongo

COUNTRYSIDE 1 country, yountry   2 Also see *BACKWOODS*

COURAGE gumption, heart, talawah

COURAGEOUS bad, out an bad, no easy, tuffa, talawah, bentasome

COVER 1 (n) cova   2 (v) kibba, cova, shut

COVET 1 (v) grudge   2 Also see *CRAVE; ENVY*

COVETOUS badmind, red yeye, grudgeful, craven, dry yeye, cubbitch, co<u>vee</u>tchous, licky licky

COWARD weakheart, soffaz, saps, duppy bat, fraidy puss, bait, mantu

COWARDLY saaf, saps, fraidy fraidy, fenkeh fenkeh, pyaa pyaa

CRACK 1 (n) line 2 (adj. *full of cracks*) line line, liney liney, crack up crack up 2 (v. *to crack; rupture*) pop

CRACK UP 1 (*laugh hysterically*) pop up, buss up a laaf, ded wid laaf, kin ova a laaf 2 Also see *GO CRAZY*

CRACKED (adj. *having a crack*) av line 2 (*full of cracks*) liney liney, crack up crack up

CRAMP 1 (n *side cramp*) stitch pain, stitchiz 2 (n. *abdominal cramps*) gripe, bad belly 3 (v. *cramp someone's style*) flop X style, cole X up

CRASH 1 (n. *accident*) lickup 2 (v. of computer) seize up 3 (*crash into*) buck, bunks, boof, baff 4 Also see *SLEEP*

CRAVE 1 (v) henka fi 2 (*greedily crave*) graff afta

CRAYFISH janga, lobsta, black hog

CRAZY 1 (*not quite sane*) touch, no righted, no balance, head no good, head lick, maddy maddy 2 (*totally insane*) mad, full mad, gaan, head gaan, head tek waata, drink mad puss piss, nyam mad puss brain 3 (n. *crazy person; insane person*) madix 5 Also see *GO CRAZY; DRIVE CRAZY; UNRULY*

CREATE pr: kriet

CREDIT 1 (n. *recognition*) mention 2 (vt. *acknowledge; recognize*) mention, call up 3 (v. *buy on credit*) truss

CRIME 1 (n. *crookedness; crime in general*) bandulu, (*violent crime*) badness, (*theft*) tiefry 2 (n. *a robbery; a specific criminal act*) jooks

CRIMINAL 1 (n) badlaw, steppa, mafia 2 (n. *fugitive*) hot steppa, road runna 3 Also see *THIEF; THUG; GANGSTER; CON MAN*

CRINGE 1 (*recoil*) quinge 2 (*make a facial expression of disgust*) kin up yu face, mek up yu face 3 (*cause person X to cringe*) nedge X teet, put X teet pan edge - *That sound makes me cringe*: Da soun deh a nej mi tiit

CRISIS hottaclapse

CRITICAL (*judgemental*) judge judge, mekam pekam

CRITICIZE 1 (vt. of person: *judge; harp on*) hype pan 2 (of idea or behavior; *decry*) bun 3 Also see *PUT DOWN; CONDEMN*

CROCODILE (*native Jamaican crocodile; Crocodilus acutus*) aligeta

CROOKED 1 (*unaligned*) cyaas, offish 2 (*illegal; devious*) bandulu, samfai, alias 3 Also see *DISHONEST*

CROSS 1 (v. of a gap or river) come ova, cut ova 2 (v. of a street) cross, cut cross, cut ova 3 (v. *cross one's legs*) cut ten

CROSS-BREED ryal

CROTCH 1 (n) crotches 2 (v. of female: *show crotch*) skin out

CROWD 1 (n. *multitude*) massive 2 (n. *unruly crowd; throng*) jing bang 3 (vt. *overcrowd*) crowd up, full up, chuck up, chock up 4 (vi. *congregate*) run een, rush een, fly dung come een

CROWDED 1 (adj) pack up, chuck up, craab up 2 (*packed; super crowded*) lock dung, ram, pack up, cork, chock up, chuck up

CRUDE 1 (*primitive*) raw chaw, wackle an dawb, bitch-up 2 (*vulgar*) butu, brawlin, raw chaw, unmannersable, cruff, crebbeh, screbbeh, streggeh, hoggish, renk, outa aada, nassy, slack, slacka, zutupeck, zutupeng, boogooyaga, boogoo boogoo

CRUEL 1 (of person) cruwel, cowl, dog heart, ugly, daak, turble, evilous, misareble, dry yeye, ded yeye, pagan, heathen 2 (of act or behavior) cruwel, cowl, evilous, dog-heart, misareble, ugly, turble

CRUELTY ugly, ugliness, dog heart

CRUMBLED crush up crush up, mash up mash up

CRUMBLY frocky, brickle, sheddy sheddy

CRUMBS dregs, dribblinz

CRUSH 1 (v) mash, crunge 2 (v. *have a crush on*) pree, penny, check fi, like off 3 Also see *DEFEAT* or *DESTROY*

CRUSHED 1 (*crushed into small pieces*) mash up, chunk up, crunge up 2 Also see *DESTROYED*

CRUTCH arm stick

CRYBABY (adj. *like a crybaby; prone to crying excessively*) bawli bawli

CUCUMBER kukumba

CUDDLE 1 (vi. *cuddle up together*) squeeze, wrap up 2 (*cuddle with*) wrap up wid

CUNNILINGUS 1 (n. *oral sex on female*) bow, swipe, numba chree 2 (n. derogatory: *one who performs cunnilingus*) bowcat, bowaz, nyammaz, swipah, cannibal, nyamatan, eatan, oral, lappa, licka, nyammara, nyamma 3 (v. *perform cunnilingus*) see *EAT OUT*

CUNNING 1 (adj) trickify, chicaney, deceptious, cunny, no easy 2 (n) ginnalship, trickify, bandulu-ness, chicaney, cunny

CURB (n. *roadside*) bankin

CURDLE hard up, sleep up

CURE pr: kyor

CURSE 1 (n. *hex*) guzu, buzu 2 (vi. *use foul language*) cuss badwud, fling badwud, chip badwud; (vulgar): cuss rass, cuss claat, buss two claat, chip two claat, fling two claat 3 (vt cuss out) trace, wile up, rax up, run up yu mout pan, trow wud pan 4 (vt. *condemn*) kuss, badmout, bun out 5 Also see list of expeletives in Appendix

CURSORY hastey, shaat-han

CUSS 1 (*use foul language*) cuss badwud, fling badwud, chip badwud (vulgar) cuss rass, cuss claat, buss two claat, chip two claat, fling two claat 2 Also see *CUSS OUT* and see list of expeletives in Appendix

CUSS OUT 1 trace, wile up, rax up, run up yu mout pan, trow wud pan, cuss claat pan, cuss bad wud afta, fling bad wud afta 2 Also see *INSULT; BERATE; CURSE*

CUSTOMER cussomaz

CUT 1 (n. *slit; laceration*) cut 2 (n. *reduction*) cut 3 (v. *to cut*) cut, lass, plaw, huff 4 (v. *cut roughly*) saaka, nyaka nyaka, chamba 5 (v. *cut in half*) pop 6 (v. *cut into a cue*) bore 7 (v. *cut classes; ditch school*) skull 8 (adj. *severed*) lass off, bobbit - Also see *CUT DOWN; CUT UP; CUT OFF*

CUT AT (*slice and slash at*) lass up, nyaka nyaka, saaka saaka, malahack, bill

CUT DOWN 1 (v. as a tree) cut dung, chop dung 2 (*beratingly insult*) trace

CUT OFF 1 (*sever*) wap, lass off, bobbit 2 (adj. *severed*) lass off, bobbit 3 (*missing the end; having the end chopped off*) tumpy, tumpa

CUT UP 1 (*to cut into pieces*) chunk up, chop up 2 (of person: *slash up violently with knife or weapon*) lass up, chamba chamba up 3 (of person: *slashed up by knife or sharp object*) lass up, macheted, nyaka nyaka, saaka saaka, chamba chamba

DAMAGE (v) mash, brok

DAMAGED (adj) mash up, brok up

DAMN 1 (adj) dyam, rahtid, Also see list of expletives in Appendix 2 (*Damn!*) Cho!, Cha!, Wat a stress!, Woy!, Lawd!, Lawdamassy!, Also see list of exclamations in Appendix

DAMN! Cho!, Cha!, Wat a stress!, Woy!, Lawd!, Lawdamassy!, Also see list of exclamations in Appendix

DANCE 1 (v) brok out, drop foot, kick up, pudung a piece a dancin 2 Also see *FREAK or TWERK*

DANGEROUS (of situation) danjarous, sticky, hot, rhygin

DARE 1 (n) tess, seh-fi 2 (vt. *to dare person X to do Y*) tess X fi Y, seh X fi Y 3 (*I dare you to Y*) mi seh fi Y 4 (*if you dare*) ef yu bad

DASTARDLY dutty, nassy, ceitful, low run, low, ugly, evilous, wikid, turble, slack, pagan, heathen, cussid, custed

DATE 1 (vi. *be in a dating relationship*) deal, deh, inna dealinz, carry straw 2 (vt) deh wid, a go rung wid

DAUNTING deep

DAWN 1 (n) daylight, fuss light, day cut, gunfayah, day break 2 (v) light

DAY OF RECKONING Ben Johnson day

DAYBREAK fuss light, day light, day cut, gun faya

DAYCARE CENTER creech

DAZED stontid (from *stunned*), tontid, head craab up, frass

DEAF 1 (adj) deaf iez, mumu 2 (n. *deaf person*) deaf iez, mumu

DEAL 1 (*arrangement*) dealinz, runninz 2 (*fair deal*) coco fi yam 3 (*useless or pointless exchange*) black dog fi monkey 4 (*raw deal; unfair exchange*) bum rap, basket fi carry waata 5 (v. *buy and sell*) juggle 6 (*make a big deal out of nothing*) fuss, mek mickle out a muckle 7 Also see *DEAL WITH*

DEAL WITH 1 (*sort out; resolve*) look about, look bou, look afta, clear, maths out 2 (as profession: *work with*) deal wid, juggle, look afta, canchol, govern 3 (*contend with; put up with*) deal wid, shape up tu, tek, angle, run wid, liv out 3 (*deal with it; improvise; make do with it*) deal wid it, run wid it, liv it out, get on, push on chu, try a way, tun yu han mek fashion, fadge

DECADENCE slackness, nassiness, dutty livity, luu ting, freaky bizniz, freakiness

DECADENT freaky, funky, slack, slacka-slacka, luu, mud up, leggo, outlaw

DECEIT jinnalship, luu, deceptiousness, twin-mout, twin-coat, back-an-belly, chicaney, cramoojin, samfai, almshouse, camaroun, come-aroun

DECEITFUL ceitful, deceptious, shakey, sipple, sipple an lie, trickify, jinnal, samfai, bandulu, switchy, back and belly, two mout, twin mout, twin coat

DECEIVE (*trick; swindle*) jinnal, bait up, fool up, draw cyaad pan, cyaad, bandulu, lamps, craff, samfai, maringle, pop

DECENT (adj. of person) heartical, bonafide, deestant, goody goody, goodup goodup

DECEPTION jinnalship, luu, olo, banduulu, back-an-belly, twin mout

DECEPTIVE 1 (adj) deceptious, trickify, sipple, shakey   2 Also see *DECEITFUL*

DECIDE (*make a decision to do something*) mek a flex, mek a move

DECIDED (adj. *already established; already determined*) set, lock

DECISION (v. *make a decision*) mek a flex, set a plan

DECORATE pretty up, artify, primps up

DECORATIONS see *ORNAMENTS*

DECORATIVE artify, splendacious

DECREASE 1 (n. *reduction*) dropoff, ease-up, cut-dung   2 (v. to *decrease*) come dung, drop off, cut dung, ease up, reduce

DEDICATE (Rasta terms) livicate, Idicate

DEDICATION 1 (*commitment*) gumption, trong eye   2 (*tribute*) livication, Idication

DEFAME (v) wash yu mout pan X (X=person being defamed)

DEFEAT 1 (*heavy defeat*) shelldung, kuffin, tumpinz, murderation, floggin   2 (v) shell dung, lick, lick fi six, slew, wyah, tump, clawt, duss, vank, trample

DEFICIENT waan fix up

DEFINITELY 1 (fronted adv) no muss   2 (pred adv) fi chu, fi sure, yes - *It will definitely fail*: It no mos a go flap, It a go flap fi chruu, It a go flap yes, It a go flap fi shuor   2 Also see *YES; TOTALLY!*

DEGENERATE see *WORTHLESS; IMMORAL; TROUBLEMAKER*

DELAY 1 (*a delay of time*) lay lay   2 (v. *linger; procrastinate*) linga, lay lay, hitch, diggle daggle, tarry   3 (*hesitate*) hitch, tan

DELETE ex out

DELICIOUS eat-nice, nice, sweet, boonoonoonoos

DELIGHT 1 (*joy*) pleasuration, fulljoy, fullyjoyment   2 (vt. *please*) sweet

DELUSIONAL 1 (adj) luu, no righted inna yu head, no righted, no balance, touch, sheg up, no heng on right   2 (v. *to be delusional*) av no sense, liv luu, drink mad puss piss, nyam mad puss brain

DEMAND (v) bawl fi - *They are demanding better pay*: Dem a baal fi a riez

DEMENTIA (v. *to suffer from dementia; be demented*) head tek waata

DEMOLISH (v) mash dung, mash up, lick dung, dungstroy

DEMON pr: diiman 1 (*demon or ghost in the form of a beastly animal*) rollin calf 2 (*demon in the form of the folkloric Old Hag*) Di Ol Hige, Di Ol Suck

DEN see *BURROW*

DENOUNCE lickout gainst, bun, bun out, chant dung

DENSE 1 (adj. of solid material) tight, pack up   2 (adj. of liquid or syrup) clammy

DEPEND ON 1 (*be relative to*) depend pan   2 (*make a living from; survive on*) live pan, depend pan   3 (adv. *dependending on*) base pan, tu how

DEPENDABLE 1 (of person: *trustworthy*) goodup, artical, ites, conscious, cool   2 (of thing) goodup, quality, tuff, name brand, bonafide

DEPORT 1 (v) dip   2 Also see *KICK OUT*

DEPORTEE dippy

DEPRAVITY badness, fuckry, sheggry, muckry, neckry, luu, almshouse bizniz, almshouse, ugliness, ugly, buzu

DEPRESSED 1 (adj) spirit low, frass out, frazzle out, spirit no right   2 (*feel depressed*) feel low, feel wutliss, feel pwoko pwoko, feel dash weh, spirit low, spirit no right

DEPRESSING (of place: *dreary*) deddy deddy, done out

DEPRESSION 1 (n) nerve prablem   2 Also see *DEPRESSED*

DEROGATORY diragiteri, bad minded, insultive

DESERT 1 (*arid landscape*) dezert   2 (v. of person: *walk out on*) gwaan leff, run leff, cut leff, splurt pan, cyaad   3 (v. of place: *leave*) leggo, leff

DESERVE (*deserve to*) good fi - *You don't deserve to get the money*: Yu no gud fi get di moni

DESIRE see *WANT; CRAVE*

DESK deks

DESPARATELY (pred adv only) bad bad, des

DESPERATE 1 (adj) des   2 (*desperate for sex*) oily-back

DESPICABLE dutty, nassy, ceitful, low run, low, ugly, evilous, wikid, turble, slacka, pagan, heathen, cussid, custed

DESPITE no mind, no care

DESTINATION endz

DESTITUTE des, dry, puckro 2 (*in need*) inna wantin 3 (v. *to be destitute*) suck salt thru wooden spoon, band yu belly an bawl

DESTROY /DESTROYED mash dung, dungstroy, mash up 2 Also see *ERADICATE*

DETACHED 1 (*broken off*) pop off 2 (*unfeeling*) donkya, dry yeye

DETERGENT fab

DETERMINATION see *RESOLVE*

DETERMINED 1 (adj. *persistent*) no easy, ambitionable, trong mind, trong eye, crabbit 2 (*determined by; governed by*) set by, canchol by, govern by 3 (ppl. *decided; established*) set, extablish

DETEST 1 (v. of things and ideas and behaviors) bun, bun out, cyaa tek 2 (v. against persons) no love, cyaa tek

DEVELOP devil up, divelin up - *develop it*: devil it up

DEVELOPMENT (*develoment as a person; process of becoming someone*) smaddyfication

DEVOTEE fallarah, tetes

DIABETES pr: dayabiitis (n) shuga, sweet blood

DIALECT lingwah

DIAPERS /DIAPER pampaz, nappy

DIARRHEA runnin belly, belly come dung, belly wok, shittinz, operation

DICK see *PENIS* or *DOUCHEBAG*

DICTATOR ginigog, guineagog, gorgon

DIDN'T 1 neva, neh 2 (in questions: *Didn't X...?*) Den X no - *Didn't I give you the answer?* Den mi no gi yu di ansa?

DIDN'T EVEN neven, nevn, neevn

DIE 1 (v) ded, pass off, step off, drop off, drop out, yeye lock 2 (*die suddenly*) cut off, drop out

DIFFICULTY 1 (*level of difficulty*) haadness 2 Also see *PROBLEMS; HARDSHIP*

DIG OUT (v) grabble out

DILAPIDATED brok dung, pop dung, rookoondung, chaka chaka, nyaka nyaka, buss up, waan fix up

DILEMMA prekeh, puru, crosses, dog corn piece (meaning *dog's corn field*)

DIRECT pr: dairek 1 (*straightforward; blunt*) strait, no easy, facety, widout folly, coas, dry yeye 2 (v. *be direct*) talk di tingz dem, no skin teet, no skin up, no lotion, no pet nor powda

DIRECTION pr: dairekshan

DIRTY 1 (*not clean*) dutty, nassy 2 (*soiled*) dutty up, mud up, putto putto, plaka plaka, mekeh mekeh, pyaka pyaka 3 (v) mud up, dutty up, nassy up 4 Also see *DASTARDLY; CORRUPT*

DIS see *DISRESPECT; INSULT; REJECT*

DISABLED 1 (*handicapped*) invalid 2 Also see *BROKEN*

DISAGREE 1 no gree 2 (*not see eye to eye*) no tek tea, no plant peas 3 (*disagree with*) see *OPPOSE*

DISAGREEMENT 1 (*a personal disagreement*) cass cass, confusion, parangles (see *FIGHT* for more) 2 (*general public disagreement*) see *CONTROVERSY*

DISAPPEAR 1 (v. of thing) gaan, gu weh, juss gu weh so, tek weh itself 2 (v. of person) gaan, duck an gaan, juss splurt, juss gu weh so, tek weh yuself 2 (v. of things) tek weh demself, gaan, gu weh, gu weh so

DISAPPOINT (v) let dung, shooks - *You disappointed me*: Mi luuz aaf a yu

DISAPPOINTED 1 (adj) sheg up, ben, bex 2 (v. *be disapointed in*) lose off a - *I'm disappointed in you*: Mi luuz aaf a yu

DISAPPOINTING see *LAME*

DISAPPOINTMENT feelinz, bexation, bextation

DISAPPROVE OF no check fi, no defend, no caytah to, no promote, no love, bun, bun out, bun faya pan, dash faya pan

DISASTER see specific type of natural disaster or see *CALAMITY*

DISC JOCKEY selektah

DISCOURAGE 1 (*advise against*) no defend, no caytah to, no promote 2 (*dishearten*) kill X vibes (X=person)

DISCOVER 1 (*find*) discoba, buck up pan, buck up, buck 2 (*get to the bottom of*) suss out

DISCRIMINATION iniquity, partiality

DISCUSS (v) talk out, reason bout, hol a vibes bout, hol a medz bout

DISCUSSION 1 (*a single discussion about a topic*) a reason, a reasonin 2 (*general discussion; controversy*) ray ray, passa passa, labba labba, yabba yabba, bagga argument, bagga chat 3 Also see *CONTROVERSY* for more

DISGRACE 1 (n) joke, alms-house 2 (vt) mud up, dutty up - *You're disgracing the company's reputation*: Yu a mod up di kompani niem

DISGRACEFUL see *DESPICABLE*

DISGUST 1 (n) sick stomach, sick belly 2 (v. *to disgust person X*) sick X belly, sick X stomach 3 (of person and their behavior: *be disgusted by*) lose off a - *I'm disgusted by you*: Mi luuz aaf a yu 4 Also see *ANGER* or *UPSET*

DISGUSTING 1 (of person or body part) nassy, crawny, scabby, renk 2 Also see *LEWD*

DISH plate

DISHES crockery

DISHEVELED 1 frazzle, frazzle out, frass, streggeh, chaka chaka, nyaka nyaka, raggy, ragga ragga 2 Also see *UNKEMPT*

DISHONEST too lie, sipple an lie, trickify, ceitful, deceptious, sipple, two mout, twin mout

DISHONESTY (n) lie an story, jinnalship, luu, olo, olo gyow, deceptiousness, twin mout, chicaney, cramoojin, samfai, almshouse

DISLIKE 1 (n) feelinz 2 (v) no love, no rate, no defend, no promote

DISLOYAL 1 (adj. *treacherous*) ceitful, deceptious, back-an-belly, twin coat, twin mout 2 (v. *be disloyal; go against the plan*) dis di program

DISMISS see *RELEASE; REJECT; TERMINATE*

DISOBEDIENCE hard yeye, hard ears

DISOBEDIENT 1 (of children) hard yeye, facety, brite, fresh, outta aada, unmannersable, hard ears 2 (n. *disobedient or unruly children*) leggo beast, jing bang

DISORDER see *MAYHEM; CLUTTER*

DISORDERLY see *DISORGANIZED* or *UNRULY*

DISORGANIZED 1 chaka chaka, chak an peckle, nyaka nyaka 2 Also see *CLUTTERED*

DISORIENTED stonted, head craab up

DISPARAGE (v) class, violate, dis, tek step wid, style, hype pan, pop style pan, skin up yu nose pan, cut yu yeye afta, low count, reduce

DISPICABLE 1 (adj) dutty, low, low run, nassy, ugly, evilous, pagan, heathen, daak 2 (n. *dispicable male*) fassy, fassyhole, pussyhole, culprit, crowbait, cacafawt, pagan, heathen 3 (n. *dispicable female*) butu, streggeh, waste gyal, batta ears gyal, eedyat gyal, pazaart, parasite, credell

DISPLAY 1 (*expose*) flash 2 (*flaunt*) see *FLAUNT*

DISPUTE 1 (n) cass cass, confusion, prekeh, puru, mixup, passa passa, ruction, parangles, fandangles, bangarang 2 (v. *to question or reject*) no gree wid, bun 3 Also see *DISAGREEMENT; ARGUMENT; CONTROVERSY; REJECT*

DISREGARD see *NEGLECT; PUT ASIDE; WAVE OFF*

DISRESPECT 1 (n) violation, donkya 2 (vt) violate, dis, tek step wid, tek liberty wid, coas up, low count, reduce, skin up yu nose pan, cut yu yeye afta, tek X mek pappy show, tek X mek prekeh (X=person)

DISRESPECTFUL (adj) bright, fresh, insultive, renk, outa aada

DISRUPTION 1 (n. *cut in supply*) cut 2 Also see *COMMOTION*

DISTANT 1 (adj) fohr fohr 2 (n. *distant place*) woy woy, chuku, moko 3 Also see *FAR AWAY; REMOTE*

DISTRESSED 1 (adj) all sheg up, fret up 2 (v. *be distressed*) belly bottom a bun yu - *I'm distressed*: Mi beli batam a bon mi

DISTURBANCE see *COMMOTION*

DISTURBING 1 (*upsetting*) deep, daak, bexashous, fretrashous 2 (*shocking*) frightenatious

DITCH 1 (n) gully, colbut (from *culvert*) 2 (v. *ditch a person*) gwaan leff, run leff, cut leff, splurt pan, cyaad 3 (*ditch a place or thing*) leggo 4 (v. *ditch school*) skull

DIVE (v. *dive from; jump off*) chuck off

DIVIDE UP share up share up

DIVINE 1 (adj) hyah 2 (v. *interpret omens or signs*) sight, penetrate

DIZZY stonted (from *stunned*)

DJ (*disc jockey*) selectah

DO du - Also see *DO IT!*

DO IT! Dweet man!, Dweet noh!, Gwaan noh!, Gwaan!, Gwaan chu!, Go deh!, Gi dem!, Go een!, Go inna it!, Run it!, Tek di miggle!

DO NOT see *DON'T*

DO WELL 1 (in a competition or on a test) see *KICK ASS* 2 (financially) liv good, step up

DODGE 1 (vt. *duck to avoid*) site 2 (vi. *dodge questions*) buckshuffle, bob an weave, site kwestian

DOES du

DOESN'T 1 (v) no 2 (*doesn't he?; doesn't she?; doesn't it?*) see *ISN'T THAT SO?*

DOESN'T EVEN no even, deven, not even - *She doesn't even know you*: Shi no iivn nuo yu, Shi nat iivn nuo yu, Shi deven nuo yu

DOGGYSTYLE (n. sex position) backass, backshot

DOLL (n) dolly

DOLLAR 1 (*a one-hundred Jamaican dollar bill; a US one-dollar bill*) a bills 2 (*dollars*) frockles

DOLPHIN dalfin, paapas, pampas

DOMINATE (v. in a relationship context) mantrol, mantrol up, hancuff, mek figaree out a, tek X tun figaree, spin X roun (X=person)

DOMINEERING trong eye, miserable

DON'T 1 (v) no, doan 2 (*don't you?; don't we?; don't they?*) see *ISN'T THAT SO?*

DON'T EVEN no even, deven, not even - *I don't even know you*: Mi no iivn nuo yu, Mi nat iivn nuo yu, Mi deven nuo yu

DON'T GET ME STARTED! No draw mi out!, No draw mi tongue!

DON'T TAKE IT PERSONALLY No feel no way, No watch no face

DON'T YOU THINK? see *ISN'T THAT SO?*

DONATE let off, lek off

DONATION freeness

DONE see *ALL GONE; FINISHED*

DONKEY jabby, jackass

DOORSTOP door cotch, cotch

DOORWAY door mout

DORK see *NERD*

DOUCHEBAG (*obnoxious male*) fassy, fassyhole, pussyhole, pussymout, bomboclaat, bombohole, curr, bait, crowbait, cacafawt, pussyfawt, dutty johncrow, heathen, pagan, chapunko

DOWN AND OUT 1 (adj) salt, bawlin, cornah dark 2 (v. *to be down and out*) cornah dark, suck salt chu wooden spoon, band yu belly an bawl - *He's down and out*: Him saalt; Him kaana daak

DRAGONFLY batimamselle, needle case, needle pointer

DRAMA (*interpersonal issues or public controversy*) bare tings, mix up, passa passa, ray ray, confusion, cass cass, bangarang, parangles, fandangles, worries, chubbles, fuss an fight, bag a argument, palangarang, palangaranga, palam pam

DRAMATIC 1 (of situation: *intense*) deep, heavy, sticky, ruff 2 (of personality: *overly emotional*) too much, gwaan too much, extra, cry cry, bawly bawly

DRAW ATTENTION TO (v. of misdeed or controversy) loud up, rinse, show up, talk up

DREAD 1 (*terror*) frightration 2 (*person with dreadlocks*) dreadlocks, dread, dready, natty dread, natty, dread head 3 Also see *RASTAMAN*

DREADLOCKED 1 (adj) natty, dread up, nat up 2 (n. *dreadlocked person*) dreadlocks, dread, dready, natty dread, natty, dread head

DREARY deddy deddy, daak, bleaky

DRESS 1 (*skirt*) frock 2 Also see *DECORATE* or *WEAR*

DRESS UP (v) kris up, primps up, (in flashy clothes): shock out, flash out, trash out

DRESSED WELL shot, hype, tun up, tun ova, buck, fabilocious, trash an ready, trash, kris up, dress tu puss foot

DRINK 1 (n. *alcoholic beverage*) watahs, juice 2 (*a non-alcoholic refreshment*) a drinks, a long drink 3 (v) jrink, swips, quail 4 (v. *gulp down*) swips off, gwap, gwat

DRIVE 1 (*motivation*) ambition, gumption, trong eye 2 (vt. of vehicle) jive, run, operate 3 (*take a drive*) mek a tracks 4 (*drive person X crazy*) mad X, mash up X head, craab up X head 5 Also see *DRIVE OFF*

DRIVE OFF /DRIVE AWAY (vt. *chase off*) run, run weh, jive weh - *Drive them off!* Ron dem!, Ron dem weh!, Jraiv dem weh! - *Drive off the enemy*: Ron weh di enemi, Ron di enemi

DRIZZLE 1 (n) dew rain   2 (v) dew   - *It's drizzling*: rien a jyuu

DROOL 1 (n) lele waata, mout waata   2 (*is drooling*) mout a waata

DROOPY fluxy

DROUGHT waata-dry, dry

DRUM pr: jo 1 (*nyabinghi bass drum*) kette, tondah   2 (*nyabinghi middle drum*) funde   3 (*nyabinghi small drum*) repeatah   4 (*shekere; gourd and bead drum*) shaka   5 (*oil drum*) drum pan, joe pan

DRUNK 1 (adj) jrunk, red, black up, gaan, cherry, unda yu liquor, unda yu waataz, unda yu juice, eena yu waataz   2 (*buzzed*) tipsy, sweet   3 (v. *make drunk*) drunk   - *Rum will get you drunk*: Rom wi jronk yu

DUCK 1 (v. *duck from*) site   2 (v. *duck in reaction to gunfire*) get flat   3 (*duck questions; equivocate*) bob and weave, buckshuffle, site question

DUCKLING dill dill

DUDE bredrin, bredda, umbre, yout, brogad (from *bro god*)

DUE TO 1 sake a, count a, caz a, chu   2 (*Due to how...*) To how   - *Due to how dark it was, we couldn't see a thing*: Tu ow it did daak wi kudn si a ting   3 (*Especially since...*) Wuss laka how   - *Especially since you're ugly, nobody cares*: Wos laka ow yu ogli, nobadi no kieta

DUEL 1 (n) war, clash   2 (v) war, clash

DUET combination

DULL 1 (of knife or tool) dullish   2 (of place or situation) deddy   3 (of person) so so, deadstock   4 (n. *dull person; dullard*) ded stock

DUMB 1 (*mute*) mumu   2 Also see *STUPID* or *FOOLISH*

DUMBFOUNDED tie-tongue

DUPLICITOUS switchy, back and belly, two mout, twin mout, twin coat, samfai

DWARF puchin, kunchin, dungrow, dufidaya, timini

DWELL ON (v. *ruminate about*) tink pan, penny, wok yu head ova

DYE 1 (n) kolah   2 (v) kolah   3 (v. of hair) X up yu hair (X=any color)   - *Dye your hair pink*: Pink op yu hier

DYNAMITE dandimite, boom, bomb

EACH (*per item*) a one   - *The patties are two hundred dollars each*: Di pati dem tuu onjrid dala a wan

EACH OTHER wi one anedda, unu one anedda, dem one anedda - *You love eachother*: Unu lov unu wananeda

EARLY ON early out

EARRING iez ring

EARS ieziz (from *earses*)

EARTHQUAKE grungshake, shaky shaky

EASE UP balance, cool, sekkle, simma dung

EASY 1 (*It's easy*) A saps, A no nuttn - *That's* easy: Dat a saps, Dat a no notn   2 (*easy girl*) see *SLUT*

EAT 1 (v) nyam   2 (*eat hastily*) cut an swalla   3 (*eat sloppily*) chamba chamba   3 (*eat fastidiously; pick and choose*) pinch an bite   4 (*overeat*) ovanyam   5 (*eat until completely full*) ketch yu lent   7 Also see *EAT OUT; EAT UP*

EAT OUT 1 (*go out to eat*) nyam a road   2 (*perform cunnilingus*) bow, suck, eat, lick, swipe, go low, go dung, nyam unda table, eat unda sheet, do numba three, wash, (vulgar): suck pussy, nyam bush, labba juice   3 (*give cunnilingus to*) nyam out, suck, swipe, bow dung pan, bow pan, go dung pan, wash

EAT UP 1 (v) nyam off   2 (v. *gobble up very quickly*) fups off, flups off

ECCENTRIC (adj) maddy maddy, diffrant, supm else, no easy

EDUCATION pr: edikieshan

EEL kwamin

EFFEMINATE 1 (of woman: *excessively feminine; prissy*) prussy, bessy   2 (of man) funny, fruity, mampala   3 (n. *an effeminate man*) funny man, fella, salad, guy, mantu, mama man, mampala, gyalips, Miss Cooba, Miss Lashey, Miss Jane

EFFORT 1 (n) gumption   2 (v. *make a great effort*) kill up yuself, hackle yuself, buss yu shut (from *bust your shirt*), buss yu skin, pudung a piece a X (X=anything effort is to be expended upon)

EGG YOLK red

EGGPLANT gyaadn egggarden egg

EGGSHELLS egg trash

EGRET (n) gaulin

EITHER 1 (in negative sentences) neida, too - *I don't love you either*: Mi no lov yu tuu, Mi no lov yu niida   2 (*Either way; Either one*) eeda idah

EJACULATE buss a juice, pop

ELASTIC laskit

ELBOW han-elbow

ELDERLY 1 (adj) ripe, ageable 2 (n. *elderly person*) oldsta, ol foot, ol head

ELDERLY MAN 1 (n) elda, elda head, oldsta, ol head 2 (terms of address for an elderly man) Eldah, Fadda 3 (n. *tough elderly man; old goat*) tuffy ram, taffu ram, tufu ram 4 for derogatory terms see *OLD MAN*

ELDERLY WOMAN nana, granny, auntie, (derogatory): ol foot lady, ol foot 2 (terms of address for an elderly woman) Madda 3 for derogatory terms see *OLD WOMAN*

ELECTRICITY current, lectric

ELEGANT 1 (of woman's appearance or clothing) criss, stush, itey titey 2 (of place) stoosh, itey titey

ELEPHANT asunu

ELIGIBLE pr: elijibl 1 (adj) paas, fit 2 (*of age*) ageable

ELIMINATE x out

ELUSIVE sipple, trickify, cunny

EMACIATED (adj) mawga, meega, suck weh, winji, pyanji, crenky, wenya wenya, parra parra

EMBARRASS (vt. *to embarrass*) mek look bad, bait up, nassy up

EMBARRASSED (v. *feel embarrassed*) feel shame, feel a way, lap yu tail

EMBARRASSING (adj) no luk good

EMERGE 1 (v) brok out, buss out, buss, pop 2 (v. *emerge from*) brok out a, buss out a, pop out a

EMOTIONAL 1 (of personality: *overly sensitive*) cry cry, bawly bawly, extra, too much 2 (of current mood: *joyful; emotional*) heart full 3 (of situation or issue: *touchy*) technical, sticky

EMPTY (v. of bucket: *to empty*) throw

EMPTY HANDED wid yu two long han dem

EMPTY PROMISES bag a mout, gyow

ENABLE 1 (*enable bad behavior of a child or loved one*) uphol 2 (*allow; make possible*) low

ENABLER (*mother who enables bad behavior of a child*) upholance mumma

ENCORE! More dat!, Faawud!, Bo! Bo! Bo!, Det! Det! Det!

ENCOURAGE (vt) hype up, gi chrent tu, gi a hype, rate up, liff up - *Don't encourage them*: No gi dem no aip

ENCOURAGEMENT see *PRAISE; SUPPORT*

END 1 (*terminus*) en 2 (*v. to conclude; finish up*) done 3 (*put an end to*) done, radicate

ENDURANCE 1 (*stamina for physical exercise*) long bret, donkey bret 2 Also see *STAMINA*

ENDURE 1 (v. *last*) tan 2 (*undergo*) suffah, go chu, deal wid, cross ova, pass chu, liv out, get chu, angle, clear

ENEMY (adj. or n.) pagan, fassy

ENERGY pr: enaji (n. *positive energy*) vibes, upliffment, upfulness, niceness

ENJOY 1 (vt. *take pleasure in*) fulljoy, live up, sree, walla inna 2 (vi. *enjoy oneself; have fun*) fulljoy yuself, lively up yuself, go haad, spree

ENJOYABLE vibesy, full a vibes, sweet

ENJOYMENT vibes, funjoy, fulljoyment, fulljoy, pleasuration

ENORMOUS 1 (adj) helleva, big big, wagga wagga, (attributive only): raatid, raas - *That's a huge fish!* A wan raas fish dat! 2 Also see *FAT; MUSCULAR*

ENOUGH nuff

ENTANGLED 1 (adj) ketch up 2 (of troubles: *entangled in*) ketch up inna, mix up inna, blen up inna

ENTHUSIASTIC 1 (of personality) full a vibes, vibesy 2 (*excited*) full a vibes, well ready

ENTIRE full, whole

ENTRAP bait up

ENVIOUS red yeye, shine yeye, craven, badmind, grabalicious, grudgeful, cramoojin, cubbitch, coveechous

ENVY 1 (n) grudgeful, craven, red yeye 2 (v) grudge, cubbitch, red yeye

EPILEPSY fits

EQUAL 1 (n. *peer*) quabbs 2 (adj. *comparable in size, strength, social status*) size - *You and I are not equals*: Mi an yu no saiz 3 (v) mek, match - *Three plus three equals six*: Chrii plos chrii mek six - *They don't equal each other*: Dem no mach dem wan aneda

EQUIVOCATE buckshuffle, bob an weave

ERADICATE radicate, bun out, x out, kill out, done out

ERASE 1 (of handwritten text) groundz out, rub out, x out 2 (of action) tek weh, x out 3 Also see *ERADICATE*

ERASER rubba

ERECT 1 (adj) cock up 2 (vt) raise up 3 (v. of penis: *become erect*) tan up, stiff up

ERECTION 1 (n) stiffaz, cockstand, piece a stone, stick a weed 2 (v. *get an erection*) buddy tan up, wood tan up, buddy stiff up, wood stiff up

EROSION washweh

ESCAPE 1 (vi) get weh, sef weh 2 (*escape from*) site, get weh fram, sef weh fram

ESPECIALLY 1 peshally 2 (*Especially since...*) Wuss laka how - *Especially since you're ugly, nobody cares*: Wos laka ow yu ogli, nobadi no kieta

ESSENTIAL crucial

ESTABLISH (vt) set up, set, extablish, pudung (*from put down*)

ESTABLISHED 1 (adj. of institution or tradition) well extablish, foundation, original, roots 2 (adj. of person) veteran, well extablish, foundation, original, artical, heartical 3 (adj. or ppl. *decided and confirmed*) set, lock, suttn, muss an boun

ESTUARY bogue, bogg

ET CETERA an ting, an so, an ray ray, an ray tay tay, an one bag a supm, an x-y-zed, an all a dem ting deh, an all a dem sittin deh, an all a dem supm deh, an teeri, an blar blar blar, an labba labba, an yabba yabba, an tarra warra, an warra warra, an wat nat, an rat nat

ETC see *ET CETERA*

ETERNALLY (pred adv) fi eva

EVADE 1 (v) go roun, site 2 (vi. *evade questions*) buckshuffle, bob an weave, site question

EVASIVE two mout, two side, sipple an lie

EVEN 1 (adj) level 2 (adv) all - *He even gave away his car*: Him aal gi weh him kyaar 3 (*even including*) dung tu 4 (*doesn't even; don't even*) deven, no even, not even 5 (*didn't even*) neven, neva even, neh even 6 Also see *EVEN IF* and *EVEN THOUGH*

EVEN IF all if

EVEN THOUGH aldoah, doah, no becaw, not because

EVENING evelin

EVENTS gwaaninz, happninz

EVENTUALLY howaz beat, bambye (from *by and by*)

EVER SINCE from - *Ever since I read that book I haven't trusted any politicians*: Fram mi riid dat buk deh mi no chos no palitishan agen

EVERY SO OFTEN every now an again, now an again, once awhile

EVERYBODY everybaddy, every smaddy

EVERYTHING evryting, all an all - *Everything is the same as it used to be*: Aal an aal siem laka fos taim

EVERYTHING'S COOL /ALL RIGHT Everyting cool, Everyting wow, Evryting arite, Evriting balance, Balance, Level vibes, Level, Irie, Evryting criss, All fruits ripe, Cool runninz, Cool breeze, Everyting pan ice, Evryting cook an curry, Evryting fit an frock, Evryting ites, Evryting a evryting

EVERYWHERE everyweh, all bout, all ova, every which paat

EVIL 1 (n) evilousness, weak heart, dark heart, black heart, dry yeye, nassiness, duttyness, slackness, ugly 2 (adj) evilous, pagan, low, ugly, cussid, custed, slacka, weak heart, dark heart, black heart, dry yeye, kramoojin

EX GIRLFRIEND /EX BOYFRIEND see *EX LOVER*

EX LOVER ole bam, ole fyah stick

EXACT 1 direck, sed - *That's the exact car I was telling you about*: Dat a di sed kyaar mi did a tel yu bout - *That's not the exact one*: Dat a no di dairek wan 2 (*the exact same*) di sed same

EXACTLY 1 same so, same one, prezackly - *That's exactly what I'm saying*: A dat siem wan mi a seh, siem so mi a taak 2 (*exactly the same*) same same 3 Also see *EXACTLY!*

EXACTLY! 1 Strait!, Tank yu very much!, A it dat!, A <u>mi</u> fi tell yu!, No <u>dat</u> mi a seh?, See it deh?, A dat mi a seh!, Desso mi a seh!, Sed speed!, Same so!, Sed way so!, Yu see it deh? 2 (*I totally agree!*) see *TOTALLY*

EXAMINE pree, check, penetrate, tek a stock a, look inna, suss out

EXCELLENT 1 (of person: *highly skilled*) mad, bad, wikid, terrible, superble, a seh <u>one</u>, artical, craab up, well skill, shot, tuff, turnt, tun up, tun ova   2 (of thing: *well made; high quality*) name brand, quality, tuff, top shelf, top a di top, toppity top, toppa top, goodup, goodup goodup, preps, original   3 (v. *to be excellent*) see *KICK ASS*

EXCEPT 1 (*except that*) part from, sep, nomo   2 (*except for*) sep fi, paat from, puttin weh - *I'll eat anything except for raw fish*: Mi wi nyam eniting putn weh raa fish

EXCESSIVE extra, ova-du

EXCITE 1 (v) hype up, vibes up, mad up, wile up   2 Also see *ANGER; AROUSE*

EXCITED well hype, full a vibes, well ready, (*extremely excited*) glad bag buss - *I'm so excited!* Mi glad bag bos!   2 (*sexually excited*) see *AROUSED*   3 Also see *GET EXCITED*

EXCITEMENT 1 (n) hype, vibes   2 Also see *COMMOTION*

EXCLUDE kip out

EXCUSE (n. *lame excuse; fabrication*) lie an story, unchute   2 (v. *forgive*) 'low, figive   3 *Don't give me any excuses!* No bada tel mi bout aas ded an cow fat!

EXCUSE ME 1 (*May I say something?*) Jus a word, Oy deh, Aks pardon   2 (*Forgive me*) Manners, hush   3 (*Allow me to pass by*) Beg yu pass, Beg yu some way deh, Beg yu likkle way, Gi mi likkle pass deh, Gi mi pass no?, Gi mi way no?, Mek mi pass chu, Move deh likkle, Mek mi go chu no?, Mek mi go chu, Shif up yuself no?, Shif up, Free mi up likkle, Free mi up deh, Draw up yu foot, Move no?, Move yuself, Hot wata!, Hot soup!, Go ova deh, Av mi excuse   4 (*Make some room for me in here*) Small up yuself, Shif up yuself, Shif up, Squeeze up yuself, Mind yuself, Draw up yu foot

EXHAUSTED 1 (*used up*) done out, nyam off   2 (*very tired*) mash up, frazzle out, pop dung

EXIT 1 (v. from building or room: *to exit*) leggo, leff, come out, buss out   3 (v. from road or highway: *to exit*) leggo, leff, come off - *Exit the road at Spanish Town*: Kom aaf a di ruod a Spanish Town

EXPEL (v) run, tun out, put out, drive weh, dish X dirt (X=person)

EXPENSIVE 1 dear - *The food is expensive*: Di fuud diir   2 Also see *HIGH QUALITY*

EXPERIENCE 1 (n. *life experience and knowledge*) sabi-so, trod   2 (n. *personal experiences*) troddinz   3 (v) go chu, live out, touch, sample

EXPERIENCED 1 (adj) een deh, deh pan top, notchilous   2 (v. *to be experienced; to know what's up*) know bout, know wa clock a strike, know wat o'clock, know di runninz, know di trod, no baan wen yu big, no baan back a cow, no juss fall out a ih truck

EXPLICIT 1 (pred. adj. *unambiguous*) strait, well clear, widout folly 2 (*uncensored*) naked up, raw chaw 3 (*sexually explicit*) slack, dutty, luu, outlaw

EXPLODE buss (fram *burst*), boom

EXPOSE 1 (*physically expose*) show up, flash 2 (v. of misdeed or controversy: *expose to the public*) rinse, show up, talk up, loud up

EXTEND 1 (vt. *thrust out*) cock out, push out, tretch out, shub out 2 (vi. *protrude*) cock out 3 (vt. of object: *lengthen*) long out 4 (vt. *prolong*) draw out 5 (vi. *extend to*) reach tu, trech out tu, cova, kibba 5 (*extend to; continue until*) reach tu

EXTENDED 1 (*protruding*) cock out 2 (*prolonged*) long out, draw out

EXTERMINATE 1 (v) bun out, x out, kill out, radicate, done out 2 Also see *KILL*

EXTINGUISH 1 (as fire or candle) out 2 (*temporarily extinguish and put aside a cigarette or joint for later use*) bruise

EXTRA (*a little something extra*) brawta, mek up, likkle more

EXTREMELY 1 (adv) well well 2 (*to the extreme*) bad, bad bad, like wow, like wah, cyaa done, so till, gaan tu bed, tu X (X=expletive) - *They are extremely tired*: Dem wel wel tayad, Dem tayad bad, Dem tayad laik wow, Dem tayad tu blodklaat, etc.

EXTROVERTED vibesy, full a vibes, irie, jolly

EYE 1 (n) yeye 2 (v. *lock eyes*) yeye mek four - *We locked eyes*: Fiwi yai mek fuor 3 (v. *examine; stare at*) pree, penny, eyes, clock

EYELID yeyeskin

FABRICATION (*deception; false excuse*) lie an story, layad story, make-up story, gyow, bag a lie, unchute, olo

FABULOUS see *EXCELLENT* or *STYLISH*

FACE UP TO shape up tu, deal wid

FACETIOUS play play

FADE (vi. *wane*) jrap off

FAIL 1 (*not succeed*) flop 2 (vi. *stop working*) pop dung, brok dung, seize up 3 (vt. of test: *fail to pass*) flop

FAILURE 1 (of attempt) flap, flop 2 (of person) floppaz, double blank, waste man, waste gyal

FAINT (v. *pass out*) drap dung, pitch ova, feneh

FAIR 1 (of person: *impartial*) strait, conscious, Ites 2 (of action) rightful

FAKE 1 (of thing: *not genuine*) carbon 2 (of brand name: *not genuine*) casco, bashco 3 (*fake Rasta*) wolf, rasta impostah, pork ras, pork dread 4 Also see *WANNABE*

FAKENESS gyow

FALL 1 (v.) drap 2 (*fall down*) drap dung, pitch, tumble dung 3 (*fall over*) kin ova, tip ova, pitch ova, pitch, tumble dung 3 (*fall off*) drap off

FALL ASLEEP jrap asleep

FALL BACK ON (v) run to

FALLOW ruinate

FALSE 1 (of thing: *not genuine*) carbon 2 (*false Rasta*) wolf, rasta impostah, pork ras, pork dread 3 Also see *WANNABE*

FAME hype

FAMILY 1 (n) fambly 2 Also see *RELATIVES*

FAMOUS 1 (adj) hype, buss, big, laaj, name gaan abroad 2 (v. *become famous*) buss, name gaan abroad 3 Also see *CELEBRITY*

FANCY see *CLASSY; STYLISH; FLASHY*

FANTASTIC see *AWESOME; EXCELLENT*

FAR (sometimes pr): fohr - see *FAR AWAY; AS FAR AS*

FAR AWAY 1 (pred adj /pred adv) way ova so, quite ova so, fohr, chock out deh, quite out deh, chock a chuku 2 (*faraway*) fohr fohr 3 (n. *faraway place*) woy woy, chuku, moko

FARM 1 (*small farm or horticultural plot*) grong, cultivation 2 (*farm for animals*) pen

FARMER farma, cultivatah

FASHION (*the latest fashion*) di lick, di shot, di hype, di ray, di ray an di tay

FASHIONABLE see *STYLISH*

FAT 1 (*obese; very fat*) helleva, slabba slabba, flabba flabba, blubba blubba, swaaty (from *swarthy*), mampy, sour, bufu, bufutu, busu busu, bufu bufu, wusu wusu, wagga wagga, luggo luggo 2 (of woman: *attractively fat*) fluffy, fluffalishous, flufflilous, buffy, bufflilicious, bufflilous, tick, tickarous, fat, trong, roun, boo<u>noo</u>noos, boonoo<u>noo</u>noos 3 (of man: *tolerably fat; stocky*) broad, bigga 4 Also see *FAT MAN; FAT WOMAN; GET FAT*

FAT MAN 1 (*tolerably fat man; stocky man*) big man, bigs, biggis 2 (*very fat man*) fattoon, fattis, fatta, mampy, blab, sowaz (from *sours*), bufutu

FAT WOMAN 1 (*fat but sexy woman*) fluffy, fat girl, fatty, round girl, trong girl, tick girl, tickarous, fluffalishous, flufflilous, buffy, bufflilicious, bufflilous, boo<u>noo</u>noos, boonoo<u>noo</u>noos 2 (*excessively fat woman*) mampy, blab, fatty boom boom, boom boom, barrel ooman, Miss Woodbine, bufutu 3 Also see *VOLUPTUOUS*

FATHER 1 (n) fadda, pupa, tata, babba 2 (v. *sow the seed of a child*) breed - 3 (*raise*) grow

FATTEN 1 (vt. *make fat*) fat, fat up, increase - *Bread will make you fat*: Bred wi fat yu, Bred wi uncrease yu, etc. 2 Also see *GET FAT*

FAUCET pipe

FAULT 1 (*It's my fault*) A mi   2 (*It's not my fault*) A no mi

FAVORITISM curry-fayva, partiality

FAWNING (adj) licky licky

FEAR (n) fraid, frightration

FEARFUL (*phobic*) fraidy fraidy, fraid fraid, fretful - Also see *AFRAID; WORRIED*

FEARLESS bad, out an bad, talawah

FEAST (n. *feast for a social gathering*) boat

FEBRUARY pr: Febri or Febiweri

FECES didi, doodoo

FEEBLE pyaa pyaa, fenkeh fenkeh, crenky, wenya wenya

FEEL 1 (v. *grope*) grab up, touch up, feel up, fingle, fingle up, fingle fingle, feel up feel up 2 (*feel for*) cry fi, feel a way fi, sorry fi 3 (v. *feel bad about*) feel a way bout 4 Also see *FEEL LIKE DOING SOMETHING*

FEEL LIKE DOING SOMETHING fiil fi X (X=action/verb) - *I don't feel like talking*: Mi no fiil fi chat

FEELING 1 (n. *ambience*) medz, vibez 2 (n. *personal emotional state*) medz 3 (n. *hunch*) rake

FEET foot, hoof

FELLATIO 1 (n) buff, headaz 2 (vi. *give blowjobs*) gargle, clean rifle, shine rifle, sing pan mic, gi head, gi neck 3 (*give a blowjob to*) clean, buff, fluff, clean X rifle, shine X rifle, sing pan X mic, gi head tu, gi neck tu (X=person)

FEMALE 1 (adj) ooman - *I have six female friends*: Six uman fren mi av 2 Also see *WOMAN* or *GIRL*

FEMININE see *EFFEMINATE*

FERMENT (v) draw

FERTILE 1 (adj) fruitful, good fi breed 2 (n. *fertile woman*) breedin grong

FESTER (v) festa, brok out, gyadda information

FESTERING (adj) a festa, full a corruption

FESTIVAL jamminz, bashment, jollification

FEW 1 (*not many*) likkle, likkle a, dinky 2 (*a few*) two chree, couple chree

FIBROIDS growth

FIELD (*field of crops*) piece - *corn field*: kaan piis

FIGHT 1 (n. *physical fight; brawl*) bam bam 2 (*verbal fight or quarrel*) cass cass, cuss cuss, war, mixup, blenda, cobell, powda house, ruction, preke, puru, bangarang, parangles, fandangles, palangarang, palangaranga 3 (*fight physically*) brok fight, ketch fight, grabble 4 (*fight verbally*) wild up, trow wud, fling wud, cuss cuss, trace, war out, war 5 (*fight to achieve something; struggle*) kill up yuself, buss yu shut bust yu shirt

FIGHT AGAINST (v. *struggle against*) fight gainst, lickout gainst, bun out, bun, bun faya pan, fling faya pan, dash faya pan, chant dung

FIGHT BACK (v) lick it back, chuck it back

FIGHT OVER IT war it out

FIGURE OUT 1 (as a problem: *successfully resolve*) sort out, maths out, clear, suss out 2 (*figure out that...*) maths out seh, sight seh, pree seh, penetrate seh 3 Also see *TRY TO FIGURE OUT*

FILL (v) full up

FILL OUT 1 (v. as a form or application) full out 2 (*gain weight; gain muscle*) increase, improve

FILM 1 (n. *camera film; thin layer*) flim, filim 2 (v) flim, shot 3 Also see *MOVIE*

FINAGLE inveegle

FIND A WAY (*improvise a solution*) try a ting, try a way, tun han mek fashion, fadge

FIND OUT get fi know, sight

FIND OUT ABOUT 1 (*research*) look inna, pree, suss out 2 (*come to know about*) get fi know bout, sight, penetrate

FINE see *OKAY* or *GOOD QUALITY* or *SEXY*

FINE QUALITY (adj) name brand, quality, goodup goodup

FINGER 1 (n) finga 2 (*forefinger; index finger*) lickpot finga, lickpot, sweet finga 3 (*little finger*) chi chi muss 4 (*ring finger*) married finga 5 (*thumb*) big finga, tumpy 6 (v. *touch with the fingers*) fingle 7 (*identify with accusation*) pick out, cry pan

FINGERTIP finga head

FINICKY picky picky, fussy fussy, mekam pekam, fenkeh fenkeh, preke preke

FINISH 1 (v) done, box off 2 (of food) nyam off

FINISHED 1 (*all gone*) done, box off, (of food) nyam off, (of weed) smoke off, (of drinks) drink off 2 (*sold out*) sell off

FIRE 1 (n) faya 2 (*small bush fire; blaze*) fyabun, bun 3 (v. of gun) blaze, buss, clap 4 (of bullet) buss, lick 5 (*dismiss from a job*) leggo, run, tun out

FIRECRACKER clappaz, squibz

FIREFLY peeny wally, blinky, blinky blinky, moonie, blinkitty, kitibu,

FIREWOOD 1 (n) logwood 2 (*twigs for fire kindling*) ticky ticky, fyah stick, creng creng, jag jag

FIREWORKS 1 (*bottle rocket or aerial fireworks*) fyah rocket 2 (*sparkler*) starlight 3 (*firecracker*) clappaz

FIRM 1 (*solid*) tuff, tight, pack up 2 (of muscles) trong, tick, pack up

FIRST 1 (adj) fuss 2 (adv) fuss 3 (*the very first*) di fuss fuss 4 (*the first time*) di fuss - *It's the first time I've seen her*: A di fos mi si har

FISH 1 (n) swimmaz - (n) see specific types such as *MACKEREL; SURGEON FISH; etc* 2 (*school of small fish*) ticky ticky 3 (v) ketch fish

FIT (v. *fit inside of*) hol inna 2 (v. *fit with*) see *GO WITH*

FITTING (adj) fit, mek sense - *It's fitting of him that he didn't come*: It fit him seh him neva kom

FLACCID fluxy, pyaa pyaa, plekeh plekeh, flaa flaa

FLAKE 1 (*unreliable person*) bad bargain 2 (v. *not show up*) poas, post 3 (v. *not follow thru*) dis di program

FLAKY (of person: *unreliable*) shakey, switchy, fenkeh, fenkeh fenkeh

FLAP (v. as a bird, with its wings) chop, knock

FLASH 1 (n. *flash of light*) gyash 2 (vi) gyash

FLASH FLOOD river come dung

FLASHY 1 (of apparel and jewelry) blingy 2 (of person: *overly flashy*) gwaany gwaany, stushilous, stushous 3 (v. *wear flashy clothes and jewelry*) bling out, shock out, Also see *FLAUNT*

FLATTER 1 (vt. *compliment*) sweetmout, sweet up 2 (vt. *butter up; kiss up to*) curry fayva wid, skin teet wid, powda, pet, sweet up, hug up

FLAUNT 1 (*flaunt one's appearance or clothes*) moggle, profile, pose off, palaav, hype, shock out, trash out 2 (*flaunt one's status or wealth*) flass, palaav

FLEDGELING quabz

FLIGHTY (*unreliable*) shakey, switchy, fenkeh, fenkeh fenkeh

FLIMSY (adj) flimmy, fluxy, fenkeh fenkeh

FLINCH (v. *move to avoid getting hit*) site

FLING 1 (n. *romantic or sexual fling*) go-rung 2 (v. *have a fling with*) talk wid, dance wid, av a go-rung wid

FLIP 1 (n. *somersault*) pupalick, bum flick, flick, kincat, cuffin 2 (n. *back flip*) bum flick 3 (v. *flip over*) kin ova 4 (*do flips*) kin pupalick, flick

FLIP FLOPS juta, clappy, samplata, sampata, shampata

FLIP OUT 1 (v. *lose your temper*) flip up, rail up, wile up, lick out, get ignarant, get ig, gwaan a way, get red 2 (v. *flip out on*) flip up pan, rail up pan, hype up pan, wile up pan, run up yu mout pan, lash yu mout pan 3 Also see *TRIP*

FLIRT 1 (v. male with female) gyalant 2 (v. female with male) temp, draw cyaad

FLOG (v) lick, cord, batta batta, fum

FLOOD 1 (n. *flash flood*) river come dung 3 (vt) flood out - *The rain flooded the house*: Di rien flod out di ous 4 (vi) flood out 5 Also see *OVERFLOW*

FLOOR (n. *tiled floor*) taris

FLOUR (old term rarely used today) flaa flaa

FLOWER flowaz, roses - *Give her a flower*: Gi har flowaz, Gi har a ruoziz

FLUENTLY (v. *speak fluently*) cut - *He can speak Spanish fluently*: Him kyan kot Spanish

FLUSH see *PURGE*

FLUTE fife

FLY (*any species of small fly; fruit fly; gnat*) jinjy fly, mini mini

FLYCATCHER (*type of bird*) pitcheary

FOAM (v) frat upfrath up

FOCUS 1 (vi. *focus mentally; concentrate*) medz, penetrate 2 (*focus on*) tink pan, study, medz, pree, program, penetrate, penny

FOLLOW 1 (v) falla backa - *Follow me!* Fala bak a mi! 2 (*adhere to*) falla, caytah to 3 (*live according to*) defend - *They follow Rasta*: Dem difen Rasta

FOLLOWER 1 (*disciple; believer*) fallarah, tetes 2 (*one who lacks originality and self-determination*) falla-fashion, falla-fashion monkey, yes man

FONDLE (v) touch up, fingle up, fingle fingle, feel up feel up

FOOD 1 (*cooked food*) bickle, ninyam, nyam 2 (*Rasta health food*) Ital 3 (*dry snacks*) dry food 4 (*food to go; takeout*) box food 5 Also see *LEFTOVERS*

FOOL 1 (n. *foolish person*) claffy, prekeh, menkeh, poppy show, dunce bat, kunumunu, coco head, yam head, iddyboo, eedyboo, sample, goose, salad, cuffy, kwashi 2 (v. *to playfully or harmlessly trick*) fool up, cyaad 3 (v. *to harmfully fool; scam*) jinnal, bandulu, lamps, craff, maringle, samfai 4 Also see *GULLIBLE; LAUGHING STOCK*

FOOLISH fool fool, foo fool, eedyat, claffy, dunce, follygrung, poppy show, chupid, yam head, coco head

FOOLISHNESS chupidness, foolinish, folly grong, poppy show, foolooloops, choopity, eedyat bizniz, alms house bizniz, alms house, fuckry, sheggry, muckry, carry go bring come, parangles, runkus, nyamps - Also see *NONSENSE*

FOR 1 (*when followed by another word*) fi 2 (*when followed by nothing*) fah - *I came here for breakfast*: Mi kom ya fi brekfos - *That's what I came for*: A dat mi kom fa

FOR A LONG TIME 1 (*for a long stretch of time*) fi a long while 2 (*since quite some time ago*) long time, from time, from how long, from nineteen how long, from Wappy kill Phillup, from saltfish a shingle housetop, from di devil was a bwoy, from God mek morning, from before God build Adam, from before God mek, donkey years

FOR A WHILE 1 (*for a good stretch of time*) fi a good while 2 Also see *FOR A LONG TIME*

FOR GOOD (adv. *permanently*) fareva, fi eva, for all time, cyaa done

FOR REAL (pred adv. *no joke*) fi real, strait, big man ting, yes - *They're going to kill him for real!* Dem a go kil im yes!, etc

FOR SURE! see *YES* or *TOTALLY!*

FOR THE HELL OF IT fi so so

FORAGE (v) prog

FORCE 1 (n) foas 2 Also see: *STRENGTH; ENERGY; EFFORT*

FOREHEAD pr: farid

FOREST bush

FOREVER fareva, fi eva, for all time, cyaa done

FORGET figet, figot, lef out

FORGIVE (v) 'low, figive, gi bly tu, gi X bly (X=person)

FORWARD 1 (adv. *in a forward direction*), frontway, faawud 2 (*brash; uninhibited*) facety, bright, no easy, coas, dry yeye

FOUL see *DISGUSTING* or *VULGAR*

FOUL-SMELLING 1 (adj) renk - (like body odour): green, ripe - (like dirty socks): cheesey - (like fish or eggz or raw meat): raw 2 Also see *MUSTY*

FOUND find - *Diamonds are found in Africa*: Daiman fain a Africa

FRACTURE 1 (n) bone-pop 2 (v) pop, buss, brok

FRAGILE 1 fenkeh fenkeh, pyaa pyaa, brickle 2 Also see *FEEBLE; FRAIL*

FRAIL 1 (*emaciated*) mawga, meega, suck weh, winji, pyanji, crenky, wenya wenya, parra parra 2 (adj *brittle*) frocky, brickle

FRAME see *ENTRAP*

FRAME OF MIND (n) medz

FRAUD 1 (n. *fraudulent activity*) bandulu bizniz, bandulu, samfai bizinz, skyamminz, chicaney, gyow 2 (n. *a person engaging in fraud*) skyamma, alias man, samfai man, bandulu, gyowa

FRAUDULENT (adj) bandulu, skyammify, samfai

FREAK (v. *dance in a grinding humping way*) dagga, bubble, chruggle

FREAKY see *HIDEOUS; PERVERTED; SCARY*

FREE 1 (adj. *liberated*) free up   2 (vt. *liberate*) free up, leggo, fly

FREEZE (v. of computer or cell phone) seize up

FREQUENTLY 1 (pred adv) all di while, regulah   2 Also see *A LOT; USUSALLY*

FRESH 1 (*clean; new*) criss   2 (*cool; breezy*) cool

FRIEND 1 (n) fren, linki, chargie, bro gad, dupa, dups, pardi, parry, parrin p, spar, bonafide, road runnah, artical, quabz, combolo, passero, compa, kolo, ites; (male only): bredrin, Idren, dads, soljie, dawdie; (female only): sistren, goodie, goodie goodie, Donna   2 (*best friend*) key, shadow, goodie goodie, (male only): bro gad (from *bro god*)   3 (*false friend*) frenemy, toy fren, tingz fren   4 (v. *be friends with*) par wid, flex wid, move wid, keep fren wid   5 Also see *BEFRIEND*

FRIENDLY 1 (*friendly by nature*) irie, jolly, heartical   2 (*eager to make friends*) skinteet, edge up   3 (*too friendly; overbearing*) extra, edge up, eggz up, ova-du   4 (*on good terms*) good, cool, balance, irie, a mesh, artical, kinteet, grounds   5 (v. *be friendly to*) gwaan good tu

FRIGATE BIRD scissors tail

FRIGHTEN 1 (v) frightn, giv fraid   2 Also see *STARTLE*

FRIGHTENED 1 (adj) fraid, jumpy, bummy   2 (v. *get frightened*) ketch yu fraid, get jumpy, get bummy   3 Also see *WORRIED*

FRIGHTENING (v. *to be frightening*) mek yu fraid, mek yu ketch yu fraid, mek yu get jumpy, mek yu get bummy - *This house is frightening to me*: Dis ous ya a mek mi fried, Dis ous ya a mek mi kech mi fried, Dis ous ya a mek mi get jompi, etc.

FRIZZY 1 (adj) dry, root up   2 (n. *frizzy hair*) dry head, kaya, bad head

FROM THE START fram mawnin, fram di fuss

FROND (*leaf of a palm tree*) bow

FRONT 1 (*in front of*) front a, outta, before   2 (v. *put on a facade*) shape, pose, form

FROWN 1 (n) screw, screw face, monkey face   2 (v) screw up yu face, screw, long out yu mout, mek up monkey face

FROZEN tuff

FRUGAL 1 (adj) cave-headed, cavey head, cavey, (*cheap*) chinky   2 (n. *penny pincher*) chink

FRUSTRATING bodderashous

FRUSTRATION bodderation

FUCK 1 (vi. *to fuck; to have sex*) sort out, fix up, hook, slam, ram, grine, touch, knock, frig, nazzle, rooks off, suss, dugu dugu, digi digi, get a likkle piece, kech up yu stomok, stir it up, cook stew peas, dance, bubble, weld, soldah, change oil, sawka sawka, play ketchy shooby, do X, go pan a X (X=word for intercourse or sex act) 2 (vt. *to fuck; to have sex with*) sort out, fix up, ride, sheg, frig, rooks off, dance wid, bubble wid, sleep wid, hook, get a likkle piece off a, (from the man's perspective only): stab, slam, ram, knock, slap, stamp, taze, tump up, jook, nazzle, lick dong, dig out, rev out, chubble, fan, change yu oil wid 3 (n. *a fuck*) a slam, a slap, a touch, a sort out, a fix up, a stab, a stamp, a ram, a jook, a taze, a grine, a stabbin, a daggarin, a lashin, a strappin, a nazzlin, a waxin, a weldin, a solderin, a oil change, a changin of oil 4 Also see *ONE NIGHT STAND; QUICKIE; SEXUAL PLEASURE*

FUCK AROUND 1 (*tinker*) panka panka, hanka panka 2 (*joke around*) ramp, mout, draw cyaad, sheg roun, skin up, jesta, gi laff fi peas soup 3 (*waste time doing bullshit*) du fuckry, jesta, sheg roun, skylark 4 (*NOT fuck around; not take any shit*) no ramp, no tek check, no skin teet, no skin up 5 Also see *HANG OUT; FUCK WITH*

FUCK OFF! 1 Suck yu mumma! 2 Also see *GO AWAY!*

FUCK OVER (v) soak, salt, flop X show, dis X program, nyam X suppa, brok X foot (X=person)

FUCK UP 1 (vi. *make a wrong move*) du madness, du fuckry, du eedyat ting, du folly, du follygrung 2 (vt. *ruin*) mash up, sheg up, mud up, rooks up, nassy up, sawka sawka, kaba kaba, soak 3 (*beat up*) lick up, sheg up, beat tu X (X=expletive) - *The bad guys fucked that kid up*: Di badman dem biit dat bwai deh tu blodklaat

FUCK WITH 1 (*harass; antagonize*) fass wid, ramp wid, tek step wid, sheg wid, hackle wid, draw cyaad pan, bait, chuck it pan, chuck pan, rooks wid, mell wid 2 (*tamper with*) fass wid, ramp wid, sheg wid, rooks wid, mell wid 3 Also see *KID; TEASE*

FUCKED UP 1 (*emotionally disturbed*) all sheg up 2 (of situation: *not right*) daak, damp, dusty, deep, low, sheg up, ugly 3 (ppl. *sabotaged*) soak, flop, mash up, sheg up 4 (n. *a fucked up situation*) alms-house, sheggry, fuckry, folly grong

FUCKING see list of expletives in Appendix

FUGITIVE (*escapee from prison*) hot steppa, road runner

FULFILL (of promise or prophecy or purpose) live out

FULL 1 (adj) full up 2 (*unable to eat more*) belly buss 3 (v. *eat until full*) ketch yu lent 4 Also see *PACKED* or *CROWDED*

FULL OF SHIT /FULL OF IT (adj) full a lie, full a gyow, full a mout, a chat foolishness, a chat bare lie, a chat bay lie, a chat peer lie, a chat pure lie, a mek up story, a sell gyow, a gyow

FULLY 1 (fronting adv. *wholly; quite*) well, full 2 (pred adv. *thoroughly; all the way*) done, full, full stop, full hundred, tu di fullness, til ih buck, clear, clean clean

FUN 1 (n) vibes, funjoy, fulljoyment, fulljoy, jollification 2 (adj) vibesy, full a vibes 3 (v. *have fun*) hol a vibes, fulljoy yuself, spree

FUNERAL pr: finaral (n. *funeral wake*) setup, ded yaad, nine nite

FUNGUS junjo

FUNNY 1 (of person: *having a good sense of humor*) laffy laffy, no easy, jokify 2 (of thing or situation: *That's hilarious!*) Dat no easy!, Dat mash up!, Dat sheg up!, Wat a X! (X=expletive) 3 (n. *a funny person*) brinjah 4 (n. *very funny thing; something hilarious*) laafin' spwoil 5 (*LOL; ROFL*) DWL (ded wid laaf), BOAL (buss out a laaf)

FURTHER farah

FUSSY (*finicky*) picy picky, fussy fussy, mekam pekam, fenkeh fenkeh, preke preke

FUTURE TENSE 1 (For affirmartive future tense the following future tense markers can be used before almost any verb other than the modal verbs *kuda; maita; mosa; mosi; shuda; wi; wuda*): a, a go, gwen - *I'm gonna go tomorrow*: Mi a go tumaro; Mi a go go tumaro; Mi gwen go tumaro 2 (For negative future tense the following markers can be used in the same way): naa, naa go

GADGETS see *TRINKETS*

GAIN 1 (v. *achieve*) hol, reach, ketch, touch 2 (v. *gain weight*) improve, increase, swell, buff out, fat up, sprawl out

GAIN WEIGHT increase, swell, buff out, fat up, sprawl out, improve

GAME 1 (*personal technique*) style, flex 2 (*the game; the hustle*) di program, di rungles

GAMEY (adj. *smelling like eggz or raw meat*) raw

GANG RAPE (n) batchry

GANGSTA see *GANGSTER*

GANGSTER 1 (n) gyangsta, mafia, shotta, kwenga, knockist, gangalee, speng 2 (*gang leader*) don, dadz, dada, notch, gorgon

GARBAGE 1 gyaabage, rubbish, ruggage 2 (*garbage bin*) gyaabage pan, rubbish pan, ruggage pan

GARDEN pr: gyaadn (n) grong, cultivation

GARLIC (n) gyaalics

GAS 1 (n) gyas 2 (*gasoline*) petrol, gyas

GATHER 1 (as a group or crowd: *come together*) gyadda roun, gyadda tugedda, rally, rope een, fall een 2 (vt. *gather around X*) fall roun X, rally roun X 3 (vt. *gather up; bundle*) ketch up, callek, gyadda, gyadda up, prah prah

GATHERING (n. of people) gyaddarin, linkup, buckup - (*Rasta ritual gathering*): groundation, grounation

GAUDY blingy plus tax, cargo dung, ovah-du

GAY 1 (adj) fishy, fruity, funny, gaan 2 (n. *gay man*) batty man, batty bwoy, chi chi man, chi chi bwoy, fish, bugga man, mama man, funny man, anti-man, beeps, beenix, battis, punga man, fruit, priest, fella, guy, men, doodle, hoodini, gaylord, rod man, digalow 3 (n. *gayness; gay sex*) numba two, batty bizniz, battism, funny bizniz, fishy bizniz, fishiness, fruitiness 4 Also see *LESBIAN*

GECKO croaking lizard

GENERATOR Delco

GENITALIA 1 front, sinting, ting, warra warra, kunumunu, whatsitnot 2 Also see *PENIS; VAGINA*

GENRE pattan, stylee

GENTLE genkle, saaf

GENTLEMAN genkleman

GENUINE 1 (of person in terms of origin and background) artical, raw born, bonafide, name brand 2 (of person in terms of personality and honesty) artical, bonafide, good-up good-up 3 (of thing) bonafide, name brand, artical

GET 1 (v. *receive*) ketch, hol - *He gets a big applause every time*: Him kech a haip evri taim 2 (v. *grab*) paan, paan up, paan up pan, kalla up 3 (vt. *gather up*) paan up, look - *She went to the forest to get firewood*: Shi gaan a bush fi luk faya stik 3 (v. *become*) tun, kom, X up - *It's getting dark*: It a daak op 4 Also see *GRAB*

GET ALONG 1 (*be compatible*) mesh, grounds, go dung good, flex good, move good 2 (*not get along*) no mesh, no grounds, no plant peas, no tek tea

GET ANGRY bex, screw, bringle, chaw fyah, rail up, flip up, puff up, get cross, get raatid, get ignarant, get ig, get dark, get red, hot up, rue

GET ARRESTED get bite, get hol

GET BY 1 (vi. *make ends meet*) nyam a food, eat a food, get on, get chu, try a way, run wid it, liv it out, tun yu han mek fashion 2 (vt. *sneak past*) screechy chu, screechy pass, jim screechy 3 Also see *HUSTLE*

GET CAUGHT UP IN 1 ketch up inna 2 (of trouble or complications) ketch up inna, get mix up inna, mix up yuself inna, get blen up inna, blen up yuself inna, eggz up yuself inna, crowd up yuself inna 3 (of the moment: *get lost in*) get weh inna

GET CONFUSED tun fool

GET EVEN 1 (v) sekkle di score 2 (*get even with person X*) ketch X back 3 Also see *RETALIATE*

GET EXCITED 1 (*get enthusiastic*) rail up, vibes up, mad up, mad, wild up 2 (*get sexually excited*) see *AROUSED* 3 Also see *GO WILD; GO CRAZY*

GET FAMOUS see *FAMOUS*

GET FAT (of person or animal only: *get fat or get fatter*) fat up, increase, improve, swell up, buf out, sprawl out

GET INVOLVED 1 (vi) link up, hitch up, run een, rope een, penetrate, fullticipate, fall een, chune een 2 (vi. *begin a romantic relationship*) hitch up, link up

GET LOST! see *GO AWAY!*

GET LOST IN (of the moment or the music or the mood) get weh ina

GET MIXED UP IN ketch up inna, get mix up inna, mix up yuself inna, get blen up inna, blen up yuself inna, eggz up yuself inna, crowd up yuself inna

GET NAKED (v) skin out, naked up

GET OFF 1 (from work) leff, buss out, leggo from 2 (from punishment) get weh, buss, get bly 3 (*dismount; exit*) come off a - *Get off my bed*: Kom aaf a mi bed

GET ON 1 (*mount; board*) jump pan, jump on pan, hop, hop pan 2 Also see *GET ALONG*

GET OUT 1 (*leave a building or room*) come out 2 (*get out and go somewhere*) du road, brok out

GET PAID eat a food, get a raise

GET READY 1 (vi) strap up yuself, set up yuself 2 (vt: *get something ready*) set up X, strap up X

GET RID OF 1 (of thing) tek weh, dash weh 2 (of person X) get X out, ex out X 3 (*eradicate*) radicate, done out, ex out - *They can't get rid of us*: Dem kyaa get wi out; Dem kyaa ex wi out

GET SHOT get shoot, shoot, get tump, collect shell, pick up grainz, pick up corn - *He got shot by police*: Him shuut bai poliis

GET SICK 1 (*become ill*) tek sick, bad breeze tek - *I'm getting sick*: Bad briiz a tek mi 2 (*become nauseated*) feel funny

GET STUCK faasn, kotch, kotch up, ketch up

GET THE HANG OF IT ketch on, get it, deh pan top - *I've got the hang of it now*: Mi deh pan tap now

GET THROUGH 1 (vt. *bear and overcome*) get chu, pass chu, pass, liv out, clear, cross ova 2 (vi. *succeed*) get chu, liv it out, mek it, clear it, pass, cross ova, cross it, push on chu, gaan clear

GET TO (*arrive at*) reach, ketch a, touch

GET TO THE POINT! No bada tell mi bout horse ded an cow fat!

GET TOGETHER 1 (*meet socially*) link up, buck up, get tugedda 2 (*unite*) kom tugedda, gyadda tugedda, rally, rope een, fall een, (Rasta): I-nite Iself, I-nite

GET YOURSELF TOGETHER fix up, sort out yuself, dechakalize yuself, balance, liff up yuself, raise up yuself, set up yuself

GET-TOGETHER 1 (n. *a social meet-up*) linkup, buckup, gyaddarin 2 Also see *GET TOGETHER*

GHETTO RIG (v. *cobble together*) bitch up

GHOST 1 (n) duppy, shadow, (in the form of a calf) rolling calf 2 Also see *DEMON*

GIGGLE 1 (n) keke 2 (v) keke

GIGGLY laffy laffy

GIGOLO mantel, (of the dreadlocked variety) rent-a-dread

GIMME A BREAK! see *GIVE ME A BREAK!*

GIMME WHAT YOU GOT! Mek mi see it!, Run it!, Sen on!, Up wid it!, Bring ih come!, Sen ih come!, Go inna it!

GIRL 1 (n) gyal pickney, girl pickney 2 (*female adolescent; very young woman*) jubie, dawta 3 (*sexy teenaged girl*) fresh vegetable, filly, prison bait 4 (*dorky young girl*) girls guide 5 Also see *WOMAN*

GIRLFRIEND 1 (*female romantic partner*) princess, empress, lioness, queen, spoogy, spoogz, superintendant, bibi, (*a new girlfriend*) preps 2 Also see *SWEETHEART*

GIVE 1 (v) gi, let off, leggo, faawud up - *I'll give you some spare change*: Mi wi let aaf a smaalz pan yu, Mi wi lego a smaalz pan yu 2 (*send*) run, send on

GIVE A BREAK 1 (*take it easy on person X*) 'low X, tek time wid X, ease X, ease up X, leff X alone, gi X a ease, gi X a ease up 2 (*give X an opportunity*) ease X up, gi X a bly

GIVE A CHANCE (*give person X an opportunity*) let een X, ease X up, gi X a bly

GIVE AWAY (v) let off, lek off

GIVE BACK gi back, leggo back, lek off back

GIVE IT A TRY try a way, gi it a try, gi it a tase

GIVE IT TO ME Gi ih tu mi, Gi mi, Lek off, Leggo, Sen on, Up wid it, Bring ih come, Sen ih come

GIVE ME A BREAK! 1 (*Get serious!*) Wappn to yu?, Wah tek yu?, Wa du yu?, Weh yu a defen?, Res mi! 2 (*Take it easy on me!*) Low mi, Come off a mi case, Tek time wid mi, Ease mi up, Leggo mi head, Leff mi alone

GIVE ME ROOM free me up, small up yuself

GIVE UP 1 (*admit defeat*) bow 2 (*abandon*) leggo, dash weh 3 (*quit* + verb) done - *I gave up cigarettes*: Mi lego di sigaret dem - *I quit smoking*: Mi don smuok

GIVEAWAY (*a giveaway; a handout*) freeness

GIVEN THAT chu, afta, az, since az how, sake a dat

GIZZARD giznick

GLAD 1 (adj) heart full, irie, vibesy, inna yu ackee, inna yu gungo 2 (*extremely glad*) glad bag buss, full a vibes 3 (v. *make person X glad*) sweet, full X heart

GLANCE 1 (n) prips 2 (v) prips 3 (v. *glance at*) prips pan

GLASSES yeye glass, glass, speticle, peticle

GLITCHES parangles

GLOOMY 1 (adj. *overcast*) bleaky, daak up, black up, a set up fi rain 2 (adj. of future outlook or prospects) daak, bleaky

GLOSSY shine

GLUTTON wanga gut, wanga belly, big belly, lang belly, lang gut, lang maw

GLUTTONOUS licky licky, nyami nyami, wanga gut, wanga belly, big eye, big belly, lang belly, lang gut

GLUTTONY licky licky, nyami nyami, wanga gut, wanga belly, big eye, big belly, lang belly, lang gut

GNAT (n) jinjy fly

GO 1 (*proceed*) mek a flex, mek a move, faawud, go chu 2 (v. *function*) run, tracks 3 Also see *GOING; GOING TO; GONNA; GO AWAY; GO AWAY!; GO BACK; GO*

EASY ON; GO FOR IT; GO HOME; GO OFF; GO ON; GO OVER; GO OUT; GO WITH

GO AWAY see *DISAPPEAR* or *LEAVE*

GO AWAY! Gu weh!, Gweh!, Tek weh yuself!, Move!, Leggo bou ya!, Move ya!, Kirrout!, Clear off!, Chuck off!

GO BACK 1 (*return*) faawud back, return back, rally back   2 (*turn around and go back*) tun back, rally back   3 (*back up*) back back, dress back

GO BACK HOME (v) fine yu gate, faawud back a yu yaad, go back a yu yaad, rally back a yu yaad, rally back a yu gate, touch back a yu yaad, touch back a yu gate

GO CRAZY 1 (*lose your sanity*) mad, head a tek yu, head a tek waata, lose yu head tu necks covah, drink mad puss piss, nyam mad puss brain - *They're going insane*: Dem hed a tek dem   2 (*get excited; party wildly*) rail up, brok wile, brok out, go haad, gwaan buckwile   3 (*take it too far; act excessively wild*) go luu, luu, gwaan a way, run up and dung

GO EASY ON 1 (*go easy on person X*) low X, tek time wid X, ease X, ease up X, gi X a ease, gi X a ease up - *Go easy on her*: Low har, Tek taim wid har, Iiz har, Iiz har op, Gi har a iiz, Gi har a iiz op

GO EASY ON 1 (v) low, tek time wid   2 (*be too forgiving*) pet

GO FOR IT 1 go fi it, go inna it, go een   2 Also see *GO FOR IT!*

GO FOR IT! Gwaan noh!, Gwaan!, Gwaan chu!, Go deh!, Gi dem!, Go een!, Go inna it!, Run it!, Tek di miggle!, A it dat!

GO HOME go a yu yaad, faawud a yu yaad, find yu gate, find yu yaad, touch yu yaad, touch yu gate, touch home, faawud back, rally back

GO MAD see *GO CRAZY*

GO OFF 1 (*explode*) buss, pop   2 (v. as an alarm) sound   3 (as a party: *rage*) shell dung, shot, happn

GO ON see *CONTINUE*

GO OUT 1 (*go out and meet up with people*) du road, go pan a flex, go pan a endz, flex   2 (*go out all night*) bleach   3 (*date*) deh, deal, go rung   4 Also see *EXIT* or *LEAVE*

GO OUT WITH see *DATE* or *GO OUT*

GO OVER 1 (*look over*) pree   2 (*revisit and discuss*) pree back

GO WILD 1 (*party wildly*) rail up, brok wile, brok out, go haad, gwaan buckwile   2 (*take it too far*) go luu, du luu ting, gwaan a way, run up and dung

GO WITH 1 (*match; compliment*) mesh wid, help, go dung good wid - *Red wine goes with dark chocolate*: Red wain go dong gud wid chaklit - *The jacket goes with the shirt*: Di jakit a help di shot, Di jakit a mesh wid di shot   2 Also see *GO OUT*

GO! Gwaan!, Galang!, Move supm!, Move ya!, Mek a flex!, Flex! - Also see: *GO AWAY!* or *GO FOR IT!*

GOAT pr: guo 1 (*male goat*) rammy, ram goat 2 (*female goat*) nanny goat

GOBBLE UP 1 (v) nyam off   2 (v. *gobble up very quickly*) fups off, flups off

GOING 1 (adj) a go, deh go   2 Also see *GOING TO*

GOING TO 1 (*is/are going to* + verb) a go, deh go, gwen   2 (*was/were going to* + verb) did a go, en a go, go fi go

GOLDEN APPLE (*Spondius dulcis*) june plum, jew plum

GONE 1 (*finished; all gone*) done, (of food) nyam off, (of weed) smoke off, (of drinks) drink off   2 (*sold out*) sell off   3 (*not home; not here*) gaan a road, out a road

GONNA see *GOING TO*

GOOD 1 (of person or thing: *generally good*) wow, goodup, blessed, Godbless   2 (*good-hearted*) goodup goodup, irie, heartical   2 (*well-behaved*) balance, goody goody, mannersable, Godbless   3 (*skillful*) shot, bad, skill, artical, mad, wicked, craab up   4 (of thing: *well made; useful*) goodup, tuff, quality, name brand   5 (*good news*) big tingz   6 Also see *EXCELLENT*

GOOD EVENING! Good night, Good evelin

GOOD JOB! A it dat!, Big up yuself!, Bare ratings!, Mad ting!, Mad!, Wikid!, Ray!, Up!, Up mi seh!, Way up!, Up! Up! Up!, Brap! Brap!, Det! Det! Det!, Large up yuself!, Wowatu!

GOOD MORNING! Maanin!, Maki!

GOOD TO GO (adj. of things only: *all set and accounted for*) lock, set, strap up, deh pan ice, chock an belay, fit an frock, cook an curry

GOOD VIBES 1 (*positive signals*) a good vibes, a positive vibes   2 (*good feelings*) gladness, niceness, upliffment, upfulness, Iyah ites

GOODBYE (Also see *I'M LEAVING*) 1 (polite terms) Walk good, Mannaz, Respeck, God go wid yu, Irie, More life, Keep trong, Keep di trong, Cool runninz, Til wi buck again, Wen mi si yu, Inna di morrows, Tek kya, Ef life spare   2 (casual) Likkle more, Laytah, Earlyah, Inna di laytaz, Eazy, Bless, Movements, Linkage, Cool, Boom, Aah, Likkle bit, Inna di likkle bit, More time, Kech yu pan di strangz, Mi wi see yu, Mi wi kech yu wan nex time, Big up yuself   3 (rootsy and Rasta) Bless, Blessed Love, Iyah Ites, Ites, Roots, Jah roots, Jah Love, Jah guide, Jah guidance, Guidance, Fullness, Rasta Love, Love Rasta, Keep ih trong   4 Also see *I'M LEAVING*

GOOF OFF /GOOF AROUND ramp, skin up, draw cyaad, skylark, jesta

GOOFBALL (n) bubu, cartoon, bobo, clown, acrobat, menkeh

GOOSEBERRY (*Phyllanthus acidus*) jimbilin, cherrymeena

GOOSEBUMPS goose pimple

GOSSIP 1 (n. *hearsay*) mix up, passa passa, ray ray, su su, seh seh, labrish, labba labba, chatinz, chat chat, hearso, carry-go-bring-come, come-come-seh, yabba yabba 2 (v. *to gossip*) labrish, su su, sus, carry go bring come, labba labba, yabba yabba

GOSSIPER long tounge, labrisher, nuttn-fi-du, madda radio, carry-go-bring-come

GOURD 1 (*large gourd*) calabash, gordy 2 (*small gourd*) packy 3 (*shekere gourd drum*) shaka

GOVERNMENT (*the government*) di gobamen, di system, Babylon

GRAB 1 (*pick up*) tek up, palmz, pawn, pawn up 2 (*snatch; sieze*) palms, pawn 3 (*clutch*) hol on pan, grap on pan, have up 4 (*grab by the collar*) collar, drape

GRACKLE (*Greater Antillean Grackle*) cling cling

GRADE (*level in school*) form - *the sixth grade*: di six faam

GRADUALLY likkle likkle, one one, bit bit

GRANDCHILD granpickney

GRANDFATHER granfadda, granpupa, papa, tatafk

GRANDMOTHER granmadda, granmuma, nana, gang gang, nen nen

GRAPEFRUIT 1 (*pomelo*) shaddock 2 (*tangelo*) ugly fruit, ugly

GRAPPLE (*wrestle*) grabble, rassle, ketch up

GRATE (v) grater

GRATITUDE (n) appricialove, love

GRAVE (adj. *serious*) real, deep

GREAT see *EXCELLENT* or *AWESOME* or *HUGE*

GREAT! see *AWESOME!*

GREED craven, payaka, licky licky

GREEDY 1 (adj. *grasping; avaricious*) grabbalicious, grabby grabby, crabbit, payaka, licky licky, nyammy nyammy, harbour sharkin, hogganeerin 2 (*craving;*

covetous) craven, cubbitch, shine yeye, red yeye, wanty wanty, licky licky, beggy beggy, co<u>vee</u>tchous 3 (n. *greedy person*) harbour shark, payaka, bella, wanga gut 4 also see *GLUTTONOUS*

GREET hail, hail up, big up, bless up, ites up

GREETINGS hail, hail up, big up, bless up, Ites up 2 (*Send my greetings to X*) Hail up X fi mi, Big up X fi mi, Shout up X fi mi, Sen a shout tu X fi mi

GRIEVE 1 (vi) ceremone 2 (v. *grieve for*) fret pan, cry fi

GRIM see *HOPELESS; PESSIMISTIC*

GRIMACE 1 (n) screw, monkey face 2 (v) screw, mek monkey face

GRIN 1 (n) skin teet, kinteet 2 (v) skin teet, kin teet

GRIN AND BEAR IT liv it out, run wid it, angle it, push on chu, press on chu, ban yu belly

GRIND AGAINST (*grind against while dancing*) wine pan

GROPE (v) grab up, touch up, feel up, fingle, fingle up, fingle fingle, feel up feel up

GROSS 1 (*disgusting*) renk 2 Also see *RUDE* or *VULGAR*

GROUCHY misareble, cantankarous, cramoojin, crampify

GROUND 1 (n) grong, dutty, dut 2 (adj. *crushed*) crush up, mash up, chunk up

GROUP 1 (n) set 2 (*social clique*) posse, crew 3 (*category*) set, class

GROUPER 1 (*giant Goliath grouper fish*) june fish, jewfish 2 (*rock grouper*) rock fish

GROVE (n. of fruit trees) walk

GROWN UP 1 (adj. *physically mature*) hard back 2 (adj. *responsible*) balance, av sense 3 Also see *GROWNUP*

GROWNUP 1 (n. *mature person*) big smaddy, big people 2 (n. *grown man*) big man, hard back man 3 (n. *grown woman*) big ooman, hard back ooman 4 Alse see *GROWN UP*

GRUDGE (v. *hold a grudge*) carry feelinz, carry belly, keep malice, av up 2 (vi. *hold a grudge against*) carry feelings fi, carry belly fi, keep malice fi

GUARD 1 (n) gyaad 2 (n. *prison guard*) bosun 3 (v. *watch over*) mine, look afta, govern, canchol

GULLIBLE 1 (adj) simple, easy, no know bout, no know di time, grow wid yu granny, no know di Schweppes 2 (n. *gullible person*) salad, simpleton, sample, goose, press-button, remote, cuffy, kwashi, bongo, moko

GULP gwap

GUM (n. *chewing gum*) wriggleys, ching gum

GUN 1 (*handgun*) iyan, nine, leng, hamma, piece, enfossa, choppa, hot tool, tool, knockinz, john, skeng, shoes, (*38 revolver*) speshi, (*automatic pistol*) matic, tic 2 (*rifle*) long gun, tall up tall up, chiney K, carbine 3 (*shotgun*) pumpie

GUNK (n) matta matta, kuru kuru, koro koro, nyaka nyaka, plekeh plekeh, screbbeh

GUNMAN shotta, steppa, kwenga, knockist, bandolero, gundolero

GUNSHOT 1 (*a single gunshot*) shot, clap 2 Also see *GUNSHOTS*

GUNSHOTS shot, coppashot, teflon, blue steel - *Gunshots are being fired*: Shat a faya, Shat a bos, Shat a bliez, Shat a biit, Shat a klap, etc.

GUT 1 (*pit of the stomach*) belly bottom 2 (*intuition*) belly bottom 3 (*paunch*) belly gut 4 (*intestines*) tripe, guts

GUTS 1 (*courage*) gumption, heart, talawah 2 (*intestines*) tripe

GUTTER guttah, colbut (from *culvert*)

GUY bredrin, bredda, umbre, (*young guy*) yout

GUZZLE 1 (v. gulp) gwap 2 Also see *USE UP* or *CONSUME*

HACKED UP (adj) chop up chop up, lass up, macheted, nyaka nyaka up, saaka saaka up, malahack, mammick

HAD 1 (v) did av, en av, did ha, en ha 2 Also see *HADN'T*

HADN'T (in past perfect tenses) neva eva, neva, neva did, neva en - *I hadn't visited Florida before I moved there*: Mi neva eva vizit Flarida bifuo mi muuv deh, Mi neva vizit Flarida bifuor mi muuv deh, Mi neva did vizit Flarida bifuor mi did muuv deh, Mi neva en vizit Flarida bifuor mi en muuv deh

HAG 1 (n) hygue, hige 2 (*The Old Hag*) Di Ole hygue, Di Ole Hige, Di Ole Suck - *The Old Hag is gonna get you!*: Di Uol Haig a go get yu!

HAGGLE higgle, bawl dung di price, talk dung di price

HAIR pr: ier 1 (*a strand of hair*) a locks 2 (*head of hair*) head - *Her hair is short*: Har hed shaat 3 (*patchy hair; clumpy hair*) dry head, picky picky head, peppa seed head 4 Also see *FRIZZY; KINKY; STRAIGHT HAIR; STRAIGHTENED*

HAIR BAND bandu

HAIRCUT trim

HALF see *MIXED RACE*

HALF-ASSED hastey, short han, haaf staff

HALFWAY haafweh, paatweh

HAMMER pr: ama 1 (v. *hit once with a hammer*) baff, pung, fum 2 (v. *hammer repeatedly*) tum tum, fum fum, mala mala

HAMMERHEAD SHARK (n) shevil-nose shark

HAND DOWN (*bequeath*) ded leff gi - *My grandfather handed the house down to me (when he died)*: Mi granfaada ded lef gi mi di ous

HAND OVER leggo, let off

HANDCUFFS prison bangle, maggie

HANDKERCHIEF henkichi

HANDLE 1 (n) angle 2 (v. *resolve; manage*) canchol, look afta, deal wid, angle, govern, hol dung, saat out 3 (v. *can't handle*) cyaan tek, cyaan manage, cyaan angle, cyaan deal wid, cyaan run wid, cyaan liv wid, cyaan canchol, cyaan govern

HANDOUT (n. *a handout; something given out of charity*) freeness

HANDSOME 1 (adj) dappa, look good, sauly, chraptin (from *strapping*) 2 (n. *p*

HANG ABOUT see *LOITER*

HANG AROUND see *LOITER* or *HANG OUT*

HANG BACK 1 (vi. *sit back and watch; keep out of the action*) watch an pree, hol yu corner, tan so back, cotch and watch, mass out, mass 2 Also see *RELAX*

HANG ON see *HOLD ON*

HANG OUT 1 (*spend time; chill*) bill, endz out, eazy, bill back, medz out, medz, flex, jooks, quat (from *squat*), hol a vibes, cool, cool out, breeze out, eaze, eaze out, mek up time, lime, satta, cotch 2 (v. *hang out regularly*) par, flex, move tugedda, jooks, lime, cotch 3 Also see *CHILL OUT WITH; ASSOCIATE WITH; HANGOUT*

HANGER (n. for shirt or pants) rack

HANGOUT (n. *meetup spot*) endz, chill spot

HAPPEN (v) gwaan, appm, happn, go, go so

HAPPENING 1 (adj. of place or party: *jumping; lit; hot*) hot up, mad up, a happn, a apm, a shot, tun up, a sell off, craab up   2 (adj. *in session*) a kip, a gwaan   3 (n. *an event*) a gwaaninz, a happeninz

HAPPENINGS (n) gwaaninz, happeninz, runninz

HAPPINESS gladness

HAPPY 1 (of current mood) glad, irie, vibesy, heart full, inna yu ackee, inna yu gungo   2 (*extremely happy right now*) glad bag buss, full a vibes   3 (of personality: *always happy*) irie, vibesy, upful, jolly   4 (v. *make person X happy*) sweet, full X heart

HAPPY GO LUCKY 1 (adj) gladdy gladdy 2 (*happy-go-lucky female*) gladdis, frightn Friday, neva-see-come-see   3 (*happy-go-lucky male*) gladstan

HARASS (v) hackle, hackle up, tek set pan, hitch up pan, draw dung pan, chuck ih pan, cold up, coas up, t orment, presha, udge

HARASSMENT hacklinz

HARD 1 (*firm*) tuff, pack up   2 (*difficult*) ruffa, deep, sticky, sipple   3 (*harsh*) coas, ruffa, deep, dread   4 (adv. *diligently*) a no likkle - *I try hard*: A no likl mi chrai

HARDCORE 1 (adj. *uncompromising*) no easy, militantly   2 Also see *EXPLICIT*

HARDEN cake up

HARDSHIP chubble, chubbles, trials, crosses, hacklinz, bodderation, sufferation, tribulation

HARDWORKING ambitionable, trong eye, haad back

HARSH (of weather or punishment or situation) daak, deep, coas, dread, wikid, rhygin, haad bad

HAS see *HAVE*

HASN'T see *HAVEN'T*

HASSLE 1 (*a hassle*) a stress, a bodderation, a tax   2 (vt. *to hassle*) badda badda, hackle, hackle wid, fass wid, mell wid, tek set pan, hitch up pan   3 (v. *be a hassle to do something*) cost, tax - *It's gonna be a hassle for you*: It a go kaas yu, It a go tax yu

HASSLES hacklinz, bodderation, chubbles, parangles

HAT 1 (*woven thatch hat*) trash hat, tatch hat, wa-fi-du   2 (*nice straw hat; panama hat*) jippy jappa   3 (*knitted tam to cover dreadlocks*) tam, crown   4 (*cap*) cyap, snapback, fitted   5 (*fedora*) rim hat   6 (*beret*) berit   7 (Rasta bowler hat) bowl hat   8 (*stovepipe hat*) bunpan hat

HATE 1 (n. *hatred*) badmind, hateridge 2 (v. *not enjoy; not tolerate*) cyaa tek, cyaa manage 3 (*despise*) bun, bun out, bun faya pan - *I hate cold weather*: Mi kyaa manij di kowl - *I hate violence*: Mi bon voilens

HATRED (sometimes pr): ietrij - (n) hateridge, badmind

HAUNT (v. *as a ghost*) tek set pan

HAUNTED 1 (adj) tek set pan by duppy 2 Also see *POSSESSED*

HAVE 1 (v) av, ha, hol, got 2 (*not have; don't have; doesn't have*) naav, naa 3 (*of a party or event: host*) keep, put on - *They're having a party on Hope Road*: Dem a kip a paati op a Hope Road, Paati a kip op a Hope Road 4 (for present perfect tense) *I have visited Florida*: Mi vizit Flarida aredi 5 see *HAVEN'T*

HAVE A HOLD ON (*have a hold on somebody*) av X a way - *Your sweet talk has a hold on me*: Fiyu lirix av mi a wie

HAVE FUN hold a vibes, fulljoy yuself, go haad, sree, par, spar

HAVE MERCY ON 1 (*go easy on*) tek time wid, 'low 2 (*be too forgiving*) pet

HAVE SEX 1 sort out, hook, slam, ram, grine, touch, knock, nazzle, frig, rooks off, suss, dugu dugu, get a likkle piece, kech up yu stomok, stir it up, cook stew peas, dance, weld, bubble, soldah, change oil, sawka sawka, play ketchy shooby, do X, go pan a X (X=word for a sex act (see *SEX*)) 2 Also see *HAVE SEX WITH*

HAVE SEX WITH sort out, ride, sheg, frig, rooks off, dance wid, bubble wid, sleep wid, hook, get a likkle piece off a, (from the man's perspective only): stab, slam, ram, knock, nazzle, slap, stamp, taze, tump up, jook, lick dong, dig out, rev out, chubble, fan, change yu oil wid

HAVEN'T 1 (for present perfect progressive tense: *haven't been* + *-ing*) naa - *I haven't been sleeping lately*: Mi naa sliip fram weh die 3 (for present perfect tense) no - *I haven't done my work yet*: Mi no du mi wok yet

HE 1 im 2 Also see *IS; ISN'T; WAS; WASN'T*

HEAD (*very top of head*) mole

HEADSTRONG purpose, crabbit, trong-eye, facety, haad iez, warify

HEALTHY 1 (adj) hearty 2 (Rasta term for vegetarian salt-free lifestyle) Ital

HEAR 1 (of sound) ear 2 (of information) sight, ear

HEARSAY see *GOSSIP* or *RUMOUR*

HEART ATTACK (*have a heart attck*) ketch heart attack

HEART DISEASE bad heart

HEARTBURN (*acid reflux*) bad stomach, bun stomach, mauli gripe an fluxy complaint

HEARTLESS 1 (of person) cowl, dog heart, ugly, daak, evilous, misareble, dry yeye, ded yeye, pagan, heathen, donkya 2 (of act or behavior) evilous, dog-heart, dutty, misareble, pagan, heathen, donkya

HEAT 1 (n. only when source of heat is indicated or implied) hot 2 (v) hot up

HEAT UP hot up

HEATED (adj. of air or food, etc) heatify - *The pool is heated*: Di puul hiitifai

HEATHEN (n) back-slider

HEAVEN pr: ebm

HEAVY 1 (*large and heavy; unwieldy*) wagga wagga, lagga lagga, lugga lugga, bufu bufu, bufutu 2 (*hard to face*) deep, dread 3 Also see *FAT*

HEDGE (n) bush fence

HEDONIST (derogatory term) heathenist, heathen, soft hand bwoy

HEDONISTIC (of person) gyalantin

HEEL (n) heelback

HELLO Greetinz, Blessinz, Blessed love, Bless, Bless up, Respeck, Hail, Ites, Ites up, Yes - (more casual or slang) Yah man, Yow, Blow, Boom, Big up, Rrrr, Wikid, Yaga, Yush 2 (*Say hello to X for me*) Hail up X fi mi, Big up X fi mi, Shout up X fi mi, Sen a shout tu X fi mi

HELP OUT 1 (vi. *give financial assistance or food*) gi a bly, let off supm, let off sittn 2 (vt. *help person X out; pull X together*) sort X out, draw X up, liff X up, raise X up

HEM AND HAW bob an weave, buckshuffle

HEMORRHOIDS pile

HER 1 (pronoun) har 2 (possessive) har, fi-har, (rural only): him, fi-him

HERBS (for seasoning) legginz

HERE 1 (n. *this place*) yasso 2 (adv) ya 3 (*right here*) right ya so 4 (*in here*) in ya, een ya 5 (*on here*) on ya 6 (*Here I am*) Si mi ya 7 (*Here X is/are*) Si X ya - *Here it is*: Si it ya - *Here they are*: Si dem ya

HERE AND THERE (adv) yasso an desso, one one, kyatta kyatta

HERE YOU GO See it ya, Canchol dis, Tek dis

HERMAPHRODITE shim, he-she

HERON gaulin

HERNIA boasin, bossun

HERS fi-har, (rural only) fi-him

HERSELF 1 (n) harself 2 (adv for emphasis) same one - *Didn't she herself tell you to go?* No shi siem wan tel yu fi go?

HESITANT (adj) bummy

HESITATE 1 (v) hitch, jesta, tek check 2 (*hesitate to speak or admit something*) block a soun, hitch, buckshuffle, bob an weave 3 (*NOT hesitate to*) no ramp fi, no hitch fi, no skin up fi - *He won't hesitate to take a man's life*: Him no hich fi mek dopi

HEX 1 (*magic curse*) guzu, buzu, obeah 2 (v. *put a hex on*) mark, fix, bun bad cyangle fi, bun bad light fi, wok pan, put obeah pan, set obeah pan, set goat mout pan, gi X foot (X=person), set sittn fi

HI see *HELLO*

HIBISCUS shoe flowaz, mahoe

HIDE 1 (vt. *obscure*) mas 2 (vi. *hide out*) mas out, mas, cool out

HIDEOUS (adj. *unsightly*) crawny, zutupek, hoodias 2 (n. *hideous looking person*) zutupek, baboon face

HIGH 1 (*high on weed*) frass, head craab up, black up 2 (*tall*) long, gara gara

HIGH CLASS 1 (of person) stoosh, uptong, hitey titey, society, risto, top rankin, tapanaris 2 (of place) stoosh, quality, cris, hitey titey

HIGH QUALITY (adj) name brand, quality, tuff, top shelf, top a di top, toppity top, toppa top, goodup, goodup goodup, preps, original

HIGH SOCIETY 1 (n) society, uptong, di uptowna dem, di tapanaris dem, di risto dem, di top rankin dem 2 (adj) stoosh, society, uptong, cris, hitey titey, risto, top rankin, tapanaris

HILARIOUS 1 (adj) no easy 2 (n. *something hilarious*) laafin spoil

HIMSELF 1 (n) himself 2 (adv for emphasis) same one - *Didn't he himself tell you to go?* No him siem wan tel yu fi go?

HINT 1 (n) prips 2 (v. *hint at*) drap wud bout 3 (*tip off*) prips off

HIP see *COOL*

HIS 1 (adj) him, fi-him 2 (pred adj) fi-him (Note: the m in *him* is usually nasalized)

HISTORY pr: ischri

HIT 1 (*hit song*) scorcha, big chune 2 (v. *strike*) lick, lash 3 (*collide with*) bunks, buck, buff, baff, lick inna 4 (v. of stage or road) touch - *They are expected to hit the stage soon*: Dem fi toch di stiej suun 5 Also see *SLAP; PUNCH; HIT ON; HIT IT OFF*

HIT IT OFF 1 (*find oneselves compatible*) mesh, go dung good - *She and I hit it off*: Mi an shi did go dung gud 2 (v. *not hit it off*) see *INCOMPATIBLE*

HIT ON 1 (*try to seduce*) lyrics, drap lyrics pan, look argument wid, look 2 (*continue hitting on someone who is not interested*) put argument tu, put words tu

HIT THE ROAD du road, touch di road, crush di road, mek a trod, mek a tracks, mek a flex

HIT THE STREETS du road, touch di road, crush di road, mek a trod, mek a tracks, mek a flex

HO see *SLUT*

HOARSE (of voice) oase, cratchy

HOBO dutty bungle, boogooyaga

HOLD 1 (v. *grasp, hold onto*) hol on pan, have up, canchol 2 (v. *detain*) clamp dung

HOLD A GRUDGE carry feelings, carry belly, keep malice, av up

HOLD BACK 1 (vi. *restrain yourself*) hol yu corner, hol out, put yuself pan pause 2 (vi. *hesitate to speak*) hol back yu chat, block a soun, hitch

HOLD ON 1 (*not let go*) hol on, grab on 2 (*physically hold on to*) hol on pan, grab on pan, have up 3 (*keep*) control, conchol - *Hold on to your money*: Kanchuol yu moni 4 (*Stay right there; I'll be right back*) No move, No go noweh, Tan tuddy, Tan deh

HOLD STILL tan tuddy

HOLD UP (v. *impede; block*) cold up, hinda

HOLE 1 (n) hol 2 (*sinkhole*) singket, stonehole, bung 3 (*animal lair*) bung

HOLY hola

HOME yaad, grong, creech

HOMOSEXUAL 1 (adj) fishy, fruity, funny, gaan 2 (n. *gay man*) batty man, batty bwoy, chi chi man, chi chi bwoy, fish, bugga man, mama man, funny man, anti-man, beeps, beenix, battis, punga man, fruit, priest, fella, guy, men, doodle, hoodini, gaylord, rod man, digalow 3 (*lesbian*) sodomite, man royal

HOMOSEXUALITY numba two, battism, batty bizniz, funny bizniz, fishy bizniz, fishiness

HONEST 1 (*straightforward*) strait, no easy, coas, dry yeye, widout folly 2 (*trustworthy*) heartical, bonafide, good up good up

HONESTLY 1 (*Honestly…*) Big man ting, Big ooman ting, Big an seerous 2 (pred adv. *in an honest manner*) strait

HONOR /HONOUR 1 (n. *reputation*) name, knowinz 2 (v. *acknowledge*) gi respeck tu, mention 3 (v. *praise*) big up, large up, sallute, liff up, count, wowatu

HOOD 1 (n. of car) bonnet 2 (n. of jacket or sweater) hoodie

HOOLIGAN tuggz, hot skull, rudebwoy, starbwoy, guineagog, tegereg, screwface, ruffneck, ruffian, russian, war monga, sluggard, scufflah, baddaz, chucky, radge, tuff, bullbucka, badlaw, baddy boo

HOORAY! Mad ting!, Mad!, Wikid!, A it dat!, Ray!, Up!, Up mi seh!, Way up!, Up! Up! Up!, Brap! Brap!, Det! Det! Det!

HORN 1 (n. *animal's horn or conch shell used for blowing*) abeng 2 (n. *brass horn or car horn*) haan

HORNY 1 (of female: *sexually aroused*) ready fi wine, hot up, staat up, stir up 2 (of male: *desperate for sex*) back up, des, hungry, ready

HORRIBLE see *BAD; HIDEOUS*

HORRIBLY (when intensifying negative-connotation adjectives such as *angry; difficult; damaged; disfigured*) bad, bad bad - *It's horribly damaged*: It mash op bad; It mash op bad bad

HORROR see *FEAR* or *DISGUST*

HORSE 1 (n) haas 2 (*elderly horse*) namprel

HOT 1 (*spicy*) peppa 2 (*What a hot day!*) Wat a day hot! 3 (*Wow, the sun is hot!*) Di sun a seh one!, Di sun a talk!, Di sun no ramp fi hot! 4 Also see *SEXY*

HOT CHOCOLATE OR COCOA cocoa tea, chocolate tea

HOT TEMPERED ignarant, ig, cross, hot skull, warify, wassy, crabbit, mizarebl

HOTEL pr: otel (n. *inn*) lodgin house, lodginz, guest house

HOUSE 1 ous 2 Also see *HOME*

HOUSEKEEPER (*cleaner; maid*) helpa

HOUSING COMPLEX scheme, housin scheme

HOW 1 how 2 (*how many*) how much 3 (*how much*) how many 4 (*Look how X the Y is!*) Wat a way X Y!, Wat a X Y! - *Look how big the moon is!* Wat a wie di muun big!, Wat a muun big!

HOW ARE YOU? /HOW ARE THINGS? Yu good?, Yu arite?, How tingz a gwaan?, Yu cool?, How yu stay?, How yu du?, Evriting balance?, Evryting cool?, Irie?, Evryting criss?, All fruits ripe?, Cool breeze?, Evryting cook an curry?, Evryting fit an frock?, Evryting ites?, Everyting pan ice?

HOW MANY how much - *How many dollars do you have?* Umoch dala yu av?

HOW OLD ARE YOU? Yu a how much?, Yu a wa age?, How ol yu be?, Wah age yu be?

HOWEVER 1 (*but*) still, yet 2 (adv) how so eva, howsomeva - *however you want to do it*: owsomeva yu waan dwii

HOWL (v. of dog) hound, houn

HUG 1 (n) squeeze 2 (v) squeeze, ugg up 3 (v. *hug and cuddle with*) rap up wid

HUGE helleva, big big, wagga wagga, raatid, raas

HUMILIATE (v) violate, dis, cold up, reduce, tek X mek prekeh, tek X mek poppy show, tek liberty wid, send a shop

HUMMING BIRD (*doctor bird; large species of humming bird that is the national bird of Jamaica*) doctah bud, scissors tail

HUNG OVER (adj) mash up

HUNGER 1 (*desire for food*) hungry 2 (*lack of food*) hungry 3 (v. *hunger for; long for*) enkafi 4 (*die of hunger*) ded fi hungry

HUNGRY 1 (adj) ungry 2 (*extremely hungry*) raw, squally, des 3 (v. *be extremely hungry*) ded fi hungry - *I'm hungry*: Onggri a lik mi beli, Mi beli a yaan - (exaggerated) Mi a ded fi onggri, Wait skwaal a kil mi, Mi chraip a nat op, Worm a dig out mi chraip

HUNTER huntaman

HURRICANE big breeze, breezeblow, staam

HURRY 1 (v) mek hase, pick up foot 2 (*to be in a hurry*) deh pan hase 3 (*Hurry up!*) Mek ase!, Pick up yu foot!, Faya Faya downtown!, Bun tyah!

HURT 1 (adj. *wounded*) mash up, pop up 2 (*emotionally hurt*) ben, ben up, cut up, hut, sheg up 3 (v. *injure*) mash, pop, buss 4 (*to ache*) bun, hot, (of stomach only) gripe, (of teeth only) edge, nedge 5 Also see *UPSET; STING*

HUSH 1 (vt. *make quiet*) quayat 2 (vt. of baby: *soothe to sleep; rock to sleep*) baya 3 (*Hush!*) Oy!, Tapinize! (from *Stop the noise!*)

HUSK 1 (n) trash, huks 2 (v) trash, huks

HUSTLE 1 (*do informal business to survive*) run road, juggle, nyam a food 2 (*hurry*) pick up foot, mek hase

HUT 1 (*little house*) hutch ranch, patta 2 (*thatched hut*) tatu

HUTIA coney

HYMN (n) sankey

HYPE (v. of event or entertainer X: *hype up*) mad up, loud up, send X a road

HYPERTENSION presha

HYPOCRITE 1 wagonist 2 Also see *TRAITOR*

I mi, a, I an I

I AM (when followed by a noun) mi a - *I am a fisherman*: Mi a fishaman 2 (when followed by an adj) mi - *I am tired*: Mi tayad 3 (when followed by a verb) mi a, mi deh - *I am kidding*: Mi a ramp; Mi deh ramp 4 (+ location) mi deh - *I am here*: Mi deh ya 5 (when completing a phrase that contains *how*) mi stay, mi tan - *That's how I am*: A so mi tan 6 (when completing a phrase containing *what* or *who*) mi be, mi is - *You know who I am*: Yu nuo a huu mi bi; Yu nuo a huu mi iz 7 Also see *I AM NOT*

I AM NOT 1 (when followed by a noun) mi a no - *I am not a doctor*: Mi a no dakta 2 (+ adj) mi no, mi doan - *I'm not satisfied*: Mi no satisfai; Mi duon satisfai 3 (+ verb) mi naa - *I'm not joking*: Mi naa ramp 4 (+ location) mi no deh - *I am not here*: Mi no deh ya

I DON'T BELIEVE YOU A lie yu a tell, A lie, Wheel and come again, Tek weh yuself, Gweh, Peer lie, Bay lie, Bare lie, Pure lie, Lie an story, Lyad story

I DON'T CARE Mi no business, Mi no biniz, Mi no matta, Mi no cater, Mi no cya - *I don't care what happens*: Eniting a eniting, Evriting a evriting

I'LL BE RIGHT THERE Soon faawud, Soon reach, Soon touch, Soon ketch, Mi a come, Mi a faawud

I'M LEAVING Mi a shoob out, Shoob out, Mi wi see yu, Mi a galang, Mi a cut, Mi a dip, Mi a leave out, Mi a lef out, Mi a splurt, Mi a bonks, Mi gaan, Mi a go step now, Mi a mek a step, Mi a tek weh miself, Mi a flash out, Mi a go now, Mi a go weh now, Mi a du so, Mi a go mek a trod now, Mi a mek a trod, Troddinz, Mi a go du road now, Mi a du road, Mi a go mek a tracks now, Mi a mek a tracks, Mi a leggo di endz, Mi a go shake out, Mi a shake out, Shake out, Mi a go tief out, Mi a tief out, Save sopm fi laytah, Mi wi kech yu wan nex time

I'M NOT CONCERNED Mi naa fret, Mi naa hot up mi head, Mi naa watch nuttn, Mi naa watch no face, Mi naa feel no way - Also see *I DON'T CARE*

I'M ON MY WAY Mi a come, Mi a faawud

IDENTICAL same same

IDIOT 1 eedyat, claffy, kunumunu, prekeh, menkeh, poppy show, dunce bat, yam head, coco head, salad, iddyboo, eedyboo, cuffy, kwashi, kwaco 2 Also see *LAUGHING STOCK; LOSER*

IDLE 1 (*lazy*) wukless, igle, cruff, crebbeh, donkya, unambitionable, mafeena 2 (v. *loiter*) igle, hitch, klutch, skylark, tan bout, diggle daggle, linga linga, tarry

IDLER iglaz, loaftah, cruff, crebbeh, donkya man, donkya bwoy, donkya, come aroun, dutty bungle, long seed bwoy, long seed man, grey tone man, boogooyaga, budger

IF 1 ef 2 (*even if*) all ef, all if 3 Also see *CONDITIONAL TENSE*

IGNORANT 1 (adj) daak, simple, no know bout, no know di time, no know wah clock a strike, no know what o'clock, no know di Schweppes, born back a cow, born when yu big, juss fall out a di truck 2 (n. *an ingnorant person*) simpleton, goose, cuffy, kwashi, kwaco, bongo 3 Also see *UNCULTURED; STUPID*

IGNORE 1 (*not respond to*) no ansa, fan off, no seh nuttn tu 2 (*not bother with*) no bizniz wid, no fret pan, no feneh pan 4 (*Please ignore X*) Lef out X, No watch X, No mind X, No chubble yuself wid X

ILL 1 (adj) sick out, poorly, mash up 2 (*nauseated*) sick stomach, sowa stomach, high stomach, sick belly, sowa belly 3 (*mentally ill*) touch, mad, no righted, no balance, head no good, head lick, no heng on right

ILL INTENTIONED see *UNTRUSTWORTHY* or *MALEVOLENT*

ILL MANNERED see *UNCOUTH*

ILLEGITIMATE CHILD outside pickney, out chile, (if father doesn't know it's not his own) jacket

IMAGINE imaginate

IMITATE 1 (vi. *follow what others do*) falla fashion 2 (v. *mimic*) pattan - *Birds immitate eachother's songs*: Bod patan dem wananeda sang 3 Also see *PRETEND*

IMITATION 1 (n. *a fake product*) carbon, casco 2 (adj. of clothing brand or other brand name: *fake; knockoff*) casco, bashco

IMITATOR 1 (*one who copies the style of others*) falla-fashion, falla-fashion monkey, carbon 2 (*imposter; one who pretends to be*) wagonist, wolf

IMMATURE 1 (of person) picknify 2 Also see *UNRIPE*

IMMEDIATELY 1 same time, sed time, jus so, slam bam 2 (pred adv only) same time, quick time, quick stick, quick quick, swips, braps, slam bam - *Tidy up your room at once!*: Pran op yu ruum kwik taim! 3 Also see *RIGHT NOW*

IMMOBILIZE clamp dung, fassn, fastn

IMMORAL dutty, slack, luu, freaky, nassy, ugly, sheg up, evilous, slacka, pagan, heathen, wikid, payaka

IMMORALITY slackness, nassiness, dutty livity, luu ting, freaky bizniz, freakiness, payaka

IMPACT 1 (n. *physical force of impact*) lick, baff, boof   2 (v. *affect*) touch, reach

IMPATIENT jumpy, swiff, impatiance

IMPERTINENCE (n) renkness, brightness, facetyness, freshness, outa orderness, dragupsy

IMPERTINENT (adj) renk, bright, fresh, facety, outa aada

IMPLICATE cyaad, point pan

IMPOLITE see *RUDE ; VULGAR*

IMPORTANT 1 (of person) big, laaj, big an large, big an supa, notchilous, supa dupa   2 (of topic) big an serious, crucial   3 (n. *important man*) notch, general, big supa, supa dupa, bigga head

IMPOTENT (*unable to have an erection*) ded wood, porridge, fluxy, pop dung

IMPREGNATE breed, gi belly, fat up

IMPRESSIVE 1 (of person in terms of talent) bad, mad, shot, wikid, terrible, superble, artical, crucial, craab up, well skill, no easy   2 Also see *AWESOME*

IMPROPER see *INDECENT*

IMPROVE 1 (vt) step up, level up, fix up, sort out, dechakalize, raise up, draw up   2 (vi) level up, step up, fix up, move up, sort out, dechakalize, liff up yuself, set up yuself, raise up yuself

IMPROVISE 1 (of story or lyrics, etc) mek it up, run wid it, mek up ih   2 (of shelter or structure) bitch up   3 (*adapt; get by*) try a ting, try a way, tun han mek fashion, fadge, run wid it

IMPROVISED 1 (of story or lyrics) mek up   2 (of shelter or structure) bitch up, wappm bappm, kabba kabba

IN 1 inna, eena   2 (when lacking an object or when preceding *deh* or *ya*) een - *You're in trouble*: Yu ina chobl, Yu iina chobl - *Please come in*: Du kom iin

IN A LITTLE WHILE likkle fram dis

IN ADVANCE beforetime

IN GOOD SHAPE 1 (adj. of woman) fit, ready, elty, elty baddy 2 (adj. of man) fit, ready, sauly, chaptin

IN SHAPE 1 (adj. of woman) fit, ready, elty, elty baddy 2 (adj. of man) fit, ready, sauly, chaptin

IN SPITE OF no mind, no care

IN STYLE 1 (of fashion or product) hype, shot, shot a road, a du road, a run road, a lead, a happn, sell off, slap weh, a slap, a clap, a lick, big, craab up, tun up, buck, bashy - *Skinny jeans are in style right now*: Chriet jiinz a slap ya now 2 Also see *POPULAR*

IN TERMS OF far as, bout, bou

IN THE FIRST PLACE fram mawnin, fram di fuss

IN THE KNOW (adj. *aware of what's up*) know bout, know di ting, know di schweppes, know di runninz, deh pan top, know wha clock a strike, know what o'clock

IN THE OLD DAYS 1 fuss time, long time, dem time deh, before time, wen mi yeye deh a mi knee 2 Also see *LONG AGO*

IN THE PAST see *LONG AGO* or *IN THE OLD DAYS*

IN THOSE DAYS dem time deh

INCAPABLE no ready, cyaa paas, cyaa go chu

INCITE set on, call dung

INCLUDE count

INCLUDING (*even including*) dung tu

INCOMPATIBLE 1 (of objects) no mesh 2 (of people) no tek tea, no mesh, no plant peas - *He and I are incompatible*: Mi an him no tek tii; etc

INCOMPETENT no ready, dibby dibby, nyamps, crebbeh crebbeh

INCOMPLETE 1 (of task) no done yet, no ready, no finish, ongle halfweh deh, halfweh done, gyow out 2 Also see *INSUFFICIENT*

INCONSIDERATE coas, donkya, pomptious

INCREDIBLE 1 (adj) mad, wikid, terrible 2 Also see *EXCELLENT*

INDECENCY slackness, dutty livity, luu ting, ugly, nassiness, freakiness

INDECENT (adj. *sexually vulgar*) slack, slacka slacka, dutty, outlaw, luu, nassy, freaky

INDECISIVE fenkeh fenkeh, (*ambivalent*) two mind

INDEED fi chu

INDEED! see *EXACTLY!* or *TOTALLY!*

INDIAN 1 (*person from India or of Indian ancestry*) coolie, (derogatory): baboo 2 (*man from India or of Indian ancestry*) coolie man, Missa Singh 3 (*woman from India or of Indian ancestry*) coolie ooman, coolie gyal, Mrs Singh, mawi 4 (adj. of thing or person: *from India or Indian background*) coolie 5 (*little girl of Indian parentage*) betty

INDIFFERENCE donkya

INDIFFERENT donkya, dry yeye, nigretful

INDIGESTION 1 (n) bilious 2 (v. *cause indigestion*) ride - *That soup will give you indigestion*: Da suup deh wi raid yu

INDIGNANT ignorant, ig

INDULGE 1 (vi) go haad, live up, spree, full-ticipate, walla walla 2 (vt. of healthy and useful activities: *indulge in*) hol, tek een, penetrate, full-ticipate inna 3 Also see *PARTICIPATE*

INEFFECTIVE 1 (of thing or person) wutless, no ready, fenkeh fenkeh, pyaa pyaa, dibby dibby, fluxy 2 (of policy or method) no wut, wutless

INFECT (vt) poison, carrup (from *corrupt*)

INFECTED 1 (adj) full a corruption, brok out 2 (v. *get infected*) brok out, festa, ketch germs, gyadda infamation

INFERIOR 1 (*lacking ability*) wutlis, wuklis, saaf (*soft*), too fenkeh, fenkeh fenkeh, dibby dibby, crebbeh, crebbeh crebbeh, kabba kabba, chamba chamba, nyamps, pyaa pyaa, sopsy, fluxy, pissy tail, half inch, half staff, no wut, no use, pop dung 2 (*poorly made*) crebbeh crebbeh, tufenkeh, fenkeh fenkeh, fluxy, dibby dibby, wutlis, wuklis, batta foot, batta ears, sketel, streggeh, screbbeh screbbeh, kaba kaba, chamba chamba, boogooyaga, butu, common, half inch, half staff, knockoff, riff raff, casco, tikki tikki, jingbang, pyaa pyaa, no wut, no use, pop dung, ol bruck, nyamps

INFERTILE 1 (*infertile woman*) mule 2 (*infertile man*) round seed, man guinep, geldinz 3 (*infertile tree*) man tree

INFIDELITY (n. *sexual infidelity*) bun

INFLAMMATION information

INFLUENCE infilence

INFORM 1 (*give info to*) prips off, mek X know (X=person) - *They informed him already*: Dem did prips him aaf aredi; Dem did mek him nuo aredi 2 (*inform about a cheating spouse or partner*) pinch, buzz, page 3 Also see *SNITCH*

INFORMATION (*scoop; latest info*) pree, current - *What's the latest information?* A wa i prii?

INFORMER see *SNITCH*

INFURIATE see *ANGER*

INFURIATING bexashus, bextatious

INHALE draw breeze

INHERITANCE dedleff

INITIATIVE gumption

INJECTION (n. *hypodermic injection*) jook

INJURE /INJURED pop up, mash up, buss, buss up

INJUSTICE iniquity, partiality

INN (n) lodging house, lodginz

INNOCENT 1 (*pure*) goody goody 2 (*naive*) goody goody, simple, grow wid yu granny

INQUISITIVE (*nosey*) fass, nuff, eggz up, edge up, swiff, bumptious, pomptious

INSANE 1 (adj) mad, full mad, gaan, head gaan, head tek waata 2 (v. *go insane*) gaan mad, lose yu head tu necks covah, head a tek waata, drink mad puss piss, nyam mad puss brain - *They're going insane*: Dem hed a tek waata, Dem a luuz dem ed tu nexkova, Dem a jrink mad pusss piss

INSECT bugaboo

INSEPARABLE 1 (of things) hitch up tugedda, tie up tugedda, stitch up tugedda, kotch up tugedda, married 2 (of friends: *joined at the hip*) hitch up tugedda, stitch up tugedda, laka batty an bench

INSIDE OUT pan di wrong side, wrong side out

INSIGNIFICANT (adj) dibby dibby, pwoko pwoko, pyaa pyaa, so so

INSINUATE waan seh, try fi seh

INSPECT pree, tek a stock a

INSPIRATION (Rasta terms) I-spiration, Italization

INSTANTLY (pred adv only) jus so, baps, same time

INSTEAD OF sted a, in place a, more dan, (only when placed at beginning of phrase) before - *Instead of wine I'd like some beer*: Bifuo wain miida laik som bier

INSTIGATE set on

INSUFFICIENT 1 (of amount) no nuff, degeh degeh, dibby dibby 2 (of effort or ability) no nuff, tufenkeh, too fenkeh fenkeh, too dibby dibby, too palla palla, too kaba kaba, mafeena 3 Also see *SLAP DASH*

INSULT 1 (n. *an insult*) violation, dis, bulla, boof 2 (v. *to insult*) dis, violate, hype pan 3 (*berate with insults; cuss out*) trace, wild up, rax up

INSULTING (adj) insultive, renk, bad minded, low countin, coas (from *coarse*), fresh, bright, outa aada

INTEGRITY (*uprightness*) characta, ambition

INTELLIGENT (adj) intelligence, koncchos (*conscious*) - *I'm very intelligent*: Mi wel intelijens

INTEND 1 (v) intention 2 (v. *intend to*) go fi, intention fi, out fi

INTENSE 1 (of personality) no easy 2 Also see *HARSH*

INTENTIONAL /INTENTIONALLY (adv) fi purpose

INTERACT (of specific people: *hang out together*) paar, flex, move tugedda

INTERCOURSE see *SEX*

INTERESTED 1 (v. *be interested in*) eena, intress inna, pree, check fi 2 (v. *be interested in romantically*) pree, look, penny, check fi, like off - *I'm not interested in what you're interested in*: Mi no iina weh yu iina; Mi no chek fi weh yu a chek fa

INTERFERE see *MEDDLE*

INTERPRET twiss

INTERRUPT cross-cut

INTESTINES belly gut, tripe

INTIMATE 1 (adj. as friends) tick, laka batty an bench, a points, groundz 2 (as lovers) deh

INTIMIDATE see *FRIGHTEN; THREATEN*

INTO inna, (when more emphasis is needed) eena - Also see *INTERESTED*

INTRODUCE pr: inchajyuus 1 (v. *to present*) call up 2 (v. *import for the first time*) carry X come a Y - *It was Bligh who introduced breadfruit to Jamaica*: A did Bligh weh kya bredfruut kom a Jamieka 3 (vt. *bring together*) link up, plug een - *I'm gonna introduce you to each other*: Mi a link op unu, Mi a plog iin unu

INTRUDE see *MEDDLE*

INTUITION belly bottom

INVADE come een pan, go een pan - *Germany invaded Poland*: Germany go iin pan Poland

INVESTIGATE 1 (vt) pree, look inna, check, suss out 2 (*take a peek*) prips, tek a prips

INVITE (v. *summon person X*) sen fi X, sen X come, sen call X, sen come call X

INVOKE call dung

INVOLVED 1 (adj. *participating*) hitch up, involve, link up, een deh, rope een, chune een 2 (*heavily involved*) deep inna it 3 (*involved in a sexual or romantic relationship*) deh, in a dealinz, carry straw 4 Also see *GET INVOLVED*

IRONED (adj. *pressed; having no wrinkles*) criss

IRONY joke - *The irony is that his car broke down just after he bought a new engine for it*: Di juok a seh him kyaar pop dung suun aafa him bai a nyuu injin fi it

IRRATIONAL 1 (adj. *delusional*) luu, no righted inna yu head, no righted, no balance, nervous, touch 2 (v. *be irrational*) av no sense, luu, liv luu, drink mad puss piss

IRRESPONSIBILITY donkya

IRRESPONSIBLE (*not dependable*) donkya, nigretful

IRRITATE 1 (of the skin: *inflame*) bun 2 Also see *PESTER; UPSET; ANGER; CRINGE*

IRRITATED 1 (of the skin: *inflamed*) hot 2 (*annoyed*) pan edge

IRRITATING 1 (*irritating to the skin*) scratchy 2 (of personality) disgustin, fassy, fassyhole, pissy tail 3 (of personality: *whiny and bitchy*) ningy ningy

IS 1 (when followed by a noun) a - *She is my friend*: Shi a mi fren 2 (+ adj) Ø - *John is crazy*: John mad 3 (+ verb) a, deh - *He is kidding*: Him a ramp; Him deh ramp 4 (+ location) deh - *It is on the warf*: It deh pan di waaf 5 (when terminating a phrase that contains *how*) stay, tan - *That's how she is*: A so shi tan 6 (when terminating a phrase containing *what* or *who*) be - *I don't care what it is*: Mi no bizniz wa it bi

ISN'T 1 (when followed by a noun) a no - *She isn't my friend*: Shi a no mi fren 2 (+ adj) no, doan - *She isn't crazy*: Shi no mad; Shi duon mad 3 (+ verb) naa - *He isn't joking*: Him naa ramp 4 (+ location) no deh - *It isn't here*: It no deh ya

ISN'T THAT SO? donti?, doan?, no chu?, no so?

ISOLATED see *REMOTE*

ISSUE 1 (n) matta, subjek, parangle 2 (v. *publish*) push out, drop

ISSUES 1 (n. *matters*) runninz, parangles 2 (n. *interpersonal drama*) mix up, bare tings, passa passa, ray reay, cass cass, confusion, parangles, worries, chubbles 3 (*emotional baggage*) worries an chubbles, parangles, bangarang, palangarang, palangaranga

IT DOESN'T MATTER 1 (*It's not important*) Anyting a anyting, Evriting a evriting 2 Also see *MAKES NO DIFFERENCE*

IT IS 1 (~ + noun) a - *It is a country*: A wan konchri; A konchri 2 (~ + adj) it - *It is good*: It good 3 (~ + verb) it a, it deh - *It is going*: It a go; It deh go 4 (~ + location) it deh - *It is here*: It deh ya 5 Also see *IT ISN'T*

IT ISN'T 1 (~ + noun) a no - *It isn't a joke*: A no juok 2 (~ + adj) it no - *It isn't good*: It no gud 3 (~ + verb) it naa - *It isn't working*: It naa wok 4 (~ + location) it no deh - *It isn't there*: It no deh deh

IT WAS 1 (when followed by a noun or adj) a did, a en - *It was a ghost*: A did dopi, A en dopi - *It was good*: A did gud, A en gud 2 (~ + verb) it did a, it en a - *It was getting dark*: It did a get daak, It en a get daak 3 (~ + location) it did deh - *It was on the table*: It did deh pan i tiebl 4 Also see *IT WASN'T*

IT WASN'T 1 (when followed by a noun or adj) a neva - *It wasn't a problem*: A neva problem - *It wasn't good*: A neva gud 2 (~ + verb) it neh a, it neva did a - *It was not getting dark*: It neh a get daak, It neva did a get daak 3 (~ + location) it neh deh, it neva deh - *It wasn't here*: It neh deh ya, It neva deh ya

IT'S see *IT IS*

IT'S ABOUT TIME A full time - *It's about time we got paid*: A ful taim wi get a riez

IT'S ALL GOOD (*Everything is all right*) Everyting cool, Everyting wow, Cool breeze, Evryting arite, Evriting balance, Balance, Level vibes, Level, Irie, Evryting Copacet, Evryting criss, All fruits ripe, Cool runninz, Everyting deh pan ice, Evryting cook an curry, Evryting fit an frock, Evryting ites, Evryting a evryting

ITCH 1 (of body part: *feel itchy to person X*) scratch X, dig X, nyam X - *My elbow itches*: Mi elbo a skrach mi 2 (of an itch: *scratch at*) craab up - *I'm scratching at my foot but it still itches*: Mi a kraab op mi fut yet i stil a skrach mi

ITS 1 (adj) fi it, it, fi ih, ih - *Its tire is flat*: Fi it taya bos; It taya bos; Fi ih taya bos; Ih taya bos 2 Also see *IT'S*

ITSELF 1 (n) iself 2 (adv. for emphasis) same one - *The government itself doesn't know*: Di govamen siem wan no nuo

JABBER see *BABBLE; CHATTER*

JAGGED (*unevenly cut*) saka saka

JAIL 1 (n) lockup 2 Also see *PRISON*

JAMAICA Jamdung, Yaad, JA, Di Rock, Jamrock, Jahmekya

JAMAICAN 1 (n. *person from Jamaica*) yaadie, yaad man, yaad man, jamrockah, baan-ya, local 2 (adj) local, yaad, yaadie - *That's a Jamaican company*: A luokal kompani dat; A yaadi kompani dat - *It's a Jamaican thing*: A yaad ting

JAMMED 1 (adj. *wedged*) kotch, kotch up 2 (of machine or electronic device: *stuck in position*) lock, seize up 3 Also see *CROWDED*

JANUARY Janri

JATOBA (*Hymenaea courbaril*) stinkin toe

JAVA PLUM (*Syzygium jambolanum*) jamblin

JEALOUS 1 (v. *to be jealous*) grudge, badmind 3 Also see *ENVIOUS*

JEALOUSY badmind, grudgeful, red yeye - *Don't let jealousy stop you*: No mek grojful stap yu

JEANS 1 (*a pair of jeans*) a jeans 2 (*slim jeans*) strait jeans, fitted jeans, (effeminate term) tight jeans

JELLYFISH (n) bladda, blubba

JEWELRY pr: juweri 1 (n) bling bling, fandangles 2 (*gold chains and gold ornaments*) cargo

JOIN 1 (of person or group) link wid, hitch up wid, rope een wid, fall een wid 2 (of activity or event: *take part in*) run een pan, rope een pan, tek paat inna, penetrate 3 (vi. *come together*) link up tugedda, hitch up tugedda 4 (vt. of parts or pieces: *connect*) piecen, canneck 5 (vi. *take part*) run een, rope een, penetrate, tek paat, fall een

JOINT 1 (*large weed cigarette; blunt*) spliff 2 (*small joint; mini-spliff*) ziggy, rizzla

JOKE 1 (n. *bad joke*) bad cyaad 2 (*insulting joke*) cyaad 3 (v. *tell jokes*) run joke 4 (*It's no joke*) A no joke, A no joke biniz, Nah skin up, Nah skin teet 5 Also see *PRANK; LAUGHING STOCK; JOKE AROUND; PLAY A JOKE*

JOKE AROUND ramp, draw cyaad, skin up, sheg roun, mout, run joke, jesta, gimmicks, wrap up, gi laff fi peas soup

JOLLY irie, upful, jokefy

JOSTLE see *SHOVE* or *MANHANDLE*

JOY vibes, gladness, jollification, upliffment, upfulness

JUBILATION vibes, gladness, jollification, upliffment, upfulness

JUDGEMENTAL judge judge, mekam pekam

JUJUBE (*zizyphus jujuba; zizyphus mauritiana*) coolie plum

JUMP 1 (v) boom 2 (v. *jump off; dive from*) chuck off 3 Also see *ASSAULT*

JUMPY (*agitated*) bummy, kra kra

JUNGLE bush

JUNK 1 (*useless stuff lying around*) kuru kuru, koro koro, ray ray, ruggage, nyaka nyaka, boogooyaga, brokinz, riff raff, jing bang, bangarang, curroaches, carowzin, corojungo, cruchment, jeng jeng 2 Also see *GARBAGE*

JUST 1 (*just an X; just some X*) juss X, jis X, ongle X, X no more - *It's just a rabbit*: A jos rabit; A onggl rabit; A rabit no mo 2 (*you're just X because Y*) a X yu X cah Y - *They're just angry because they didn't win*: A bex dem bex kaa dem neva win 3 Also see *ONLY; STRICTLY*

JUST AS 1 (*just like how*) same how 2 (*at the same time as*) same time, so, so X so Y - *The car broke down just as we arrived*: Di kyaar pap dong siem taim wi riich; So wi riich, di kyaar pap dung; So wi riich, so di kyaar pap dung

JUST AS WELL jus as cheap, might as cheap

JUST ENOUGH 1 (*just enough to X*) nuff fi X no mo 2 (*just enough X to Y*) nuff X fi Y no mo - *I make just enough to live*: Mi get nof fi liv, no mo - *I make just enough money to live*: Mi get nof moni fi liv, no mo

JUST LIKE 1 same laka, same as - *I'm struggling just like you*: Mi a chrogl siem laka yuu 2 (*just like how*) same how

JUST LIKE THAT 1 (*exactly like that*) same so, same way so 2 (*all of a sudden*) all pan a suddn, suddn, same time, juss so, braps, baps

JUST RIGHT well kris

JUST THE OTHER DAY 1 (*Just the other day...*) Wah day, Fuss nite, Di adda day, Tadda day, Tarra day, Tedda day, Tidda day 2 (pred adv. *the other day*) weh day, fuss nite, di adda day, tadda day, tarra day, tedda day, tidda day - *Just the other day we saw Lisa at the market*: Wa die wi si Lisa a di maakit - *We saw Lisa the other day*: Wi si Lisa weh die

JUTTING see *STICKING UP* or *STICKING OUT*

KEEP pr: kip 1 (v) canchol 2 (*keep* + verb) keep on a X, no stap X - *Keep talking*: Kipaan a chat; No stap chat 3 (*Keep going*) galang galang; push aan chu (*push on thru*) 4 (*keep out of the action; keep one's distance*) watch an pree, hol yu corner, tan so back, mass out, mass (from *mask*)

KEEP BACK (vi) hol yu corner, tan so back

KEEP GOING! (*Keep it up!*) More dat!, More faya!, Faawud!, Push aan!, Gwaan!

KEROSENE (n) kurseen oil, fyah oil, lamp oil

KETTLE (n) kekkle, jesta

KICK ASS 1 (vi. *be amazing; be impressive*) a lead, slap weh, run tings, run di road, a seh one, a di ish, a di general, a di don, sell off, carry di swing 2 (vi. *do really well in a competition or performance*) shell dong, slap weh, mad up di ting, pop off, sell off, beat dem bad, lick dem fi six, kill dem, slew dem, slawta dem, wyah dem, tump dem, clawt dem, duss dem, trample dem, vank dem, mash dem 3 Also see *EXCELLENT*

KICK BACK see *RELAX*

KICK OUT (*expel*) run, tun out, put out, drive weh, dish X dirt (X=person)

KID 1 (n. *child*) pickney, pitney 2 (*adolescent*) jubie, yout 3 (vt. *playfully fool*) ramp wid, draw cyaad pan, run joke pan, cyaad, gimmicks, rungles 4 Also see *KID AROUND*

KID AROUND ramp, mout, draw cyaad, skin up, sheg roun, run joke, jesta, gimmicks, wrap up, gi laff fi peas soup

KILL 1 (vt) duss out, tek out, done, mek duppy outa, slap weh, light up, light, wyah, kweng, kuff, page, slew, pitch dung, vank 2 (vi. *kill people* (in general)) mek duppy, fly duppy, X people, X man (X=any of the terms in 1 above) - *He's not afraid to kill people*: Him no fried fi mek dopi, Him no fried fi tek out man

KILLER (n) murdarah, kwenga

KILL OFF (v) kill out, done out, x out, radicate

KILL TIME 1 (v) mek up time 2 Also see *LOITER*

KILLING (n. *slaughter; carnage*) murdaration

KILN (n) skil

KIND 1 (n. *type*) kine, saat, style, manna 2 (adj. *kind-hearted; nice*) irie, heartical 3 (v. *be kind to; treat well*) gwaan good tu, kin teet wid, hangle good

KIND OF 1 (adv. *somewhat*) kine a, go fi +adj, adj+ish - *They are kind of young*: Dem kain a yong; Dem go fi yong; Dem yonggish 2 (n. *type of*) saat a 3 (*all kinds of*) all manna a 4 (*Yes, kind of; In a sense*) Pan a level, Inna some saat a way

KINDLING (n. for fire) ticky ticky, fyah stick, creng creng, jag jag

KING BIRD pitcheary

KINKY 1 (*sexually kinky*) freaky 2 (*kinky hair*) bad head, dry head

KISS 1 (n. *simple peck*) choops, toops 2 (*French kiss*) troats 3 (*give a simple peck*) choops 4 (*make out*) wrap up, hug an kiss, suck out tongue, suck face, troats

KISS ASS 1 (n. *sycophant*) moutwaata, press-button 2 (v) curry fayva, edge up, eggz up, crowd up, beg fren

KISS UP TO curry fayva wid, fertilize yourself wid

KNEECAP knee cup

KNIFE 1 (*pocket knife*) skeng, ratchet, brokback ratchet, punyack 2 (*kitchen knife*) kitchen bitch 3 Also see *MACHETE*

KNOCK 1 (v. *hit accidentally*) bunks, buck, baff 2 (v. *knock down*) lick dung, baff dung 3 (*knock on*) nock

KNOCK KNEE(S) 1 (n) tun foot, k-foot 2 (adj) tun foot, k-foot

KNOW THE DEAL see *KNOW WHAT'S UP*

KNOW WHAT I'M SAYING? yannastan?, yovahs?, yu si mi?, yu seet?, yu no seet?, zeen?, seen?, sight?, yu see weh mi a seh?, yu see weh mi deh?, yu see weh mi a deal wid?

KNOW WHAT'S UP (v) know bout, know di ting, know di schweppes, know di runninz, deh pan top, know wha clock a strike, know what o'clock

KNOWLEDGE 1 (n. *knowledge in general*) ovastandin, full yeye, sabi-so 2 Also see *WISDOM*

KUDOS (n) ratingz, hype, big up, respeck

KUNG FU MOVIE kickaz

LABIA MAJORA (vulgar) pussy jaw

LABOR 1 (n. *employment*) wok, wuk 2 (v. *work hard; toil*) buss yu shut (from *bust your shirt*)

LABORATORY labachi

LACK 1 (v) waan   2 (adj. *lacking*) short, wantin - *It lacks salt*: It waan salt - *It's lacking a battery*: It want a bachri; It shaat a bachri

LACKING 1 (*lacking in supply*) dry   2 (*needy*) inna wantin   3 (*lacking X*) waan X, shaat a X - *It's lacking in salt*: It shaat a saalt; It waan saalt

LADDER   ledda

LADY 1 (n) ooman, lioness, empress, queen   2 (*old lady*) nana, granny, auntie, madda, (derogatory): ol foot lady, ol foot   3 See *WOMAN* for more

LADY'S MAN see *PLAYER*

LAG 1 (n. *a delay in time*) lay lay   2 (v. *fall behind*) drap aback, lay lay, leggeh leggeh   3 (*linger*) linga, lay lay, hitch, diggle daggle, dilly dally, tarry

LAGGING leggeh leggeh

LAME 1 (*having one useless leg*) drawfoot   2 (of product or event) fluxy, crebbeh crebbeh, screbbeh screbbeh, fenkeh fenkeh, tufenkeh, dibby dibby, pyaa pyaa, kaba kaba   3 (of male person: *uncool and ineffectual*) saaf, sopsy, fenkeh fenkeh, tufenkeh, wutless, wukless, no wut, dibby dibby, pissy tail, batta iez, crebbeh, screbbeh, nyamps, pyaa pyaa   4 (of female: *uncool and unworthy of respect*) dibby dibby, crebbeh crebbeh, pancoot, zutupeng, zutupeck, wutless, wukless, no wut, batta foot, batta iez, cruff, pissy tail   5 (n. *lame guy*) waste man, floppaz, saps, cruff, floops, eedyat, eedyat bwoy, double blank, image, scout, guy, fella, poppy show, prekeh, menkeh, pussyfawt, cacafawt, batta iez bwoy, pissy tail bwoy, mafeena, nyamps   6 (n. *a lame or unworthy female person*) waste gyal, eedyat gyal, pissy tail gyal, batta foot gyal, batta iez gyal, screbbeh, screbz, pancoot, zutupeng, zutupeck, crebbeh, cruff, dibby dibby gyal, girls guide

LAND 1 (*parcel of real estate*) piece, grong   2 (v. as an airplane) touch dung   3 (v. *land on*) pitch pon

LANDLORD (n) rent man

LANDSLIDE landslip, washweh, brokweh, cutweh

LANGUAGE pr: langwij - Also see *LINGO*

LANKY 1 (*excessively tall and thin*) lenga lenga, langalala   2 (n. *lanky person*) langalala, tallis, pawpaw tree, wiss, cucucum stick

LARGE see *HUGE*

LARGE AMOUNT (n) heap, whole heap, x amount

LARYNX rum bump

LASH OUT lick out

LAST 1 (v. *live on; endure*) live on, tan 2 (adj. *this past; the most recent*) *I saw her last Saturday*: Mi si har satdeh gaan, Mi si har satdeh laas

LATE 1 (*wee hours of the night*) howaz 2 (*It's getting late*) howaz a beat

LATE-BLOOMER (n. *a child who is slow to learn*) baffan, baff-han

LATELY 1 (adv. at start of sentence only) Fram wa day 2 (pred adv) fram weh day - *Lately I haven't been working*: Fram wa die mi naa work - *I haven't been working lately*: Mi naa work fram weh die

LATER 1 (*a bit from now*) likkle more 2 (*later on*) bambye, howaz beat 3 (*later than*) layta dan, layta an 4 also see *GOODBYE*

LAUGH 1 (v. *to laugh*) laaf, skin teet, skin up 2 (*laugh at*) laaf afta 3 (*laugh hysterically; crack up*) pop up, buss up a laaf, ded wid laaf, kin ova a laaf 4 (*laugh inappropriately or falsely*) skin up yu teet

LAUGHING STOCK (*one who makes a fool of themselves*) mascot, cartoon, image, acrobat, claffy, prekeh, poppy show, menkeh, eedyat, iddyboo, floops, cacafawt, pussyfawt, sample, salad

LAUNDRY DETERGENT fab

LAXATIVE (n) salt physic, brook lac

LAY LOW (v. *try to be inconspicuous*) screechy, hol ih dung, tan so back, skull (from *skulk*)

LAZY 1 (adj) wukless, igle, cruff, crebbeh, donkya, unambitionable, mafeena 2 (n. *chronically lazy person; idler*) cruff, crebbeh, creb, screbz, iglaz, loaftah, come aroun, dutty bungle, long seed man, long seed bwoy, grey tone man, pissy tail bwoy, pissy tail gyal, boogooyaga, budger

LAZY EYE (adj. *having a lazy eye or amblyopia*) cyaas eye, look a bush

LEADER 1 (*the leader; the chief*) di gorgon, di big supe, (of gang) di don 2 (*person with leadership qualities or experience*) artical, bonafide, gorgon, notch, bantan

LEAK (v) spring, jrip, pyu (from *spew*)

LEAN 1 (adj. *thin and healthy*) limba 2 (adj. *muscular*) samba 3 (v. *lean on or against*) brace pan

LEAVE 1 (*put*) leff 2 (*depart*) leff, leff out, du road, shoob out, move, splurt, step, leggo di endz, cut, dip, flash, flash out, breeze, mek a flex, mek a move, mek a trod, mek a tracks, bunks, du so, shake out, tek weh yuself, galang 3 (*leave discreetly*) tief out, Jim Screechy, screechy 4 (*exit from*) leggo, leff, come out a 5 (*walk out on*) gwaan leff, run leff 6 Also see *LEAVE ALONE; I'M LEAVING; GO!; GO AWAY!*

LEAVE ALONE 1 (*leave person X alone*) low out X, low X, come off a X case, res X, mek X tan, mek X stay 2 (*leave it alone*) mek ih stay, mek ih tan, leff ih alone

LEAVE BEHIND leff back

LEAVE ME ALONE! see *LET ME BE!; GIVE ME A BREAK!* or *GO AWAY!*

LEAVE! see *GO!* or *GO AWAY!*

LEFT leff han - *on the left side*: pan di lefan said

LEFTOVERS 1 (*leftover food*) whatlef, wa lef, bambaye, aftawuds, dribblinz 2 (*leftovers served the next morning for breakfast*) chaklata, Sunday-Monday

LEG foot

LEISURE pr: leja - see *FUN*

LEMONADE (*lemonade made with sibble orange or limes and brown sugar*) bebrage

LEND (v.) gi borrowz, len a ting

LENGTHEN long out

LEPER kokobeh man, cocobay man

LEPROSY kokobeh, cocobay

LESBIAN sodomite, man royal

LET mek, lek

LET BE 1 (*let person X be*) low X, res X, eaze X, come off a X case, mek X tan 2 (*let thing X be*) low X, res X mek X tan, mek X stay

LET BY (*let X pass by*) gi X pass, gi X way, free X up, free X up, ease X up, ease up X

LET DOWN 1 (v. *disappoint; deceive*) let dung, dis X program, shooks 2 (*be let down by*) lose off a - *I've been let down by you*: Mi luuz aaf a yu 2 (adj. *disappointed*) sheg up

LET GO 1 (*stop holding on*) leggo, leh go, let off, lek off, ease up, free up 2 (v. *liberate*) free up, fly

LET GO! Leggo!, Leh go!, Let off!, Lek off!

LET IT BE mek ih stay, mek ih tan, leff ih alone

LET KNOW 1 (*let person X know*) mek X know 2 (*Let X know about things being done behind their back*) pinch X, buzz X, page X

LET ME BE! Low mi!, Come off a mi case!, Res mi!, Mek mi tan!

LET'S GO Mek wi go, Mek wi flex, Mek wi mek a move, Come an galang

LET'S SEE IT! (*Show what you got!*) Mek mi see it!, Run it!, Sen on!, Up wid it!, Bring ih come!, Sen ih come!

LETTER 1 (n) letta 2 (*lowercase letter*) common letta 3 (*capital letter*) big letta

LEVER pr: liiva (n) angle

LEWD (adj) luu, slack, dutty, freaky, nassy, funky

LIAR liad, con<u>i</u>vah (coniver)

LIBIDO naycha, back

LIBRARY pr: laibri

LICENSE licen, plastic

LID 1 (of garbage can or drum or barrel) pan head 2 (of drink bottle) cork

LIE 1 (n) lie an story, gyow 2 (v. *recline*) lay dung 3 (*to fib; to lie*) tell lie, sell gyow, gyow 4 (*lie to*) tell lie pan 5 (*That's a lie; I don't believe you*) A lie, A lie yu a tell, Lie an story, Lyad story, Peer lie, Bay lie, Pure lie

LIE DOWN lidung

LIFESTYLE livity, way a livin

LIFT 1 (n. *car ride*) jrap, drop 2 (v) liff up

LIGHTNING 1 (n) lightn 2 (*flash of lightning*) gyash

LIKE 1 (v) rate, promote, defend, pree, check fi, penny - *I really like Mexican food*: A m<u>ii</u> seh Mexikan fuud; Mexikan fuud mi seh 2 (*similar to*) laka 3 (*similarly to*) afta - *He sings like his father*: Him sing aafa him faada 4 Also see *ADMIRE; ENJOY; LOOK LIKE; LIKE THIS; LIKE THAT*

LIKE THIS 1 so, laka dis 2 (*this way*) da way ya - *How can you live like this?* Ow yu a liv so? - *How can you live this way?* Ow yu a liv da wie ya?

LIKE THAT 1 so, laka dat 2 (*that way*) da way deh, dem way deh - *Don't act like that*: No gwaan so; No gwaan dem wie deh

LIKEABLE see *FRIENDLY* or *COOL*

LIKELY (*likely to + v*) good fi, goodly - *Glen is likely to be there*: Glen gud fi deh deh

LIMIT 1 (n) buck 2 (v. *hit the limit*) buck, zero 3 (*push to the limit*) buck 4 (*reach your limit*) buck, ketch yu lent

LIMP 1 (adj. *flaccid*) fluxy 2 (v. *hobble*) drag foot, fayva one foot

LINGO lingwah

LION FISH poison groupa, stingin groupa

LIPS see *LABIA MAJORA*

LISP liss tongue

LISTEN 1 lissen 2 (vt. *listen to*) lissen, hear - *Listen to what I'm saying*: Lisn weh mi a seh, Ier weh mi a seh, Peni weh mi a seh 3 Also see *LISTEN UP!*

LISTEN UP! Ear wa, Ear dis, Earz dis, Lissn ya, Pree dis, Check dis, Medz dis, Penny dis, Penetrate dis, Caz wa, Ear mi now, Yeery, Yu waan si

LIT 1 (adj. of candle or room) light 2 Also see *AWESOME; HAPPENING*

LITERARY wordical

LITERATE pr: litaret

LITERATURE lichicha

LITTLE 1 (*small*) likkle, lilly 2 (*not much*) few, dinky - *I have little money*: Mi ha fyuu moni 3 (*tiny*) beenie, likkle bit, lilly bit, beenie bit, uku bit, jinji, mini mini 4 (n. *a little*) a smalls, a skimps, a kimps, a toops, a choops, a quips, a kench 5 Also see *LITTLE BY LITTLE, IN A LITTLE WHILE*

LITTLE BY LITTLE likkle likkle, one one, bit bit, piece piece, peessa peessa

LIVE 1 (v. *be alive*) draw bret 2 (v. *reside*) res, black 2 (*reside temporarily; board*) stop, deh 3 (v. *live off of*) liv pan

LIVE OFF OF liv pan

LIVER SPOTS shitten cloud

LIZARD see *ANOLE; GECKO; SKINK*

LOAF 1 (v. *be lazy; do nothing*) igle, hitch, klutch, skylark, tan bout, diggle daggle, linga linga, tarry 2 (v. *loaf about*) box bout, batta bout, batta batta, gyalant, pang pang

LOAN 1 (n) borrows 2 (v) gi borrows, lend a ting

LOCK EYES yeye mek four - *We locked eyes*: Fiwi yai mek fuor

LODGE 1 (n) lodgin house, lodginz 2 (v. *stay temporarily*) cotch, stop, black

LOITER hitch, clutch, tan bout, linga bout, linga linga, skylark, diggle daggle, pang pang

LOL DWL (ded wid laaf), BOAL (Buss out a laaf)

LONG 1 (adj) tall - *It requires a long stick*: It niid a taal stik   2 (in terms of time: *long and drawn out*) langalala

LONG AGO fuss time, long time, before time, before Wappy kill Phillup, when saltfish a shingle housetop, when di devil was a bwoy, before God mek morning, before God build Adam, before God mek

LONG FOR fret pan, cry fi

LONG TIME 1 (*for a long time now; since quite some time ago*) from time, from how long, from nineteen how long, from Wappy kill Phillup, from saltfish a shingle housetop, rom di devil was a bwoy, from God mek morning, from before God build Adam, from before God mek, donkey years   2 Also see *LONG AGO*

LOOK! Ku deh!, Ku ya!

LOOK AFTER 1 (*be responsible for*) canchol, govern, deal wid, angle, run   2 (*of household or children: care for*) mind, mine, wife up, govern, canchol

LOOK AT look pan, pree, ku, ku pan

LOOK AT THAT Ku deh, Look deh, Pree dat, Ku dat

LOOK AT THIS Ku ya, Si ya, Look ya, Check dis, Pree dis, Penny dis, Penetrate dis

LOOK AWAY (v) look a bush

LOOK DOWN AT 1 (v. *scorn*) skin up yu nose pan, cut yu yeye afta, tek step wid, class, style, hype pan, reduce, low count   2 (*literally look in a downward direction at*) look dung pan, ku dung pan

LOOK FOR see *SEEK*

LOOK FORWARD TO see *EXCITED*

LOOK HOW 1 Ku how   2 (*Look how X the Y is!*) Wat a way X Y!, Wat a X Y! - *Look how big the moon is!* Wat a wie di muun big!, Wat a muun big!

LOOK INTO 1 (*investigate*) look inna, pree, suss out, tek a stock a   2 (*physically look into*) llook inna

LOOK LIKE 1 (*resemble*) fayva, come een like   2 (*it seems as tho*) come een laka seh, fayva laka seh

LOOSE 1 (of vagina) done out, rev out   2 Also see *SLACK; PROMISCUOUS; SLUT*

LOOSEN 1 (v. of knot) pull 2 (v. of strap or restraint) loose, fly

LOSE 1 (v) loss - *Careful you don't lose the key!* Main yu laas di ki! 2 Also see *LOSE WEIGHT; LOSE YOUR PATIENCE; LOSE YOUR MIND*

LOSE WEIGHT draw dung, mawga dung, suck dung, suck out, reduce

LOSE YOUR MIND see *GO CRAZY; GET ANGRY*

LOSE YOUR TEMPER see *SNAP*

LOSER 1 (*socially scorned male*) waste man, saps, cruff, floppaz, eedyat, eedyat bwoy, pissy tail bwoy, double blank, image, scout, cartoon, menkeh, acrobat, poppy show, prekeh, pussyfawt, cacafawt, guy, fella, floops, batta iez bwoy, mafeena, nyamps 2 (*loser at getting women*) gyal clown, board man, cartoon, floops 3 (*female loser*) waste gyal, eedyat gyal, dibby dibby gyal, pissy tail gyal, batta foot gyal, batta iez gyal, girls guide, pancoot, zutupeng, zutupeck, poppy show, screbbeh, screbz, crebbeh

LOST 1 (adj) laas 2 (*lost forever*) laas cyaa find

LOUD (*boisterous*) jingbang, brawlin, ballahoo

LOUSY 1 (*lacking ability*) wutlis, wuklis, saaf (*soft*), too fenkeh, fenkeh fenkeh, dibby dibby, crebbeh, crebbeh crebbeh, kabba kabba, chamba chamba, nyamps, pyaa pyaa, sopsy, fluxy, pissy tail, half inch, half staff, no wut, no use, pop dung 2 (*poorly made*) crebbeh crebbeh, tufenkeh, fenkeh fenkeh, fluxy, dibby dibby, wutlis, wuklis, batta foot, batta ears, sketel, streggeh, screbbeh screbbeh, kaba kaba, chamba chamba, boogooyaga, butu, common, half inch, half staff, knockoff, riff raff, casco, tikki tikki, jingbang, pyaa pyaa, no wut, no use, pop dung, ol bruck, nyamps

LOVE POTION tempting powda

LOW CLASS 1 (of behavior or speech) butu, sketel, raw chaw, batta foot, batta iez, boogooyaga, boogoo boogoo, streggeh, zutupeck, zutupeng, chamba chamba, hoggish, bongo, backawall, backabush, backamoko 2 (of person: *without class*) butu, raw chaw, cruff, common, crebbeh, screbbeh, streggeh, hoggish, zutupeck, zutupeng, jingbang, boogooyaga, boogoo boogoo, backawall, backabush, bongo, (female only): sketel, pancoot 3 (n. *a low class person*) butu, crebbeh, cruff, streggeh, screbbeh, screbz, dutty bungle, batta foot, boogooyaga, boogoo boogoo, zutupeng, zutupek, (male only): kwashi, kwaco, cuffy, bongo, (female only): sketel, pancoot, credell 4 Also see *VULGAR or LOW QUALITY*

LOW QUALITY 1 (adj. *cheap; poorly made*) crebbeh crebbeh, tufenkeh, fenkeh fenkeh, fluxy, dibby dibby, wutlis, wuklis, batta foot, batta ears, sketel, streggeh, screbbeh screbbeh, kaba kaba, chamba chamba, boogooyaga, butu, common, half inch, half staff, knockoff, riff raff, casco, tikki tikki, jingbang, pyaa pyaa, no wut, no use, pop dung, ol bruck, nyamps 2 (n. *low quality stuff*) see *JUNK*

LOWER 1 (vt. *physically lower an object*) ease dung, carry dung 2 (v. *reduce*) ease dung, dress dung, draw dung

LOWERCASE (n. *lowercase letters*) common letta

LOWLIFE (n. *despicable male*) fassy, fassyhole, pussyhole, cacafawt, pussyfawt, pussymout, crow bait, curr, dutty johncrow, crab inna barrel, harbour shark, heathen, pagan, chapunko 2 (*despicable and disreputable female*) dutty stinkin gyal, nassy gyal, streggeh, sketel, credell, scrcbbeh, jezibel, pancoot, pazart, parasite, kinarky, crebbeh crebbeh 3 Also see *LOSER; WORTHLESS; TRAITOR*

LOWLY see *UNREFINED* or *DISPICABLE*

LOYAL 1 (of person) heartical, goodup goodup 2 (n. *loyal male*) soljah, heartical 3 (n. *loyal female*) goody, goody goody

LUCK see *BAD LUCK* or *OUT OF LUCK*

LUCKY 1 (adj) luck, luddy 2 (v. *get lucky*) buk up, jrap inna soup 3 (*Lucky you!*) Yu drop inna soup!

LUCKY CHARM (n. *talisman*) gyaad

LUGGAGE bag dem, grip dem, bag an ting, (potentially insulting when used in reference to another person's luggage): bag an pan, karowchiz

LUMBER (n) boad

LUMP (n. *lump or swollen bump on the head*) coco, cocabola

LURK see *LOITER*

LUXURIOUS stoosh, kris, quality, name brand

LUXURY pr: logzri 1 (n) stushness, quality 2 (adj) stush, uptown, quality, ristocrat, risto

LYCHEE pr: laichii (n) chiney guinep

LYMPH NODES (*swollen lymph nodes*) wax an cannon, wax an canal, wax an kernel

MA'AM ma

MACHETE 1 (n) cutlass, lass, machett, bill, afana, combolo 2 (*small hooked machete*) hooka

MACHISMO man ting

MACHO mannish

MACKEREL (*mackerel in a tin or can*) tin makril, dutty gyal, wutliss, flash out

MAD see *CRAZY* or *ANGRY*

MADE mek

MAGGOTS magich, magidge

MAGIC 1 (n) guzum, zuzu   2 Also see *SORCERY; CURSE; SPELL*

MAHANDLE (v) ruff up, hackle, hackle up, manhangle, malahack, mammick, sawka sawka

MAID 1 (*cleaning lady*) helpa, days worka   2 Also see *GIRL; WOMAN*

MAIL (v) poas

MAILMAN poasman, poassy

MAINTENANCE mentenans, main tenants

MAKE mek

MAKE A BET run a bet

MAKE A FOOL OF (*make a fool of X*) tek X mek poppy show, tek X mek prekeh, tek X tun prekeh

MAKE A LIVING nyam a food, eat a food

MAKE BELIEVE 1 (*imaginary*) play play   2 (v. *pretend*) play play

MAKE DO see *MAKE ENDS MEET* or *GRIN AND BEAR IT*

MAKE ENDS MEET 1 nyam a food, eat a food, get on, get chu, hustle, try a way, run wid it, liv it out, tun yu han mek fashion, fadge   2 Also see *HUSTLE*

MAKE FUN OF laaf afta, draw cyaad pan, cyaad, tek X mek prekeh, tek X mek poppy show (X=person)

MAKE LOVE see *SEX*

MAKE OUT see *KISS*

MAKE PLANS set up plan

MAKE ROOM small up yuself

MAKE SENSE spell sense, fit

MAKE SURE 1 (*check around*) tek a stock   2 (*make sure about*) look about, look bou   3 (*Make sure you don't* X) Mind yu X, Tekya yu X (X=affirmative verb) - *Make sure you don't hit the wall*: Main yu bonks di waal

MAKE UP 1 (v. as an lie: *concoct*) mek up   2 (*fabricate from the imagination*) shape, form up   3 (*become reconciled*) tun back fren, tun back spoogz, leggo malice

MAKES NO DIFFERENCE Six fi a nine, Black dog fi monkey

MALEVOLENCE (n) bad mind, grudgeful, ugly, dark heart, evilousness, nastiness, duttyness, payaka bizniz, harbour sharkin

MALEVOLENT (adj) bad mind, pagan, evilous, low, ugly, cramoojin, dark heart, black heart, nassy, dutty, payaka, harbour sharkin

MALICE (n) bad mind, grudgeful, ugly, dark heart, evilousness, nastiness, duttyness, payaka bizniz, harbour sharkin

MALICIOUS (adj) bad mind, pagan, evilous, low, ugly, cramoojin, dark heart, black heart, nassy, dutty, payaka, harbour sharkin

MAN-O'-WAR (n. *portuguese man-o-war jellyfish*) manawar bladda, manawar blubba

MANAGE 1 (*supervise; deal with*) canchol, govern, look afta, deal wid, angle, run, hol dung 2 (*put up with*) tek, liv wid, deal wid, angle, liv out, run wid 3 (vi. *make do*) get on, run wid it, liv it out, get chu, hustle, try a way, tun yu han mek fashion, fadge

MANATEE sea cow

MANCHILD saps, mama man, mantu, saaf-han bwoy

MANCHINEEL TREE (*Hippomane mancinella*) swell hand

MANHANDLE (v) ruff up, bad up, hackle, hackle up, man hackle, manangle, malahack, mammick, sawka, sawka up

MANIPULATE 1 (*coerce; coax*) inveegle, trongmout 2 (as in a relationship: *dominate*) mantrol, manchol up, hancuff, mek figaree out a, tek X tun figaree, spin X roun (X=person)

MANIPULATION mantrol

MANLY 1 (*macho*) mannish 2 (of woman: *butch*) mannish

MANNERS 1 (*good manners*) balance, mannaz, behavior, broughtupsy, upbringin 2 (*bad manners*) outa orderness, dragupsy 3 (v. *mind one's manners; behave oneself*) balance 4 Also see *WELL MANNERED* or *UNCOUTH*

MANY 1 (adj) nuff, whole eap a, bans a, a bag a, a bungle a, extramount a, x amount a 2 (n) nuff, whole eap, bans, a bungle, extramount - *I have many friends*: Nof fren mi av, Woliip a fren mi av, etc. - *I have many*: Mi av banz, Mi av a bonggl, etc

MARIJUANA see *CANNABIS*

MARKET 1 (n. *open-air market; swap meet*) bendung plaza, bendung maaket 2 (vt. *advertise*) push, hype up, sen a road

MARRY (v) married, married to, tek off a di market - *He wants to marry her*: Him waan mariid har, Him waan mariid tu har, Him waan tek har aaf a di maakit

MARSH morass

MASCULINE mannish

MASSACRE massakrah

MASSES (*common people*) massive

MASTURBATE 1 (for male) back yu fist, choke di chicken, hanmiggle it, mek love tu palmela   2 (for female) fingle up yuself, fingle it, flick it   3 (n. *one who loves to masturbate*) selfist

MASTURBATION fist backin, chicken chokin, hanmiggle bizniz

MATCH 1 (n. *match for starting a fire*) matches   2 (n. *partner; equal*) quabs   3 (v. *go together*) mesh

MATERIALISTIC worlian

MATH mats

MATTRESS machras

MATTER 1 (n. *issue*) matta   2 (*matters of business or state*) runnins   3 (*complicated and controversial matters*) parangles, fandangles, bangarang, ray ray   4 (v. *be of importance*) count, mek difference

MATTERS 1 (*daily affairs*) runninz   2 (*complicated matters*) parangles

MATURE 1 (of person: *grown up*) hard back   2 (adj. *responsible*) balance, av sense   3 (n. *mature person; grownup*) big smaddy, big people   4 (n. *mature man*) big man, hard back man   5 (n. *mature woman*) big ooman, hard back ooman   6 (of fruit: *ripe*) fit, reddy   7 (v. *get older*) get big   8 Also see *RIPEN*

MAXI PAD 1 (n) pad, stayfree   2 (vulgar terms) bloodclaat, pussykclaat, bomboclaat

MAXIMUM see *TO THE MAX*

MAY see *MIGHT; CAN*

MAYBE 1 (adv) praps, paravencha   2 (*Maybe that's true*) Coulda so ih go

MAYHEM kanfusion, mixup mixup, fuckry, sheggry, pollution, corruption, palangarang, palam pam, bam bam, bodderation, parangles, fandangles, ruption, ruction, hottaclaps

MEAL (n. *quick meal*) ration, rashi, ketchup

MEAN 1 (*unkind*) misareble, oglify, waasy, dark, cramoojin, crampify (from *crampified*), cubbitch   2 (*average*) migglin   3 (v. *intend to say*) waan fi seh, waan seh   4 (*What does it/that/this mean?*) A wa name so?   5 Also see *MISERLY* or *MISER*

MEASELY deggeh deggeh, so so

MEAT salt ting, (Rasta) dedaz

MEDDLE 1 (v.) fass, meggle, mell, eggz up, edge up   3 (vt. of social affairs: *meddle in*) fass inna, push yu nose inna, eggz up yuself inna, get mix up inna

MEDDLESOME fass, nuff, eggz up, edge up, swiff, bumptious, pomptious

MEDICINE 1 bittaz bitters   2 Also see *PILL*

MEDIOCRE see *SO SO* or *INFERIOR*

MEDITATE hol a medz, hol a medi, satta, penetrate, Iditate

MEDITATION medz, medi, Iditation

MEDIUM (n. *spiritual medium*) myal man, myalist

MEDIUM SIZED migglin

MEDIUMSHIP myal

MEET 1 (*make acquaintance with*) buck up pan, buck up inna, buck   2 (vt. *encounter*) buck up, buck   3 (vi. *convene; meet up*) link up, hol a vibes, hol chapta   4 (vi. *meet with someone face to face*) mek four yeye

MEETING 1 (n. *organized meeting*) linkup   2 (n. *meeting place*) buckup, endz

MEETUP (n) linkup, buckup, gyaddarin

MEMBRANE flim

MEMORIZE membarise

MENOPAUSE change-a-life

MENSTRUATE (old rural term) moon

MENSTRUATION (old rural term) moon

MENTALLY ILL 1 touch, mad, no righted, no balance, nervous, head no good, head lick, no heng on right   2 Also see *INSANE*

MERRY irie, upful, jokefy

MESS 1 (n) mekeh mekeh   2 Also see *STUFF; JUNK; MESS UP; MESS WITH; MESS AROUND*

MESS AROUND 1 (*tinker*) panka panka, hanka panka 2 (*play*) ramp, mout, draw cyaad, run joke, skin up, sheg roun, wrap up, jesta, gimmicks 3 (*waste time doing bullshit*) du fuckry, jesta 4 Also see *HANG OUT; MESS WITH*

MESS UP 1 (vi. *make a mistake*) du madness, flop, du eedyat ting, du folly, du follygrung 2 (vt. *ruin; botch*) mash up, sheg up, mud up, nassy up, sawka sawka, kaba kaba, soak 3 (*badly beat up person X*) beat X tu Y (Y = any expletive) - *The bad guys messed that kid up*: Di badman dem biit di bwai tu blodklaat

MESS WITH 1 (*antagonize*) fass wid, ramp wid, tek step wid, sheg wid, hackle wid, draw cyaad pan, bait, chuck it pan, chuck pan, rooks wid, mell wid 2 (*tamper with*) fass wid, ramp wid, sheg wid, rooks wid, mell wid 3 Also see *KID; TEASE*

MESSED UP 1 (*emotionally disturbed*) all sheg up 2 (of situation: *unfair*) low, sheg up, ugly 3 (ppl. *sabotaged*) flop, mash up, sheg up - *Our plan got sabotaged*: Fiwi pruogram get flap 4 (n. *a messed up situation*) alms-house, sheggry, fuckry, folly grong, bum rap 5 Also see *MESSY*

MESSY 1 (of personality: *carelessly sloppy*) slacka, slacky tidy, donkya 2 (adj: of person: *messy looking*) slacka, slacka slacka, slacky tidy, chaka chaka, raggy raggy, ragga ragga, boogooyaga, nyaka nyaka 3 (of place: *cluttered*) chaka chaka, chuck up chuck up, chak an peckle, nyaka nyaka 4 Also see *DIRTY*

MIDDLE miggle

MIDDLE EAST Miggle Eas, Syria

MIDDLE EASTERN 1 (adj. *Syrian; Lebanese; Jordanian; Iraqi; Iranian*) Syrian 2 (n. *person of aforementioned nationality or ancestry*) Syrian

MIDGET puchin, kunchin, dufidaya, timini, dungrow

MIDWIFE nana, grandie

MIGHT 1 (n. *physical strength*) chrent, trang 2 (v. *may possibly*) mighta 3 (*might not*) mightn 4 (*might not have...*) mighta neva 5 Also see *MIGHT AS WELL*

MIGHT AS WELL jus as cheap, might as cheap, cheap

MILDEW junjo

MIND YOUR OWN BUSINESS see an blind

MINE fimi - *That's mine*: Dat a fimi, A fimi dat

MINGLE (v. *mingle socially*) mix up mix up, frah frah, buttafly

MISBEHAVE gwaan a way, go luu, wild up, brok out

MISCELLANEOUS 1 different different 2 (n. *miscellaneous things*) ray ray, bangarang, tarra warra

MISCHIEF fuckry, sheggry, muckry, neckry, mixup, passa passa, alms house bizniz, alms house, jinnalship, folly grong, foolooloops, bangarang, parangles, fandangles, runkus, carowzin

MISCHIEVOUS 1 (adj) trickify, trick, renk, outta aada, unmannersable, cunny, jim screechy, hard yeye 2 Also see *MALICIOUS*

MISCOMMUNICATION mix up, parangles, confusion

MISER (n. *stingy man who won't share*) chink, tight han, titus, tightaz, star apple

MISERLY (*miserly*) mean, cubbitch, geechy, tight han, tight, chinky, pinchy cubby

MISFORTUNE 1 (n) crosses, chyals, buzu 2 Also see *UNLUCKY*

MISS 1 (*yearn for*) fret pan, cry fi 2 (*lack*) waan - *It's missing a battery*: It waan bachri

MISTAKE 1 (*careless mistake*) choopidness 2 (*big mistake; major screw-up*) eedyat ting, folly grong, fuckry, sheggry 3 (v. *make a mistake*) du eedyat ting, du madness, du fuckry

MISTER Missa, Maas, Massa, Baba

MISTRESS matey, deputy, conki

MISUNDERSTANDING 1 (*a misunderstanding*) one mixup, one confusion, one parangles 2 (*general misunderstanding*) mix up, blenda, confusion, feelinz, worries, passa passa, ray ray, bangarang, parangles, fandangles, palangarang

MIX 1 (n) blem, mesh, mashup, meshup 2 (v) blem, mesh 3 Also see *MIXED RACE*

MIX UP see *QUARREL; CONFUSE; CONFUSED*

MIXED 1 (adj) blem, mesh up 2 Also see *MIXED RACE*

MIXED RACE 1 (n. *person of mixed race*) royal, half breed 2 (*person of black and white ancestry*) zebra, maranta, malatta, brown man, (female) brownin 3 (*person of black and Chinese ancestry*) half breed chaini, chiney royal 4 (*person of black and East Indian ancestry*) coolie royal, half breed indian, bad breed indian

MIXED UP see *CONFUSED; GET MIXED UP IN*

MOB (*noisy and agitated crowd*) jing bang

MOCK 1 (adj. *simulated*) play play 2 (v. *ridicule*) laaf afta, style, hype pan, pop style pan, draw cyaad pan, jeri, reduce, tek X mek pappy show, tek X mek preke (X=person)

MOCKING BIRD nightingale

MODEL 1 (n. *replica; demo*) moggle 2 (*person who demonstrates clothing*) moggle 3 (adj. *make-believe*) play play - *model airplane*: plie plie plien 4 (v. *demonstrate*) moggle, profile 5 Also see *FLAUNT; PARADE*

MOLDY frowzy

MOMBIN spanish plum

MOMMY mumi, mum

MONEY 1 (n) funds, bills, frockles, cheese, chedda, papers, butta, coil, corn, dunz, dunza, dunny, cream, ceeza 2 (*a small amount of money*) a smalls 3 (*loose coins*) loosaz, duss, coppa, silva

MONSTER 1 zutupeck 2 Also see *GHOST*

MOOCHER walk-an-nyam, henkabout, come rung, budger

MOOD 1 (n. *emotional state*) spirit, medz 2 (n. *atmosphere*) vibes, medz

MOODY see *BITCHY; EMOTIONAL; TEMPERAMENTAL*

MOON 1 (*full moon*) moon full 2 (*moonlight*) moonshine

MORAL 1 (adj. of action or intention) rightful 2 (adj. person) conscious, ites, bonafide, goodup goodup

MORAY EEL mory, snake eel

MORNING 1 mawnin 2 Also see *DAWN*

MORON see *IDIOT* or *STUPID*

MOSQUITO 1 (n) maskita, maskit 2 (*mosquito larvae*) tadpole

MOST OF THE TIME more time, more while

MOTH bat, night bat

MOTHER 1 (n) madda, muma 2 (*single mother; unwed mother*) baby madda

MOTHERFUCKER 1 (n. *despicable male*) fassy, fassyhole, pussyhole, bomboclaat, cacafawt, pussyfawt, pussymout, bait, crow bait, curr, dutty johncrow, crab inna barrel, harbour shark, heathen, pagan, chapunko 2 Also see *TRAITOR*

MOTIVATED see *AMBITIOUS* or *EXCITED*

MOULD (n) junjo

MOURN ceremone

MOUSE mus mus, mice, micey, ratta

MOVE 1 (vi: *stir*) flex, shiff 2 (*move the position of X*) shiff X 2 (*move X to another location*) carry X go 3 (*change residence*) move go, move weh gaan 4 Also see: *MOVE!*

MOVE! see *GO!* or *GO AWAY!*

MOVE AHEAD see *MOVE ALONG* or *MOVE UP*

MOVE ALONG step along, step an galang, step up, step, press along, press on chu, faawud on chu, push on, push on chu, push an go chu, go chu, galang galang

MOVE FORWARD see *MOVE ALONG* or *MOVE UP*

MOVE UP (*improve one's status or wellbeing*) step up inna life, step up, level up, liff up yuself, set up yuself, live up

MOVIE 1 (n) flim, pictures, show, movie show 2 (*martial arts movie*) kickaz 3 (*porno movie*) blue movie, blues 3 (*movie theater*) pichaz

MR. (*mister*) Missa, Maas, Massa, Baba

MRS. Mistress, Miss

MUCH 1 (n) whole heap, bands 2 (adv) whole heap 3 (adj. *not much*) no portion, no whole heap - *I don't have much money*: Mi naav no woliip a moni, Mi naav no puoshan a moni - *What are you doing? Not much*: Weh yu a du? No puoshan

MUCH LESS (adv) much more - *He doesn't eat, much less talk*: Him no nyam, moch muor taak.

MUCH MORE nuff more

MUCH OF (*much of ...*) nuff a, a no likkle a - *Much of what he says is lies*: Nof a weh him seh a lai, A no likl a weh him seh a lai

MUD (n) mud mud, puttuh puttuh

MUDDY mud up, mud up mud up, puttuh puttuh, mekeh mekeh

MUDSLIDE landslip, washweh, brokweh, cutweh

MULATTO (n or adj) zebra, maranta, malatta, brown man, (for female) brownin

MULL IT OVER tink pan ih, medz pan ih, medz it ova, medz ih, penny it, penetrate it, wok yu head, study yu head, tuddy yu head, consida yu head, tun it ovah inna yu head

MULL OVER 1 (vt) tink pan, medz, medz pan, medz ova, penny, penetrate 2 Also see *MULL IT OVER*

MULTITASK ride an whistle

MURDER 1 (n. *homicide*) murdah, murderation 2 (v. *kill*) duss out, tek out, done, mek duppy outa, slap weh, light up, light, wyah, kweng, kuff, page, slew, pitch dung, vank, ded off

MURDERER murdarah, kwenga

MUSCLE pr: moskl

MUSCULAR 1 (adj) bigga, tick, chaptin (from *strapping*), samba 2 (*short and muscular*) tuku, duggy 3 (n. *muscular dude*) bigga, ticka

MUSHROOM (*wild muschroom with broad flattened top*) Duppy umbrella

MUSHY mashy mashy, sawfy sawfy, plaka plaka, fluxy

MUST 1 (*have to*) haffi, muss haffi 2 (adv. *surely*) mussy, mussa, no muss - *You must think I'm crazy*: Yu mosi tink seh mi mad, Yu no mos tink seh mi mad

MUSTY (adj) frownzy, frowzy

MUTE 1 (adj) mumu 2 (n. *deaf person*) mumu

MUTILATE /MUTILATED mash up, lass up, saaka saaka, nyaka nyaka up, malahack

MY mi, fimi (from *for me*)

MYSELF 1 (n) miself 2 (adv for emphasis) same one - *I myself built it*: A mi siem wan bil it

NAG 1 (vi) ningy ningy 2 (vt) bodda bodda

NAIL POLISH cutex

NAIVE 1 (*innocent*) goody goody, grow wid yu granny 2 (*clueless and gullible*) simple, easy, moko, grow wid yu granny, juss fall out a di truck, no know bout, no know di time, no know di Schweppes, no know wah clock a strike, no know what o'clock 3 (n. *gullibly naive person*) simpleton, sample, claffy, dunce bat, salad, goose, menkeh, press-button, remote, cuffy, kwashi, bongo, moko

NAME BRAND 1 original 2 see *HIGH QUALITY*

NANNY (*babysitter*) nana

NAP 1 (n) shet yeye, puss nap 2 (v) hol a five, bunks yu rest, bunks, hol a shuteye

NAPPY 1 (of hair) kaya 2 (n. *nappy hair*) kaya, bad head

NARCOLEPSY dropsy

NASTY see *MEAN; RUDE; DISGUSTING; LEWD*

NATIVE 1 (fronting adj) baan (from *born*), raw baan 2 (pred adj) baan ya, baan deh, bilang ya, bilang deh, fiwi 3 (*native to*) kom fram, bilang tu, bilanx tu

NATURAL 1 (adj) nachral, (Rasta term) Ital (from *vital*) 2 (*natural lifestyle*) natural livity, Ital livity, naturality

NATURAL LIFESTYLE

NATURALLY (pred adv. *in harmony with nature*) nachral, Ital

NAUGHTY 1 hard yeye, facety, brite, outta aada, unmannersable 2 (n. *naughty children*) leggo beast, jing bang

NAUSEA (n) sick belly, sowa belly, sick stomach, sowa stomach, high stomach

NAUSEATE (*nauseate person X*) sick X belly, sowa X belly, sick X stomach, sowa X stomach

NAUSEATED (*feel nauseated*) feel bad, feel funny, av sick belly, av sowa belly, av sick stomach, av sowa stomach, av high stomach

NAVEL belly cork, nabel

NEAR 1 (prep) near to 2 (*near here*) bout ya, bou ya, roun ya so 3 (*near there*) roun deh so

NEARLY nearlymost, jus leff fi, ongle leff fi, partly, likklemost - *I nearly fell out of the chair*: Liklmuos mi jrap out a di chier

NECK neck string, necktring

NEED (v) waan - *The car needs gas*: Di kyaar waan gyas - *The car needs to be washed*: Di kyaar waan wash

NEEDY 1 (*in need*) inna wantin 2 (of personality: *needy and whiny*) ningy ningy

NEGATIVE pr: negitiv (adj. *cynical*) dungful, downful

NEGATIVITY pr: negitiviti (n) bad mind, badways

NEGLECT lef out, dash weh, leggo, brush weh, negret

NEGLECTFUL nigretful, donkya

NEGLIGENT donkya, nigretful

NEIGHBORHOOD 1 (n) corners, side 2 (n. *ghetto neighborhood controlled by a gang or cartel*) garrison

NERD 1 (n) mascot, clown, cartoon, Urkle 2 (*guy who is awkward around women*) board man, gyal clown

NERVE see *AUDACITY*

NERVOUS 1 (adj. *anxious or agitated*) bummy, jumpy, kra kra, fretful   2 Also see *ANXIOUS; ANGRY; NEUROTIC*

NETTLE 1 (*nettle bush; Urtica dioica*), scratch bush   2 (*climbing nettle; creeping nettle; Tragia involucrata*) cow itch, <u>cur</u>eech

NETWORK (v. *schmooze*) mek links

NEUROTIC touch, maddy maddy, no righted, no balance, no heng on right

NEVER (for present tense) no X eva   - *I never drink milk*: Mi no jrink milk eva

NEVERMIND no mind

NEVERTHELESS still for all, still

NEW 1 (adj) nyew, criss   2 (*brand new*) criss, fresh, clean   3 (n. *brand new thing*) preps, crispy biskit

NEWS (n. *the scoop; the latest info; the word on the street*) di current, di pree, di talk, di labrish   2 (*good news*) big tingz

NEXT 1 (adj) nex, comin   - *next Saturday*: Satdeh komin, Satdeh nex   2 (adv. *subsequently*) likkle afta dat   3 (*next to*) side a

NICE 1 (of weather or environment) sweet, ites, boonoo<u>noo</u>noos   2 Also see *FRIENDLY; FINE QUALITY; STYLISH*

NICKNAME 1 (*name given endearingly by family or close friends*) pet name, yard name   2 (*stage name; pen name; moniker*) nickname

NIGHTJAR patu

NO MATTER HOW 1 (*no matter how…*) no mind how, no mine how, no care how, no cya how   - *No matter how he tried, he couldn't succeed*: No kya ow him chrai, him kudn get chruu   2 (*No matter how much or how hard...*) All weh   - *No matter how hard he works he doesn't get any money*: Aal we him a wok, him naa get moni

NO ONE nobadi, no man, not a man

NO SOONER THAN no more   - *No sooner did I get back home than it started raining*: No muo mi riich bak a mi yaad an di rien staat

NO SUCH THING (*There's no such thing; I don't know of anys such thing*) Wha name so?

NO WAY! No sah!, Not a X! (X=any expletive), Yu mad?, Wappn tu yu?, Wa du yu?, Cyaa go so!   - (See Appendix for list of expletives)

NOBODY 1 nobadi, nombadi, no man, not a man 2 (*guy of no significance*) image, cartoon, double blank, cub, dibby dibby, crebbeh crebbeh, nyamps 3 (*girl of low status or significance*) waste gyal, batta ears gyal, girls guide, dibby dibby, crebbeh crebbeh, credell

NOISE pr: naiz 1 (*lots of noise; a racket*) one piece a noise, bag a noise, bangarang, apalangarang, palam pam, bam bam, galangin, jing bang, rig jig, ruction, ruption

RACKET 1 (*scam*) bandulu scheme, bandulu, scyam, parangles, rake, rungles, ligues, chickaney 2 (*noise*) piece a noise, bag a noise, bangarang, palangarang, palam pam, bam bam, galangin, jing bang, rig jig, ruction, ruption

NOISY (*noisy and unruly*) jingbang, roogoo roogoo, brawlin, ballahoo

NONCHALANT donkya, dry yeye

NONETHELESS still for all, still

NONI (*Morinda citrifolia*) duppy soursop, hog apple

NONSENSE 1 (*nonsensical talk; blabber*) labrish, labba labba, blar, gyow, bag a mout, fullamout, chatinz, ray ray, chat chat, su su, seh seh, talk 2 (*foolishness*) mixup, mixup mixup, passa passa, ray ray, fuckry, sheggry, muckry, alms house bizniz, alms house, chupidness, folly grong, poppy show, foolooloops, foolinish, choopity, eedyat bizniz, carry go bring come, parangles, fandangles, runkus, nyamps

NOON miggleday, sun-hot

NOR neida - *Neither the government nor businessmen support him*: Niida di govamen niida binizman bak him

NORMALLY more time, more while

NORTH naat

NOSEY fass, nuff, eggz up, edge up, swiff, bumptious, pomptious

NOSTRIL nose hole

NOT no - *Tell her not to cry*: Tel har no fi baal

NOT AT ALL nonatall, nontall

NOTE (v. *take note*) mark how

NOTHING nuttn, not a ting, no portion, nil, ducks

NOTHING BUT (*strictly*) peer, bare, bey, pure, so so, lone

NOTICE pick up pan, si, sight

NOTWITHSTANDING no mind, no mine, no care

NOUVEAU RICHE hurry come up, neva see come see

NOVICE nav nav, rooks

NOW 1 nung 2 (*right now*) now now, right nung, nung nung, eena di Iwah

NOWADAYS (adv) dem time ya, tideh day ya

NOWHERE noweh, not a weh

NUBIAN KNOTS chiney bump

NURSERY (for babies) creech

NUTMEG nutn egg

NUTS see *TESTICLES; CRAZY*

OAF see *BOOR; CLUMSY; IDIOT*

OAFISH see *CLUMSY; STUPID; VULGAR*

OATH (v. *make an oath*) nyam bible leaf, tek God off a di cross

OBESE see *FAT*

OBJECT TO fight gainst, no defend, no caytah to, no promote, no love, bun, bun faya pan

OBLIGATED (adj) muss an boun

OBNOXIOUS (of person) renk, fassy, fassyhole, naasy, butu, brawlin, raw chaw, boogooyaga, boogoo boogoo, outa aada, slack, slacka, zutupeck, zutupeng, (for female only): sketel, pancoot

OBSCENE 1 (*sexually obscene*) dutty, renk, luu, freaky, funky, outlaw, ugly, slack, slacka slacka   2 Also see *VULGAR*

OBSCENITY 1 (n. *lewdness*) luu, slackness, ugliness, freakiness, funkiness, sketelness, renkness   2 (n. *obscene word*) bad wud, ugly wud, sketel bomb

OBSEQUIOUS (adj) licky licky

OBSERVE pree, study, eyes, tek een, tek a stock a, clock, program, penny, penetrate

OBVIOUSLY! No muss!, Strait!, No dat mi a seh?

OCCASIONALLY now an agen, once awhile

OCTOPUS sea cyat, sea puss

ODDS AND ENDS ray ray, ray an tay, bangarang

ODOUR 1 (n) piece a scent   2 (*have a bad odour*) smell rude, smell green, smell renk, smell ripe, smell frowzy, smell frownzy

OF a, fi - *The sixth of March*: Di six a Maach - *The king of the jungle*: Di king fi di jonggl

OF COURSE 1 (*clearly*) still   2 (*of course*) yu done know, no muss   3 Also see *OF COURSE!*

OF COURSE! 1 (*Of course I will!*) Yah man!, How yu mean!, Yu done know!, Strait!, No worry yuself!, No fret yuself!, Yu good!   2 (*Obviously!*) No muss!, Strait!, No dat mi a seh?

OFF CENTER /OFF CENTRE (adj) cyaas, offish

OFFENDED 1 (*offended and angered*) ben up, bun up, bex, bringle, hot up   2 (*offended and deeply hurt*) cut up, sheg up   3 (v. *feel offended*) feel a way   4 Also see *ANGRY*

OFFENSIVE 1 (adj. *insulting or obnoxious*) renk, insultive, coas (from *coarse*), fresh, bright, outa aada   2 Also see *OBSCENE; OBNOXIOUS;* or *SMELLY*

OFFICIAL 1 (adj) artical, bonafide   2 (n. *person of authority*) bigga head

OFTEN more time, more while, nuff time, nuff while

OIL ile

OIL DRUM drum pan, joe pan

OKAY (*all right*) arite, wow, cool, irie, deh deh, deh ya

OKRA okro

OLD 1 (adj) ol, oul oul   2 (of person) ripe, ageable   3 (n. *old person*) eldah, elda head, oldstah, (derogatory): ol foot, ol head   4 Also see *OLD LADY; OLD MAN; HOW OLD ARE YOU?*

OLD LADY nana, granny, auntie, madda, (derogatory): ol foot lady, ol foot

OLD MAN 1 (n) eldah, elda head, oldstah, (derogatory terms): ol head, ol foot, ol foot man, long seed man, grey tone man   2 (n. *tough elderly man; old goat*) tuffy ram, taffu ram, tufu ram   3 for respectful terms of address see *ELDERLY MAN*

OMIT lef out

ON 1 pan, (when not followed by any other words): on   2 (*on here*) on ya - *It's on here*: It aan ya - *Time to move on*: Taim fi muuv aan - *They are on the ground*: Dem pan di grong

ONCE 1 (*on a single occasion*) one time 2 (*after*) fram - *Once you've seen it you don't need to see it again*: Fram yu siit yu naafi siit agen 3 (*in the distant past; once upon a time*) fuss time, long time, before time, before Wappy kill Phillup, when saltfish a shingle housetop, when di devil was a bwoy, before God mek mornin, before God build Adam, before God mek

ONCE AND FOR ALL (adv) for all time

ONCE IN A WHILE every now an again, now an again, once a while, once an now an again

ONE 1 (adj) wan 2 (subj pron) man, a wan - *One must depend on oneself*: Man mos dipen pan himself; A wan mos dipen pan wanself

ONE BY ONE one one

ONE MOMENT 1 (*I'll be right back*) No move, No go noweh, Tan deh, Tan tuddy, Mi a come, Mi a faawud 2 Also see *WHAT ARE YOU TALKING ABOUT?*

ONE NIGHT STAND (*one-time sex encounter*) one-pop, stamp an go, john pop, taze, fuck an duck

ONLY 1 (*the only*) di ongle 2 (*nothing but*) ongle, one, alone - *Only love can save us*: Onggl lov kyan siev wi, Lov wan kyan siev wi, Lov aluon kyan siev wi 3 for more uses, see *JUST* and *STRICTLY*

OOZE (v) pyu (from *spew*), fly

OPEN pr: uopm 1 (of can or bottle) pull 2 (of window or bonnet, etc) fly

OPINIONATED trong mout (from *strong mouthed*), hard ears, ears hard - *He's too opinionated*: Him tuu trang mout; Him iez tuu haad; Stik brok ina him iez

OPPORTUNITY pr: apachuuniti (n. *chance*) bly, one-go

OPPOSE fight gainst, lickout gainst, no defend, no promote

OPPOSED gainst

OPPRESSION iniquity, sentence, downpression, dungpression

OPPRESSOR iniquity worka, downpressa man, dungpressa man

OPTIMIST (n. *one who is unreasonably optimistic*) gladis

OPTIMISTIC 1 (adj) upful 2 (*overly optimistic*) gladdy gladdyf

ORAL SEX 1 (n) suck, numba three, freakiness 2 Also see *CUNNILINGUS; FELLATIO*

ORANGE pr: arinj

ORCHARD walk

ORDEAL 1 (*personal ordeal*) bangarang, parangles, bodderation, crossiz, trials, fandangles, runkus   2 (*public ordeal*) mixup, passa passa, ray ray, parangles, fandangles, runkus

ORDER 1 (n) aada   2 (v. *command*) sen, tell   3 (*buy*) aada, sen fi

OREO (n. *someone who is black on the outside and white on the inside*) roas breadfruit, coconut

ORGANIZE 1 (*coordinate*) set up, juggle   2 (*put in order*) sort out, set up   3

ORGASM extasy, agony

ORIGINAL 1 (*the original; the very first*) di fuss fuss, di original, di foundation   2 (adj. *authentic*) bonafide, name brand, artical, heartical, foundation, roots

ORIGINATE FROM kom fram, bilang tu, bilanx tu

ORNAMENTS 1 (*gaudy ornaments; trinkets*) fandangles, fandangus, parangles, bangarang   2 (*gold chains and gold ornaments*) cargo

OSTENTATION   ovah-du

OSTENTATIOUS ovah-du

OTAHEITE APPLE apple, oti iti apple, iti oti apple, eetiopi apple, eetiopia

OTHER 1 (adj) adda, edda   2 (adj. *another*) a nex, anadda, anedda, wanedda   3 (adj. *the other*) di adda, di nedda, di nex, tarra, tedda, tidda

OTHER DAY see *THE OTHER DAY*

OTHERWISE else, odda helse

OUGHT TO fi - *You ought to think it over*: Yu fi tink pan i

OUR wi, fiwi

OURS fiwi

OURSELVES 1 (n) wiself   2 (adv for emphasis) same one - *Didn't we ourselves tell him?* No wi siem wan tel him?

OUT (*not at home; not in the office*) gaan a road, out a road, deh pan a endz

OUT OF LUCK salt, corner dark, get knock, dog nyam yu suppa - *You're out of luck*: Yu saalt, Yu kaana daak, Dag nyam yu sopa, Yu get knock

OUT OF SHAPE (*physically unfit*) tyad body (from *tired body*), lazy body, pop dung, no mek it - *She's out of shape*: Shi no mek it

OUTDOORS outadoor

OUTGOING vibesy, full a vibes, irie, jolly

OUTLAW 1 (n) badlaw, mafia 2 (n. *fugitive*) hot steppa 3 See *THUG* for much more

OUTLOOK (*prognosis; scoop*) pree, current - *What's the outlook?* A wa di prii?, Wai prii?

OUTSPOKEN trong mout

OVERBEARING trong-eye, extra, misareble

OVERCAST 1 (*cloudy*) setup, bleaky, dark up 2 (v. *to become overcast*) set up, bleak up, dark up

OVERCHARGE (*overcharge person X or people X*) nyam out X, saalt out X

OVEREAT ovanyam, clide

OVERENTHUSIASTIC extra, eggz up, too nuff, nuff, bumptious

OVERFLOW 1 (n) ovamount, extramount 2 (v) flood ovah, (for river only) come dung - *The river is overflowing*: Riva a kom dong, Rivabank a flod ova

OVERSEAS Farin (from *Foreign*)

OVERSEER (*overseer of slaves*) busha, bakra

OVERTHINK buss yu brain, pree too deep, worry yu head, fret up yuself, hot up yu head, hot up yuh skull

OWL patu (technically patu is a nightjar but the word is commonly applied to owls)

OWN 1 (v) canchol (from *control*), hol 2 (*one's own X*) yu owna X - *Do your own thing*: Du yu uona ting

PACIFIER (n. for baby) sooda (from *soother*)

PACKED (*crowded to the limit*) lock dung, ram, pack up, cork, chock up, chuck up

PAID 1 (adj or ppl) pay, sen on 2 Also see *GET PAID*

PAIN 1 (n) hot 2 (v. *suffer physical pain*) hot, feneh 3 (vt) hut, hot - *It pains me!* It a hat mi!

PAIN IN THE ASS see *HASSLE*

PAINFUL hot

PAIR 1 (n. *a pair of shoes*) a shoes 2 (n. *a pair of pants*) a pants, a trouziz 3 (n. *a pair of socks*) a socks 4 (n. *a pair of gloves*) a gloves 5 (n. *a pair of shorts*) a shorts

PALE (*having a very light brown complexion*) clear, yellow

PALM 1 (n. of hand) han miggle, han belly 2 (v) palms

PAMPER (v) pet an powda, pet an pampa, caytah tu

PAN (*tall saucepan*) bunpan

PANDEMONIUM see *UPROAR; MAYHEM*

PANTIES panty, draws, baggy, (*large panties*) bingo

PANTS 1 (n) drawz, trouziz, pantses 2 (*a pair of pants*) a pants, a trouziz 3 (*slim pants*) strait pants, fitted pants, gun foot, (*effeminate term*) tight pants

PANTY HOSE stockin foot

PAPAYA pawpaw

PARADE (vi. *walk around flaunting oneself*) moggle, pose off, hype, palaav, profile, primps off, pop style, cut figga

PARANOID parro

PARDON ME 1 (*May I say something?*) Jus a word, Oy deh, Aks pardon 2 (*Forgive me*) Manners, hush 3 (*Allow me to pass by*) Gi mi pass, Gi mi way, Low mi, Mek mi go chu, Free mi up, Av mi excuse

PARKING LOT cyar park

PARKINSON'S DISEASE shakes, nerves

PARSELY paasle

PARTICIPATE 1 (v) tek paat, penetrate, come een, run een, fall een, chune een 2 (*participate fully*) full-ticipate

PARTICIPATING (adj. *involved*) hitch up, link up, chune een, een deh, on ya

PARTICULAR 1 (*specific*) direck, sed, sottn (from *certain*) 2 (*picky*) fussy fussy, mekam pekam

PARTNER 1 (*companion*) combolo, quabs 2 (*business partner; associate*) paadna, paadi 3 (*sex partner*) combolo, fren 4 (v) link up

PARTY 1 (n. *bash*) paaty, dance, session, bashment, jammins 2 (*sausage party*) bull dance 3 (v. *go out and party*) du road, brok out, rave 4 (*party wildly*) rail up, brok wile, brok out, go haad, gwaan buckwile, rave 5 (*take it too far; act excessively wild*) go luu, luu 6 (v. *party until morning*) bleach

PASS DOWN (*bequeath*) ded leff gi - *My grandfather handed the house down to me when he died*: Mi granfaada ded lef gi mi di ous

PASS ON see *BEQUEATH* or *DIE*

PASS OUT (v) drop dung, pitch ova, feneh

PASS THE TIME 1 (v) mek up time 2 Also see *LOITER*

PASSION FRUIT sweet cup

PASSIONATE (adj. *determined; fiery*) trong eye, trong mind, facety, no easy

PAST paas - Also see *RECENTLY; IN THE OLD DAYS; LONG AGO*

PAST PERFECT TENSE (for affirmative statements or questions, the past perfect tense has the same structure as the simple past tense (see *PAST TENSE*). For negative statements or questions, the past perfect uses the following words and phrases instead of *hadn't*): neva, neva eva, neva did, neva en - *I hadn't visited Florida before I moved there*: Mi neva vizit Flarida bifuor mi muuv deh; Mi neva eva vizit Flarida bifuor mi muuv deh; Mi neva did vizit Flarida bifuor mi did muuv deh; Mi neva en vizit Flarida bifuor mi did muuv deh

PAST TENSE 1 (For affirmartive simple past tense, the following past tense markers can be used before any verb other than the modal verbs such as *cyan, mighta, mussi, shuda, will, etc*): did, di, id, en, ben, den, min - *I saw you*: Mi did si yu, Mi id si yu, Mi en si yu, etc. 2 (For negative past tense the following past tense markers can be used in the same way): neva, neh

PASTRY bake ting

PATCHED (adj) pitchy patchy

PATENT pr: pieten

PATH (n) paas, pass, trod

PATIENT (adj) patience

PAVED nylon, barbagreen

PAVEMENT nylon, barbagreen

PAY 1 (n) raise, food 2 (v) let off, lek off, sen on, faawud up

PAY ATTENTION TO mind, mine, pree, eyes, watch, check, clock, study, medz, program, penetrate, penny

PAY ATTENTION! 1 (*Listen to what I'm about to tell you*) Memba mi tel yu! 2 Also see *LISTEN UP!; BE CAREFUL!*

PEANUT (n. old colonial-era term) pinda

PEDESTRIAN 1 (n) walkfoot, ten-toe turbo 2 (adj) walkfoot

PEE (v. childish terms for *urinate*) wee wee, shee wee

PEEK 1 (n) prips 2 (v) prips 3 (*peek at*) prips pan

PEEP (v) prips

PEEPING TOM doorpeep

PEG LEG tumpa foot

PELICAN pilikin, joe bud, ole joe

PEN (*animal enclosure*) crawl

PENETRATE 1 (of a barrier) brok chu, brok, buss chu 2 (*puncture*) bore, go chu, brok chu, buss chu, jook 3 (vt. *sexually penetrate*) bore, jook up inna 4 (vi. *sexually penetrate*) go chu, bore

PENICILLIN pr: peninsilin

PENIS 1 (n) buddy, wood, cocky, rifle, puppy, pem pem, pengileng, john, pipe, hose, sausage, meat, flesh dagga, flesh axe, weldin torch, solderin torch, plank, tool 2 (*large penis*) numbah nine, bamboo, plantain, sugarcane, anaconda, rifle, tud leg, third leg 3 (*small penis*) peanut, chiney banana, frog banana, chi chi finga, chi chi mus 4 (*little boy's penis*) peanut, teelie, teapot

PEOPLE 1 (n. as subject of sentence) man an man, one an one - *People should work together*: Man an man fi wok tugeda 3 (*the people; the crowd; the population of a specific location*) di massive, di people dem 4 (when following a definite article or demonstrative adj) smaddy, one - *The people up in New York*: Di smadi dem op a Nyuu Yaak - *These people here*: Dem smadi ya, Dem wan ya

PERCEIVE pick up pan, penny

PERCH (v. as a bird) pich

PERFORM pr: prifaam

PERFORMANCE pr: prifaamans

PERFUME essen

PERHAPS 1 (adv) praps, paravencha 2 (*Perhaps that's true*) Coulda so i go

PERM (n. *permanent hair treatement*) cream

PERMANENT fareva, fi eva, for all time

PERMANENTLY fareva, fi eva, for all time, cyaa done

PERMISSION pr: promishan

PERSIST 1 (v. *endure*) live on, tan 2 (v. *persevere*) strive

PERSISTENT 1 (of person: *naggingly persistent*) eggz up, edge up, argumentable 2 (*resourceful and determined*) no easy, crabbit, trong eye, trong mind

PERSON smaddy, sumaddy - *He's a good person*: Him a gud smadi

PERSUADE 1 (*try to persuade*) put argument tu, put words tu 2 Also see: *MANIPULATE; COAX*

PERSUASION argument

PERSUASIVE 1 (of personality) lyrical, sweet mout, trong mout 2 (of a particular argument) well reason, mek sense, spell sense

PERVERT (n) freak

PERVERTED freaky, funky, slack, luu, pagan, heathen, outlaw

PESSIMISTIC 1 (of personality) negative, sowa 2 (of attitude) negative, sowa

PESTER (v) badda badda, sheg wid, tek set pan, hitch up pan, ningy ningy, tyad out, udge, fiteeg

PET (v. *caress*) brush

PHARMACY docta shop

PHOBIC fraidy fraidy

PHONE 1 (*mobile phone*) celli, digi 2 (v) link, shout

PHYSIQUE bazeek, structa

PICK AND CHOOSE (v) pinch an bite, pick pick

PICK ON Also see *HARASS or TEASE*

PICK UP 1 (*grab from off the ground*) tek up, pawn, pawn up, ketch up 2 (*go get something from another location*) look 3 (*go and get a person from another location*) look tu

PICK UP ON 1 (*try to seduce*) lyrics, drap lyrics pan, look argument wid 2 (*continue picking up on someone who is not interested*) put argument tu, put words tu

PICKPOCKET (n) stickman, Jim Screechy 2 (v. *pick someone's pocket*) stick, pick

PICKUP LINES lyrics

PICKUP TRUCK open back van, van

PICKY stush, fenkeh fenkeh, itey titey, picky picky, fussy fussy, mekam pekam

PIECE porshan 2 (*tiny piece*) finga, chenks 3 (*little pieces; scraps*) nyaka nyaka, dregs

PIERCE (v) bore, go chu, brok chu, buss chu, jook

PIERCED (adj) bore

PIGGYBACK RIDE donkey ride

PILL (*pill of medicine*) phensic

PILOT pr: pailat

PIMP see *STUD; PLAYER*

PIMPLE love bump, bump

PINEAPPLE sweet pine, pine

PINKIE FINGER (n) chi chi muss

PIPE (n. for smoking ganja or marijuana) cutchie, chalice, chalwah, chillum

PISS (v. *pee*) peep

PITTANCE smalls, skimps, kimps, dregs, dribblinz

PITY (v. *feel pity for*) sorry fi, feel a way fi

PLACE (*meeting place or hangout spot*) endz, chill spot

PLAID checky checky

PLAINS (*the plains*) di flat

PLAIT plat

PLAITED 1 (adj) plat 2 (n. *plaited hair*) plat hair, plat head

PLAN 1 (*the plan*) di program 2 (v. *make plans*) set a plan, set up a plan 3 (*plan to; intend to*) go fi, intention fi

PLANT (*any herbacious organism*) bush, weed

PLASTIC BAG (*supermarket-style plastic bag*) scandal bag, scandal

PLAY 1 (v. as children or animals) ramp 2 (*play the role of*) form, shape, pattan 3 (v. of joke or sport) run - *Are you playing a joke?* A juok yu a ron? - *Let's play some football*: Mek wi ron som baal

PLAY A JOKE ON run joke pan, gimmicks, play cyaad pan, cyaad

PLAY AROUND see *MESS AROUND; JOKE AROUND*

PLAY THE FOOL form fool - *He's playing the fool*: Him a faam fuul

PLAYBOY 1 (*wealthy young male hedonist*) pretty bwoy, spree bwoy, soft-hand bwoy 2 Also see *PLAYER*

PLAYER 1 (*football player*) footballa, balla 3 (*lady's man; womanizer*) gyalis, girls man, slappa, cha cha bwoy, strikah

PLAYFUL rampify, play play

PLEAD see *BEG*

PLEASANT 1 (of weather or ambiance) sweet, vibesy, boonoo<u>noo</u>noos, ites 2 (of person) cool, irie, heartical, ites

PLEASE 1 (adv. *kindly*) du, beg yu, beg yu du 2 (pred. adv. *if you don't mind*) noh - *Have a seat please*: Sidung no 3 (pred adv. *I'm begging you*) du, beg yu - *Please help me!* Help mi <u>duu</u>! 4 (v. *delight*) sweet, mek glad 5 (*try to please; kiss up to*) curry fayva wid, kin teet wid, powda, pet, sweet up, hug up

PLEASED sweet, well sweet, cool, good, irie

PLEASURE 1 (*enjoyment*) vibes, pleasuration, funjoy 2 (*sexual pleasure*) agony, extasy

PLENTIFUL (adj) like rice, like dirt, like sand, like wow, like wah, kulu kulu, nuff fi stone dog

PLENTY 1 (n) nuff nuff, wholeap, nuff fi stone dog, kulu kulu 2 (adj) nuff nuff 3 (*plenty of*) nuff nuff 4 (pred adv. *in abundance*) inna bungle, like wow, like wah, like rice, like dirt, like sand, fi stone dog ; (following obj pronoun only) wagga wagga, lagga lagga, kulu kulu - *I have plenty of lyrics*: Mi av nof nof liriks, Mi av liriks laik rais, Mi av liriks ina bonggl, Mi av liriks fi stuon dag, Mi av dem waga waga, Mi av dem laga laga, Mi av dem kulu kulu

PLOT 1 (n. *plot of land for farming*) grong, piece 2 (v. *conspire*) set up plan, study 3 Also see *PLOY; SCHEME*

PLOY (n) rake, scyam, bandulu skeem, chicaney, ligues, rungles, gimmicks

PLURAL (Plural nouns in Jamaican Creole are usually the same as the singular noun. But the word 'dem' (from *them*) is often placed after a plural noun if that plural noun is preceded by the definite article 'di' (from *the*) or by a possessive adjective such as 'mi' or 'yu'. For example: *My friends love me*: Mi fren dem lov mi)

PNEUMONIA new mona

POKE (v) jook, jam

POLENTA tun tun

POLICE 1 (*the police*) babylon, di babylon dem, di red stripe dem, di blue bag dem 2 (*police officer*) police, squaddie, constable, lawman, corpie, red seam, blue seam, red stripe, blue bag, pan head, (derogatory): babylon, beast, woodpecka

POLITE mannersable, balance, proppa, deestant

POLITICIAN (derogatory) politricksta, follytician

POLITICS (*affairs of governance*) runninz, (derogatory): politricks, follytricks

POMEGRANATE pranganat, panganat, pomgranat

POMELO shaddock

POMP poppy show

POMPOUS 1 pomptious, poppyshow, ova-du, extra 2 (n. *pompous person; pompous ass*) dry land tourist, dry-pan tourist, poppy show 3 Also see *PRETENTIOUS; CONCEITED*

POOP 1 (*excrement*) didi, doodoo 2 (v. *defecate*) didi

POOR 1 (*very poor; destitute*) des, dry, puckro, mafeena 2 (n. *poor person*) suffara, mafeena, kwashi, kwamin, bongo

POPSICLE suck suck, icicle, kisko pop, kisko

POPULAR 1 (of person: *well-liked and well-known*) hype, a lead, a happn, shot, shot a road, a run road, slap weh, sell off, name brand, craab up, buss, big, large, criss 2 (adj. of thing: *trending*) shot, shot a road, a run road, hype, a lead, a happn, sell off, craab up, slap weh, slap, clap, a tek, a lick, bashy, criss 3 (n. *popular male*) star bwoy, kwenga 4 (*popular female*) star gyal, hot gyal, glamma gyal

PORCH (n) varanda

PORK arnold, trentan, dat

PORNO MOVIE blue movie, blues

PORPOISE paapas, pampas

POSE 1 (v. *show off*) moggle, pose off, palaav, profile, cut figure, primps off, shape 2 (v. *pose as*) shape, form, pattern, du like, gwaan like, move like, flex like

POSEUR double six

POSH 1 (of person) stoosh, hitey titey, risto, society, chest high 2 (of place) stoosh, hitey titey

POSITIVE 1 (*positive energy; positive vibes*) gladness, niceness, upliftment, upfullness 2 see *CHEERFUL; OPTIMISTIC; SURE*

POSITIVITY see *POSITIVE*

POSSESS 1 (as a demon: *control one's body*) ride 2 Also see *HAVE; OWN*

POSSESSED 1 (adj. *possessed by a spirit or demon*) haunted, duppy deh pan X, duppy a ride X (X=person) - *He's possessed*: Him aantid, Dopi deh pan him, Dopi pan him, Dopi a raid him

POSSESSION 1 (*spiritual mediumship*) myal 2 (v. *take possession of*) paan, paan up, tek up, nyam up 3 (n. *thing owned*) see *POSSESSIONS*

POSSESSIONS (*personal stuff*) bag an pan, ray ray, bangarang, curroaches, carowzin, corojungo, cruchment, jing bang, jeng jeng

POSSIBLE pr: pasibl (*That's possible; That could be*) Coulda so ih go

POST-MENOPAUSAL (*no longer able to bear children*) bear off, av out yu lot - *She's too old to have kids*: Shi bier aaf, Shi av out har lat aredi

POSTPONE 1 put off 2 (*postpone until*) nah kip til

POSTURING (n) mogglin, pozin

POT see *COOKING POT; CHAMBER POT; CANNABIS*

POTATO pitayta, Irish

POTLUCK (*a meal prepared among friends*) boat

POUND 1 (v. *pound once*) pung, fum 2 (*pound repeatedly*) fum fum, mala mala

POWER 1 powa 2 (*electricity*) current, lectric, powa

POWER OUTAGE powa cut

POX (n) Yaws

PRAISE 1 (n) ratingz, hype, upliffment, respeck 2 (v) rate, rate up, big up, large up, count, liff up, sallute, wowatu

PRANK 1 (n) gimmicks, cyaad, rungles 2 (v) run joke pan, gimmicks, play cyaad pan, cyaad, rungles

PRAWN janga

PRAYER pryah

PRAYING MANTIS duppy riding-horse, devil riding-horse, devil horse

PRECISE direck, prezack

PRECISELY 1 (adv) same so, same one, prezackly - *That's precisely what I told him*: A <u>dat</u> siem wan mi tel him, A siem so mi tel him

PRECOCIOUS 1 (adj) force ripe, fresh, brite 2 (v. *to do something precocious*) fly pass yu ness

PREDICAMENT prekeh, puru, crosses, dog corn piece (meaning *dog's corn field*)

PREFER preffa, radda

PREGNANCY breed belly, belly, breedin

PREGNANT 1 (adj) breedup, preggy, gaan 2 (v. *get pregnant*) breed, get belly, fat up 3 (v. *be pregnant*) show belly, ha belly, av belly 4 (*a pregnant woman*) belly ooman

PREPARE (vi) set up yuself, strap up 2 (vt) set up, strap up

PREPARED (*ready to go*) lock, strap up, overlap

PRESENT 1 (*here; in attendance*) on ya, deh ya 2 (adj. *current*) now - *the present generation*: di now jinarieshan 3 Also see *GIVE* or *INTRODUCE*

PRESENT CONTINUOUS TENSE 1 (in affirmative sentences) a, deh - *I am working*: Mi a wok; Mi deh wok 2 (in negative sentences) naa - *I'm not working*: Mi naa wok

PRESENT PERECT CONTINUOUS TENSE 1 (same as present continuous tense, but sometimes with words such as *fram* and *fi* added to give a context of time): *She has been drinking since ten o'clock*: Shi a jrink fram ten; Shi deh jrink fram ten - *I haven't been working these days*: Mi naa wok nowadiez

PRESENT PERECT TENSE 1 (in affirmative sentences: *have; has*) Ø - I have seen it before: Mi si it aredi 2 (in negative sentences: *haven't; hasn't*) no - *She hasn't done her work*: Shi no du ar wok

PRESS AHEAD see *PRESS ON*

PRESS ON (*continue advancing*) push an go chu, push on chu, press on chu, press along, move up, step along, step an galang, galang galang, gwaan du yu ting

PRESSED (adj. of clothes) criss

PRESSURE 1 (n. *physical pressure*) presha 2 (n. *emotional and mental pressure*) bodderation 3 (v. *to pressure; put pressure on*) hackle, push push, udge, presha presha

PRESUMPTUOUS 1 (adj) bright, bumptious, eggz up, edge up, even up, shoob-up shoob-up, extra 2 (v. *to be presumptuous*) tek liberty, tek step, eggs up yuself, fly paas yu nest, paas yu place 3 Also see *PRETENTIOUS*

PRETEND 1 (vi. *make believe*) play 2 (vi. *bluff*) gyow, sell gyow 3 (v. *pretend to be X* (X=noun)) pattern X, form X, shape X, du like X, gwaan like X, move like X, flex like X 4 (v. *pretend to be Y* (Y=adjective)) gwaan like yu, du like yu, galang like yu

PRETENTIOUS 1 (adj) hype up, gwaani gwaani, big an so-so, eggz up, bumptious, pomptious, ovadu, extra, nuff, consequential, neva-see-come-see, nyanga 2 (n. *pretentious person*) dry land tourist, dry-pan tourist, poppy show, neva-see-come-see, gyowa 3 (v. *to be pretentious*) nuff up yuself, fly paas yu nest, paas yu place 4 Also see *CONCEITED*

PRETENTIOUSNESS nuffness, bumptiousness, pomptiousness, hype, nyanga, gyow, extra, poppy show

PRETERITE TENSE see *PAST TENSE*

PRETTY 1 (of place) sweet, nice 2 (of woman) kris, pretty pretty, pretty like wow, pretty laka X (X=anything of value), pretty no Y (Y = expletive), a seh one, boonoonoonoos 3 (n. *pretty woman*) kris ting, goodaz, glama gyal, goody

PRETTY BOY face bwoy, cha cha bwoy

PREVENT block, hinda, hol dung

PREVIEW 1 (n) prips, pree 2 (v) prips, pree

PRICK (v. *poke; sting*) jook

PRICKLY jooky jooky, picky picky

PRIDE 1 (*self-respect*) ambition 2 (*conceit*) nuffness, bumptiousness, pomptiousness, nyanga

PRIMITIVE raw chaw, wackle an dawb, bitch-up, backabush, backamoko

PRISON wok house

PRISSY prussy, itey titey

PRIVATELY (*one to one*) one a way

PRIVILEGED getty getty, havi havi

PROBABLY 1 (adv) goodly, good fi 2 Also see *SURELY*

PROBLEMS 1 (*glitches*) chubbles, parangles 2 Also see *ISSUES; HARDSHIP*

PROCEED (v) push on, press on

PROCRASTINATE igle, hitch, jesta, diggle daggle

PROCRASTINATOR jestara, iglaz

PROFANITY badwud

PROFIT (n. *money earned*) raise

PROGNOSIS pree, current - *What's the prognosis?* A wa di prii?, Wai prii?

PROGRESS 1 (n) pr: pruogres 2 (v) move up, step up, go chu, tek di lead

PROHIBIT clap dung

PROJECT 1 (n) projeck, ting 2 Also see *EXTEND*

PROLAPSE body kom dung

PROLONG 1 (vt) long out, draw out 2 (vi. *prolong an argument by adding more and more to it*) falla up

PROMISCUOUS (of woman) dutty, manny manny, mud up, jezibel, cridell

PROMISE 1 (v. *make a promise; make an oath*) tek God off a di cross 2 (*break a promise; renege*) tun back, sheriff

PROMOTE 1 (*contractually promote*) back, cyarry 2 (*hype up*) mad up, loud up, send X a road (X=event or performer) 3 (*not promote; not support; not accept*) no defend, no caytah to, no low, bun, bun out

PRONG 1 (n) sprong 2 (n. of a fork) teet

PROP UP cotch up

PROPER (*uspstanding*) deestant, goody goody, mannersable

PROPS 1 (*kudos*) ratingz, hype, big up, respeck 2 (v. *give props to*) rate up, big up, large up, count

PROSTATE (*enlarged prostate and difficulty urinating*) stoppage a waata

PROSTITUTE 1 (n) rental, sportah, blue foot, man ketcha, Miss Cooba 2 (*Dreadlocked male prostitute who serves tourist women*) rent-a-dread

PROSTITUTION 1 (n) flat foot wok 2 (v. *to work as a prostitute*) wok a back road, du flatfoot wok

PROTEIN meat kind

PROTEST 1 (*react in oppostion*) lick out 2 (*react against*) lick out gainst

PROTRUDE /PROTRUDING cock out, pulp

PROUD 1 (*dignified*) upstandin 2 (*be proud of oneself*) big up yu chess 3 (*feel very proud about an accomplishment*) proud bag buss - *I'm so proud!*: Mi proud bag bos! 3 Also see *POMPOUS; CONCEITED*

PROVERB tellin

PROVIDE FOR (*give financial or other support*) carry

PROVOKE 1 (*provoke person X*) draw X out 2 (*antagonize*) hype pan, rail up pan, wile up, hackle wid, sheg wid, bait, draw cyaad pan, chuck it pan, chuck pan, cold up, coarse up

PRY 1 (*meddle*) fass, meggle, mell, eggz up, edge up 2 (*pry open*) pull

PUBERTY machure

PUBIC HAIR (n. of woman only) pum pum bush

PUBIC MOUND buff, fluff

PUBLISH jrap - *He hasn't published the book yet*: Im no jrap di buk yet

PUBLISHED (adj. or pp. of book or other work) jrap, gaan a road

PUDDING puddn, pone

PUFFER FISH 1 (*spiny puffer fish; porcupine fish*) hedgehog fish, macca fish, pracupine fish 2 (*smooth-skinned puffer fish*) bokkle fish, puff gut

PUFFY buff out, buff up, buffo buffo, puff up puff up

PULL (v) draw - Also see *PULL DOWN; PULL UP; PULL OUT; PULL OFF*

PULL DOWN haul dung, pull dung, hice dung (from *hoist*)

PULL OFF 1 (v. as a physical stont or aerial stont) cut 2 (*exit*) come off

PULL OUT 1 (vt. *remove*) draw out, draw, back out 2 (vt. *yank out; remove suddenly*) pop out 3 (*pull out of; retreat from*) leggo, back out fram, tek we yuself fram

PULL UP 1 (vt. *lift*) liff up, haul up, hice up (from *hoist*), draw up 2 Also see *STRAIGHTEN OUT; REPRIMAND*

PUMP UP 1 (of event or show: *promote; hype up*) mad up, hype up, loud up 2 (of crowd or team: *excite; motivate*) mad up

PUMPKIN punkin

PUNCH 1 (n. *a punch; a blow*) tump, kuff, lick, clap, clot, bula, boof 2 (v. *to punch*) lick, tump, kuff, clap, clot, baff, boof

PUNCTURE 1 (n) bore   2 (v) bore, go chu, brok chu, buss chu, jook

PUNISH 1 (*castigate*) put unda mannaz, deal wid, hangle   2 (*being punished*) unda mannaz - *He's being punished for what he did to the old lady*: Him anda manaz fi weh him du di uol liedi

PUNISHMENT mannaz (from *manners*)

PURE 1 (adj) pyor, lone - *That's pure liquor* A luon lika dat   2 (*virtuous and innocent*) goody goody   3 (adv. *utter*) peer, bare, bey, so so - *It's pure mayhem out there*: A pier mixop out deh, A bie mixop out deh, etc

PURGATORY (n) pokitori

PURGE 1 (n. of intestines: *a flushing out*) operation, washout   2 (v. *clear the intestines*) operate, wash out

PURPOSE 1 (adv. *on purpose*) fi purpose   2 (*What's your purpose?*) A weh yu fah?, A who yu?

PURSUE 1 (*physically chase after; hunt down*) run dung, mek afta   2 (*work toward*) run dung

PUS corruption

PUSH 1 (v) push, brace   2 (*push and jostle through a crowd*) bump an bore   3 (*push up against*) brush, brace up pan, push up pan   4 Also see *PROMOTE; SHOVE; PERSUADE*

PUSHOVER sawfaz, press-button, remote, saps, prekeh

PUSHUP pressup - *Give me forty pushups*: Gi mi faati presop

PUSHY see *AGGRESSIVE; PERSISTANT; NOSEY*

PUSSY 1 (*coward*) saps, sawfaz, bait, mantu, nyamps, fraidy puss   2 (*vagina - innocent terms*) front, miggle, ting, sinting, whatsitnot, tarra warra, coco bread, pokie, property, crotches; (more sexualized) kitty, kyatty, nookie, buff, good good, eva bless, evn gates, entrance, zum zum, Benz, glamity, glimity-glamity, cherry pie, panti pie, bammy-an-pear, pum pum, pumselle, cherry, cho cho, tomato, salad, veggie, salt ting, salt fish, fattaz, buffaz, clump; (vulgar terms) punani, nani, di nana, puni, punash, nash, nush nush, katash, kitash, fishy, tuni, tun-tuni, tun tun, chune chune, beef, renkin meat, fur burger, hairy bank, bumbo   3 (n. *very tight vagina*) neegle eye, glue, tight gift, tightness, ukubit, uku

PUSTULE (n) Yaw

PUT ASIDE (of problems or disagreements or differences) lef out, put pan pause

PUT BACK ON put on back

PUT DOWN 1 (*set down*) pudung, res 2 (*disparage*) dis, style, class, tek step wid, hype pan, coas up, col up, low count, reduce 3 Also see *INSULT*

PUT OUT (*extinguish*) out

PUT UP WITH 1 (*accept*) low 2 (*contend with*) deal wid, tek, angle, manage, suffah, go chu, pass chu, get chu

PUTTER AROUND pang pang

QUAIL partridge

QUALITY (adj. *high quality*) name brand, quality, tuff, top shelf, top a di top, toppity top, toppa top, goodup, goodup goodup, preps, original

QUARREL 1 (n) cass cass, cuss cuss, war, confusion, cobell, preke, puru, mix up, blenda, powda house, bangarang, parangles, fandangles, ruction, bag a argument 2 (v) trace, war, war out, cuss cuss, wile up, trow wud, fling wud

QUARRELING see *DRAMA*

QUARRELSOME warify, cuss cuss, ignarant, ig, cross, hot skull, brawlin, waasi, trong physic, rhygin

QUESTION pr: kwestian

QUICKIE (n. *a quick sexual encounter*) a rooks off, a sort out, a kech up, a taze, a stamp an go

QUICKLY (pred adv only) quick time, quick stick, quick quick 2 (pred adv: *with a sudden swift motion; in a flash*) swips, foops, floops - *He stole the purse in a flash*: Him skofl di purs so, swips!

QUID PRO QUO hand go han come

QUIET pr: kwayat 1 (*silent*) hush up 2 Also see *QUIET!*

QUIET! Oy!, Tappinize!, Heng up!, Hol ih dung!, Hush yu mout!, Kibba yu mout! 2 Also see *SHUT UP!*

QUIT 1 (vi. *surrender*) bow 2 (vt. *resign from*) leggo 3 (*give up a habit*) leggo - *He quit smoking*: Him lego di sigaret dem, Him don smuok

RACKET 1 (*scam*) bandulu scheme, bandulu, scyam, parangles, rake, rungles, ligues, chickaney 2 (*noise*) piece a noise, bag a noise, bangarang, palangarang, palam pam, bam bam, galangin, jing bang, rig jig, ruction, ruption

RAGGED raggy raggy, ragga ragga, reggeh reggeh, chaka chaka, nyaka nyaka, yaka yaka, yagga yagga, chak an peckle

RAGS (*tattered old clothes*) reg jegz, jeng jeng, yagga yagga, yeg yeg, rullucks, lurrucks

RAIN 1 (*gentle rain*) dew rain, white rain 2 (*incessant light rain*) ol ooman rain 3 (*heavy rain*) season rain, man rain

RAINSTORM season rain

RAISE 1 (vt) liff up, rise, hice (from *hoist*), hice up 2 (vt. of child: *nurture*) grow

RAM (v. *slam into*) bunks, buck, run ina

RAMBLE see *BABBLE; WANDER*

RANCH (*farm for animals*) pen

RANCOR see *RESENTMENT*

RANDOM (of person: *eccentrically funny*) no easy

RANK pr: rank

RASH 1 (*skin rash*) fassy, kokobeh, cratch-kin 2 (*itchy rash*) heech, kratch kratch 3 (*eczema*) Cudjo rubba 4 (*athlete's foot*) grunge

RASTA see *RASTAMAN; RASTA WOMAN*

RASTA WOMAN empress, lioness, African queen

RASTAFARI see *RASTAMAN* or *RASTA WOMAN*

RASTAFARIAN see *RASTAMAN* or *RASTA WOMAN*

RASTAMAN 1 (n) ras, rastafari, Iyah man, (of Nyabinghi order) binghi man; (of Bobo Shanti order) bobo dread, bobo 2 (title or address for a rastaman) Ras, Iyah, Lion, I, (for young rastaman) Jah son 3 (*false rasta*) wolf, rasta impostah, pork ras, pork dread

RAT ratta, mus mus, micey

RATHER 1 (v. *would rather*) preffa, radda 2 (adv. *somewhat*) kine a, adj+ish, go fi +adj - *They are rather young*: Dem yonggish; Dem go fi yong 3 (*rather than*) sted a, in place a, more dan, before

RATIONAL 1 (adj. of decision or idea) reason 2 (of person) righted, ha sense

RAVINE gully

RAY see *STINGRAY*

RAZOR BLADE razor mout

REACT (vi. *react in kind to a threat*) lick ih back

READY (*all set and ready to go*) lock, set, fit, cool, strap up, deh pan ice, chock an belay, fit an frock, cook an curry

REAL 1 (*authentic*) bonafide, name brand, fi real, strait 3 (of person: *sincere*) artical, bonafide, name brand, strait, fi real

REALIGN straitn up back

REALIZE (*realize that* X) pree seh X, sight seh X, penitrate seh X, pick up seh X, come tu yu seh X, lick yu seh X - *I just realized that it's Sunday today*: It jos lik mi seh a Sondeh tideh

REALLY 1 (when modifying a verb or adj) well - *They really want to come*: Dem wel waan fi kom - *They are really tired*: Dem wel tayad 3 (when modifying an adjective but only if placed <u>after</u> that adjective) bad, bad bad, like wow, like wah, cyaa done, so till, gaan tu bed, tu X (X=expletive) - *They are really tired*: Dem tayad bad, Dem tayad lak wow, Dem tayad kyaa don, Dem tayad tu blurdkliit, etc. 4 (*don't really; isn't really;* etc) no too - *She doesn't really care*: Shi no tuu mata

REALLY? Fi real?, Inna real life?, A chu?, Nah ramp?, A lie, A joke

REARRANGE see *REPOSITION* or *REORGANIZE*

REASONABLE 1 (of decision or idea) reason, mek sense, spell sense 2 (of personality) righted, concious, well reason 3 (v. *to be reasonable*) av sense

REBEL 1 (n) radic 2 (v) <u>rebel</u>, revolute, lick out, brok weh

REBELLIOUS 1 (of child: *disobedient*) see *DISOBEDIENT* 2 (of personality) waasi, facety, no easy 3 (*insurgent; mutinous*) brokweh

REBUILD bill up back

RECANT tek back yu chat

RECEDE (v. as water) draw

RECEIVE (v) ketch, hol

RECENTLY see *LATELY; THE OTHER DAY*

RECOGNITION 1 (n) respeck, mention 2 (*give recognition to*) gi respeck tu, mention, call up 3 Also see *PRAISE*

RECOGNIZE 1 (*identify*) pick out 2 (*give recognition to*) gi respeck tu, call up, mention 3 Also see *HONOUR; REALIZE*

RECONNECT 1 (as people) link up back 2 (of thing) hitch up back tugedda

RECOVER 1 (vi. *regain strength*) build back, bill back 2 (vt. *re-obtain*) get back

REDO du back, du ova

REESTABLISH set up back, extablish back

REFLECT 1 (*replicate*) refleck back 2 (vi. *reflect about things*) medz, hol a medz, hol a medi, hol a reason, satta

REFLECTION shadow

REFRAIN (*refrain from speaking*) block a soun, hol back yu chat

REFRESHED fresh up, well sweet

REFRESHING nice, cool

REFRESHMENT (*cold drink*) long drink, cool drink, drinks, jrinks

REFUSE (v. *refuse to*) naa - *We refuse to give up*: Wi naa giv op

REGARDING (*with respect to*) far as, wen it come on tu, bou

REGARDLESS 1 still for all, still 2 (*regardless of*) no mind, no mine, no care

REGULARLY all di while, regulah

REHEARSAL rershal, run-chu, (*soundcheck*): stringup

REHEAT (v) hot ova, hot up back

REHEATED hot ova

REJECT 1 (n. *social outcast*) waste man, double blank, cruff, crebbeh crebbeh, boogooyaga, mafeena 2 (v. *to reject socially*) run, ex out, tun out, send a shop, dish X dirt (X=person) 3 (v. of statement or idea) bun, bun out, no defend, no promote

REKINDLE ketch up

RELATE 1 (vi. *sympathize and understand*) ovastan, ovaz, penetrate, groundz 2 (*relate to*) mesh wid, grounz wid - Also see *GET ALONG WITH*

RELATIONSHIP 1 (*romantic relationship*) dealinz 2 (v. *be in a romantic relationship*) deh, carry straw

RELATIVE(S) 1 (n) fambily, generation 2 (*a blood relative*) fleshy 3 (*any relative not in the direct line*) cousin

RELAX 1 (*chill out*) easy, bill back, bill (from *build*), sekkle, level, quat, balance, cool, cool out, breeze out, satta 2 Also see *HANG OUT* or *RELAX!*

RELAX! Juss cool!, Easy Yuself!, Bill!, Balance!, Level!, Seckle!, Quat!, Cool noh!, Ease up!, Easy noh!, Breathe easy!, Satta!, Simma dung!, Go simma!, Cool yu foot!, Res yu spirit!

RELEASE 1 (*let go of*) leggo, let off, fly 2 (*unfasten*) fly, pull 3 (*liberate*) free up, leggo, fly 4 (*publish*) jrap

RELIABLE 1 (of person) goodup, heartical, artical, conscious, cool, deestant, ites 2 (of thing) goodup, goodup goodup, quality, tuff, name brand, bonafide

REMAIN 1 (*endure*) live on, tan 2 (*stay*) tan, hitch, klutch, quat, bats

REMAINDER (*the remainder*) di odda res, di res, di wah leff, di aftawuds

REMAINS 1 (n. of food: *leftovers*) wah lef, bambaye, aftawuds 2 (n. *ruins*) nyaka nyaka, wah leff

REMEMBER (v) memba, (as a warning to take note of something for future reference) mark - *Remember this number*: Maak da nomba ya

REMIND (vt) memba

REMOTE 1 (adj) backabush, backamoko, back a God back, backa beyond 3 (n. *remote area*) outlaw districk, woy woy, moko, chuku - *It's in a very remote area*: It out a woi woi, It ina di outlaa distrik

REMOVE 1 tek weh 2 (*take off*) back off 3 Also see *WITHDRAW*

RENEGE tun back, dis di program, sheriff

REORGANIZE dechakalize, sort out back, set up back

REPEL (*drive off*) jive weh

REPLENISH (of supplies or fuel) top up, full up back, chock up

REPLENISHED 1 (of person: *refreshed*) fresh up, well sweet 2 (of supplies or fuel), top up, full up, chock, chuck

REPLY 1 (v) ansa back 2 (*get back to someone*) rally back, page back

REPOSITION shiff, shake up

REPRESENT 1 (v. *signify*) mean seh, tan fi, tan fah 2 (v. *promote*) defend, back, carry, promote

REPRIMAND (v) draw up, put unda mannaz

REPROVE (v) draw up, put unda mannaz

REPRESENTATIVE representah

REPUTATION name, knowinz

REQUEST (v) sen fi

REQUIRE 1 (*necessitate*) need 2 (*oblige*) mek

REQUIRED 1 (*needed*) rikwaya 2 (*obligated*) muss an boun

RESEARCH 1 (n) studderation 2 (v) look inna, suss out

RESEMBLE fayva, come een like

RESENT 1 (*feel bitter about*) carry feelinz bout, carry belly bout, keep malice bout 2 (vt. *resent person X*) carry feelinz fi X, carry belly fi X, keep malice fi X 3 Also see *DISLIKE; BADMIND*

RESENTFUL 1 (adj) badmind 2 (v. *feel resentful*) carry feelinz, carry belly, keep malice

RESENTMENT malice, feelinz, sowa belly

RESIDENCE yaad, resident, creech

RESILIENCE (n. of people) gumption, talawah, haad back

RESILIENT 1 (of person) talawah, no easy, haad back, tuffa 2 (*durable*) trong

RESIST 1 (*tense up*) fight, chuggle 2 (vi. *retaliate*) lick ih back, chuck ih back 3 (vt. *stand up against*) fight gainst, chant dung

RESOLVE 1 (n) ambition, gumption 2 (*figure out; solve*) sort out, maths out, clear, suss out 3 (*resolve to; decide to*) decide fi, make up yu mind fi

RESORT TO (v) run to, tun to

RESOURCE pr: ri<u>zuos</u>

RESOURCEFUL skill, no easy

RESOURCEFULNESS gumption

RESPECT 1 (n) rispeck, ratinz 2 (v) rispeck, rate, count 3 (*self-respect*) ambition 4 (v. *have self-respect*) matta yuself, rate yuself, count yuself 5 (*lose respect for*) lose off a 6 Also see *DISRESPECT*

RESPECTABLE (of person) artical, bonafide, deestant, goodup, conscious, (female only): goodaz, goody

RESPECTED 1 (of male: *highly respected*) artical, shot, a lead, rankin, notchilous, toppa top, bonafide 2 (n. *a highly respected male*) notch, rankin, bantan, general, admiral, gorgon, don, bonafide 3 (n. *highly respected woman*) goodaz, goody, big ooman, empress

RESPLENDANT (adj) splendacious, splendifarous

RESPONSIBLE 1 (*in charge*) response 2 Also see *DEPENDABLE*

REST 1 (v. *relax; replenish your energy*) bill back, bill, sekkle, quat, balance, cool, cool out, breeze out, eazy, hol a medi, satta 2 Also see *NAP*

RESTAURANT (*small restaurant*) cookshop, funda

RESTLESS (adj) kra kra

RESTRAIN 1 (*hold in a bear hug*) buckle hol 2 (*immobilize*) clamp dung, fastn 3 (*restrain oneself*) hol yu corner

RETALIATE lick it back, chuck it back, serve sauce

RETREAT 1 (v) tun back, ease off, back weh, tek weh yuself 2 (*retreat slightly; back up*) dress back

RETRIBUTION du fi du, bam bam, wataloo, Ben Johnson Day

RETURN 1 (*go back; come back*) faawud back, return back, rally back 2 (*give back*) gi back, leggo back, lek off back

REVEAL 1 (*physically reveal*) show up, flash, buss 2 (of misdeed or controversy: *call attention to*) loud up, rinse, show up

REVENGE 1 (n) du fi du, vengeancy 2 (v. *get revenge*) seckle di score, chucky back, ansa back, serve sauce

REVERSE (v) reverse back, go backway

REVIEW (*revisit*) pree back

REVOLUTIONARY 1 (adj. *insurgent*) brokweh 2 (adj. *groundbreaking*) original, terrible 3 (n. *a revolutionary*) radical, roots radical, roots steppa

REWIND (v) reel back, wheel back

RIBCAGE side

RICH 1 (*weathy*) set up, pocket long 2 (n. *rich person*) money man, long pocket, risto, Missa T 3 Also see *UPPER CLASS*

RICKETY ruku ruku, rookoondung, frekeh frekeh, rickety rickety, palla palla

RIDE (n. *lift; free ride*) jrap

RIDICULE (v) laaf afta, style, hype pan, reduce, pop style pan, draw cyaad pan, jeri, tek X mek pappy show, tek X mek prekeh (X=person)

RIDICULOUS poppyshow, cartoon, alms-house, fool fool, eedyat, follygrong

RIGHT right-han - *on the right side*: pan di rait-han said

RIGHT AWAY 1 same time, sed time, jus so, slam bam 2 (pred adv only) same time, quick time, quick stick, quick quick, swips, braps, slam bam - *Tidy up your room at once!*: Pran op yu ruum kwik stik!

RIGHT NOW 1 (adv) now now, nung nung, right nung, eena di Iwah 2 (when following a command) same time, quick time, quick stick, quick quick, slam bam - *Tidy up your room at once!*: Pran op yu ruum kwik stik!

RIGHT? see *ISN'T THAT SO?*

RING OUT (v. as gunshots) beat, clap, wave - *Shots ring out in the city*: Shat a klap ina di siti, Shat a biit, Shat a wiev

RINSE wrench

RIPE 1 (adj) fit, ready 2 (*almost ripe*) tun 3 (*overripe*) pass ripe

RIPEN tun, fit - *The mangos are ripening*: Di manggo dem a fit, Di manggo dem a tun

RISE (vi) raise up, liff up

RISK (v) chance, truss

RISKY sticky

RIVER MOUTH /RIVER DELTA (n) bogue, bogg

RIVERBANK bankin

ROAM 1 (*roam aimlessly*) box bout, walk up an dung, walk an tun, tun-rung tun-rung, spin-rung spin-rung 2 (*travel and explore*) trod di lan, trod di eart

ROB tief, scuffle, borrow, pick

ROBBER (*armed robber*) steppa

ROBBERY pr: rabri (n. *a robbery*) a jooks, one jooks

ROCK 1 (*stone*) rockstone 2 (vt. *rock to sleep*) baya

ROCKY (adj) karra karra

ROFL DWL (ded wid laaf), BOAL (Buss out a laaf)

ROLL DOWN (of window, etc) wine dung

ROLL UP (of window, etc) wine up

ROLLING PAPER skin, bamboo, rizzla

ROOF housetop

ROOST (v) tek a set, pich

ROOSTER cock chicken

ROOT FOR carry, back

ROOT VEGETABLES/TUBERS grung provision, grung food, food

ROPE cord, rope, tightie

ROT (vi. as food) pwile, tun frowzy, get fluxy

ROTTEN 1 (of food) spwile, fluxy, gaan 2 (*slightly rotten; starting to go bad*) touch

ROUGH 1 (*coarse; gritty*) gritty gritty, bogro bogro 2 (*bumpy; rocky*) koro koro, karra karra 3 (*scaly*) alligator back 4 (of situation: *harsh*) coas, deep, dread

ROUGH UP (v. *mahandle*) ruff up, bad up, hackle, hackle up, man hackle, manangle, malahack, mammick, sawka, sawka up

ROUND (adj) roun, rung, pum pum

ROUTINE (n) runninz

RUB 1 (v) rub, groundz 2 (*rub up against*) brush, groundz pan

RUBBISH see *GARBAGE* or *STUFF*

RUDE 1 outta aada, facety, bright, renk, nassy, mizarebl 2 Also see *VULGAR*

RUDENESS (n. *impoliteness*) renkness, facetyness, brightness, freshness, outa orderness, dragupsy

RUIN /RUINED (adj) mash up, sheg up, mud up, nassy up, sawka sawka, kaba kaba, soak, spwile

RULE (vi. *be amazing; be the best*) a lead, slap weh, shell dong, run tings, run di road, a seh one, a di ish, a di general, a di don, sell off, pop off, carry di swing, beat dem bad, lick dem fi six, kill dem, slew dem, slawta dem, wyah dem, tump dem, clawt dem, duss dem, trample dem, vank dem, mash dem

RULER 1 (n) twelve inch rule 2 (*monarch*) big chief, gorgon, ginigog, guineagog

RUMMAGE (v) prog

RUMOUR 1 (n) talk, fame, soun, bush telegram, mout-a-gram, su su   2 (*rumours*) see *GOSSIP*

RUN 1 (v. *to sprint*) dig foot, pull foot, liff up foot, liff up, pick up foot inna han, pudung a piece a runnin, gyal up, gyallop   2 (v. of stream or river) walk   3 (vt. *manage*) canchol, govern, look afta, hol dung   4 (v. *run a traffic light*) brok stoplight, brok traffic light   5 Also see *RUN OFF* or *RUN AWAY*

RUN AFTER see *PURSUE*

RUN AROUND run up an dung, tun rung tun rung

RUN AWAY 1 (*abandon somebody or some place*) run leff, run weh, run weh leff, cut, splurt, brok weh   2 (*run away from; abandon*) run leff, run weh leff, cut leff   3 (*run off suddenly*) see *RUN OFF*

RUN DOWN (of building: *dilapidated*) brok dung, rookoondung, nyaka nyaka, chaka chaka   2 (of bike or vehicle) rev out   3 (of person: *exhausted*) pop dung, frazzle out, rev out, mash up

RUN INTO 1 (*collide with*) bunks, lick inna, run inna, buff, baff   2 (*encounter unexpectedly*) buck, buck up inna, buck up pan, run inna

RUN OFF 1 (*drain away*) run out   2 (*sprint off in haste*) splurt, flash, breeze, run weh, cut, dip, brok weh, brok, run leff, run weh, brok weh, run weh leff, cut leff pull foot, liff up foot, liff up, pick up foot inna han, dig foot an gaan, pudung a piece a runnin   3 Also see *RUN AWAY*

RUNNY mekeh mekeh

RURAL 1 (adj) country, yountry   2 (*very rural*) bush, moko, backabush, back a God, backawall, backamoko, back a God back, backa beyond   3 (adv. *in a remote rural place*) back a bush, back a wall, behind God back, back a God back, back a moko, backa beyond   3 (n. *very rural area*) outlaw districk, woy woy, moko, chuku

RUSH 1 (n) hase   2 (vi. *hurry*) mek hase, pick up foot   3 (vt. *approach; accost*) run een pan, fly dung pan, draw dung pan, harbourshark, payaka   4 (*Don't hurry me; Don't rush me*) No hase mi

RUTHLESS 1 (adj) cowl, dog heart, evilous, daak, misareble   2 (n. *ruthless leader or dictator*) ginigog, guineagog, gorgon

SABOTAGE 1 (vt. *intentionally impede person X*) badmind X, flop X show, nyam X food, dis X program   2 (*sabotage the plan*) dis di program

SACK 1 (*burlap sack*) cruckuss bag   2 (*plastic shopping bag*) bagscyandal bag

SAD 1 (*deeply sad; traumatized; deeply hurt*) cut up, sheg up   2 (v. *feel sad or bad about something*) feel a way

SAFETY pr: sie̱fiti

SALIVA (n) mout waata

SALTY salt

SALUTE (v) hail

SAME 1 (*the same*) same 2 (pred adj. *exactly the same*) same same 3 (*of the same age or status*) size 4 (*the same as*) same like, same laka 5 (pred adv. *in the same way*) same 6 (*That's the same way that* + subj + v) Same so - *These books are the same*: Dem buk ya siem - *They are exactly the same*: Dem siem siem - *This is the same as the other*: Da wan ya siem lak di ada - *I dance the same as you*: Mi dans siem laka yuu - *That's the same way that I do it!* Siem so mi du it!

SAME DIFFERENCE Six fi a nine, Black dog fi monkey

SAND DUNE sand gall

SANDAL 1 (n) sandals, slandaz 2 (*simple rubber sandal*) samplata, sampata

SANITARY NAPKIN 1 (n) pad, stayfree 2 (vulgar terms) bloodclaat, pussykclaat, bomboclaat

SAPOTE (*Sapota achras*) neesberry

SATAN Ole John

SATISFIED well sweet

SATISFY (*meet the needs of*) hol, keep

SATURDAY satdeh, satday, satadeh

SAUSAGE PARTY (n. *crowded party with mostly men*) bull dance

SAVANNA BLACKBIRD (*Crotophaga ani*) blackbud, tick eater

SAW (v) saaka saaka

SAYING (*proverb*) tellin

SCALE THE FENCE boom fence

SCALLION skellian, kellian

SCALP head top, (*top of scalp*) mole

SCAM scyam, bandulu skeem, rake, chicaney, ligues, rungles, gimmicks

SCAPEGOAT exscape goat

SCAR 1 (n. *scar from knife from ear down cheek toward mouth*) telephone cut   2 (n. *knife scars on skin*) chamba (in reference to Chamba tribe of Africans who ritually scar their skin)

SCARCE (*hard to obtain*) short, visa

SCARE 1 (v) frightn, giv fraid   2 (*startle*) giv heart attack, kil ded, lick dung flat

SCARECROW grung god

SCARED 1 (adj) fraid, jumpy, bummy   2 (v. *get scared*) ketch yu fraid, get jumpy, get bummy   3 Also see *WORRIED*

SCARF 1 (n. *head scarf*) tie-head   2 (v. *scarf down; eat hastily*) cut an swalla, swalla dung

SCARY (v. *to be scary*) mek yu fraid, mek yu ketch yu fraid, mek yu get jumpy, mek yu get bummy - *This house is scary to me*: Dis ous ya a mek mi fried, Dis ous ya a mek mi kech mi fried, Dis ous ya a mek mi get jompi, etc.

SCATTERED skyatta skyatta, kata kata

SCHEME (n. *ploy*) rake, scyam, bandulu skeem, chicaney, ligues, rungles, gimmicks

SCHIZOPHRENIC pr: skitsafriinik - Also see *MENTALLY ILL* or *INSANE*

SCHMOOZE (v) mek links, mix up mix up, frah frah, buttafly

SCHOOLBOY skoolaz

SCHOOLGIRL skoolaz

SCOLD 1 (v) draw up, put unda mannaz   2 Also see *BERATE*

SCORN (v) class, dis, style, cut yu yeye afta, skin up yu nose pan, col up, low count, reduce, send a shop

SCORNFUL misareble, stucky, cramoojin, crampify

SCOWL 1 (n) screw, mokeyface   2 (v) screw, skin up yu face, skin up yu nose, mek up monkeyface, mek up face   3 Also see *FROWN*

SCRAP 1 (n. *small piece*) chenks   2 Also see *FIGHT*

SCRAPE (vt. *rub off the skin in an accident*) crawp, bun

SCRAPS 1 (*remnant pieces of material*) dregs, nyaka nyaka   2 (*leftover food*) whatlef, wa lef, bambaye, aftawuds, dribblinz

SCRATCH 1 (n) cratch   2 (vt) crab, plaw, huff   3 (vt. as thorns to skin: *scratch up*) crawb up, crawp crawp   4 (*scratch oneself; scratch an itch*) crab up yuself

SCREAM (v) bawl out, reel

SCREW OVER (v) soak, salt, flop X show, dis X program, nyam X suppa, brok X foot (X=person)

SCROTUM seed bag

SEA CUCUMBER sea banana

SEARCH 1 (*search a place or area*) check all bout 2 (*search files or lists*) check, pree 4 (*search for*) look, check fi

SEASONING (n. *herbs for seasoning*) legginz

SECLUDED see *REMOTE*

SECOND sekan

SECOND RATE crebbeh crebbeh, tufenkeh, fenkeh fenkeh, fluxy, dibby dibby, wutlis, wuklis, batta foot, batta ears, sketel, streggeh, screbbeh screbbeh, kaba kaba, chamba chamba, boogooyaga, butu, common, half inch, half staff, knockoff, riff raff, casco, tikki tikki, jingbang, pyaa pyaa, no wut, no use, pop dung, ol bruck, nyamps

SECONDHAND 1 (esp of clothing) wear an leff, poop eena, (of item) ole brok 2 (*various used items in good condition for purchase*) ray ray

SECRET 1 (n) belly wud 2 (*Keep this a secret*) Hol it dung

SECRETION (n) matta

SECULAR worlian

SECURE 1 (*physically stable*) lock, tuddy 2 (*emotionally or financially stable and secure*) sort out, solid, tight, concreet 3 (v. *take possession of*) paan up pan, tek up

SECURED (*fastened*) lock, belay, conneck

SEDUCE 1 (v) temp, tease up 2 (*seduce person X with words*) drap lyrics pan X, lyrics X, sweetmout X

SEDUCTIVE temptious

SEE 1 si, sight, sight up 2 (v. *pay a visit to*) check, check fi 3 (vt. *date*) deh wid, go rung wid

SEE IT THROUGH live it out, run wid it, angle it, push on chu, press on chu, ban yu belly

SEE YOU LATER see *GOODBYE* and *I'M LEAVING*

SEE YOU SOON Earlyah, Likkle fram dis, Soon time

SEEING THAT chu, afta, as, since as how, sake a dat

SEEK 1 (v) look 2 (of money or other advantage: *pursue greedily*) graff afta

SEEM 1 (v) look - *That seems wrong to me*: Dat luk rang tu mi 2 (*seem like*) come een like, fayva like, tanka

SEIZE (*take possession of*) pawn up, pawn, cyaptcha, pra pra

SEIZURE (*epileptic seizure*) fit

SELF CONFIDENCE shurance

SELF CONFIDENT shurance, confidence

SELF ESTEEM 1 ambition 2 (*person lacking self esteem*) see *LOSER*

SELF RESPECT 1 ambition 2 (*person lacking self respect*) see *LOSER*

SELFISH 1 grabbalicious, grabby grabby, crabbit, payaka, harbour shark, hogganeering, cubbitch, purpose 2 Also see *GREEDY; CONCEITED*

SELL OUT 1 (*run out of stock*) sell off 2 (sell out one's integrity

SEMEN man juice

SEND 1 (v) run, send on 2 (*send thing X to person Y*) sen X gi Y - *Send them to Lisa*: Sen dem gi Lisa 3 (*send thing X to place Y*) sen X go a Y, sen X come a Y - *Send them here*: Sen dem kom - *Send them to Florida*: Sen dem go a Flarida

SEND FOR see *SUMMON*

SENSE 1 (n. *impression*) vibes 2 (*common sense*) sense, sabi-so 3 (v. *perceive*) pick up seh - *I sense something is wrong*: Mi a pik op seh sitn no rait

SENSIBLE 1 (of decision or idea) well reason, reason, mek sense, spell sense 2 (of personality) righted, concious, well reason 3 (v. *to be sensible*) av sense, ha sense

SENSITIVE 1 (*easily upset*) cry cry, bawly bawly 2 (*complicated; risky*) technical

SENSITIVE PLANT (*Mimosa pudica*) shame bush, shame lady

SENTENCE pr: sentans

SERIOUS 1 (*grave*) deep, real, daak, seerous, bleak 3 (*This is serious*) Nah skin up, Big an seerous, Big man ting, Big ooman ting

SERIOUSLY? Fi real?, Inna real life?, A chu?, Nah ramp?, A lie, A joke

SERIOUSLY! Fi real, Mad ting, Strait, Big man ting, Big ooman ting, Nah skin up

SERVE 1 (v. *help*) saav, back, promote   2 (v. *serve as; function as*) saav az, use fi

SET 1 (adj. *prepared and ready*) lock, fit, chock an belay   2 (v. *put temporarily*) ress

SET DOWN (*put temporarily*) res (from *rest*)

SET IN MOTION put about

SET UP 1 (*establish*) set up, extablish   2 (*entrap*) bait up

SETTLE 1 (vi. *establish oneself in a location*) sekkle dung   2 Also see *CALM DOWN*

SETTLE DOWN 1 (*decide to stay*) sekkle dung, pudung roots   2 (as wind or noise: *level off*) ease up, sekkle dung, sekkle, level, simma dung   3 (*to stop arguing; to relax*) sekkle, cool, balance, bill, level, quat, eazy yuself, eazy, eaze up, cool out, breeze out, satta, simma dung, cool yu foot, res yu spirit

SETTLE DOWN! Juss cool!, Easy Yuself!, Bill!, Balance!, Level!, Seckle!, Quat!, Cool noh!, Ease up!, Easy noh!, Breathe easy!, Satta!, Simma dung!, Go simma!, Cool yu foot!, Res yu spirit!

SEVERE (of weather or act) coas, dread, rhygin, haad, deep, daak

SEWER DITCH colbut (from *culvert*), gully

SEX 1 (*intercourse*) action, wuk, straight wuk, rooks, a likkle piece, vitamin S, night food, food, rudeness, nastiness, outa-orderness, dugu dugu, digi digi, dolla wine, rukumbine, bubblin, ketchy shooby, grinin, cabin stabbin, stabbin, daggerin, lashin, beatin, nazzlin, rail an drop, sawka sawka, waxin, weldin, solderin, oil change, changin of oil   2 (n. *an act of sex*) a slam, a slap, a touch, a sort out, a fix up, a stab, a stamp, a ram, a jook, a taze, a grine, a stabbin, a daggarin, a lashin, a strappin, a nazzlin, a waxin, a weldin, a solderin, a oil change, a changin of oil   3 (vi. *have sex*) sort out, fix up, hook, slam, ram, grine, touch, knock, frig, nazzle, rooks off, suss, dugu dugu, digi digi, get a likkle piece, kech up yu stomok, stir it up, cook stew peas, dance, bubble, weld, soldah, change oil, sawka sawka, play ketchy shooby, do X, go pan a X (X=word for intercourse or sex act)   4 (vt. *have sex with*) sort out, fix up, ride, sheg, frig, rooks off, dance wid, bubble wid, sleep wid, hook, get a likkle piece off a, (from the man's perspective only): stab, slam, ram, knock, slap, stamp, taze, tump up, jook, nazzle, lick dong, dig out, rev out, chubble, fan, change yu oil wid   5 Also see *ONE NIGHT STAND; QUICKIE; SEXUAL PLEASURE*

SEX APPEAL status

SEX DRIVE naycha

SEX PARTNER 1 fren, combolo, quabs   2 (*second woman; female lover on the side*) matie   3 (*second male lover*) Joe Grind, bunna man

SEXUAL INTERCOURSE see *SEX*

SEXUAL PERVERSION (n. *sexual perversion in general*) freakiness, nastiness, funkyness, kinkyness

SEXUAL PLEASURE agony, extasy

SEXY 1 (of woman) ready, hot, fit, criss, goodaz, elty badi, bokkle shape, av status, goody   2 (of man) hot, ready, sauly, chaptin   3 (*voluptuous; fat yet sexy*) fat, fluffy, flufflilous, fluffalishous, buffy, bufflilous, bufflilicious, tick, tickarous, trong, roun, boonoonoos, boonoonoonoos   4 Also see *SEXY WOMAN*

SEXY WOMAN 1 (n) goodaz, hottaz, hot gyal, criss ting, hottie hottie, glama gyal, goody goody, filly, fatty, block-traffic, boonoonoonoos   2 (*voluptuous woman; fat yet sexy woman*) fat girl, trang girl, tick girl, fluffy, see more at *VOLUPTUOUS WOMAN*   3 (*bedroom performer*) champion, stulliesha, buddy broka, ridah

SHABBY see *TATTERED* or *UNKEMPT*

SHACK tatu, wappn bappn

SHADOW shedda

SHADY 1 shade   2 Also see *SLEAZY*

SHAKY 1 (*trembling*) chimble chimble   2 (*wobbly; unstable*) ruku ruku, frekeh frekeh, rickety rickety, palla palla

SHAMAN 1 bush docta, bushman, shepherd, myal man   2 Also see *MEDIUM; SORCERER*

SHAMELESS dry yeye, donkya, bright, facety, bareface, bumptious, pomptious, eggs up, shame tree dead

SHAPE UP see *GET YOURSELF TOGETHER* or *STRAIGHTEN UP*

SHAPELY see *VOLUPTUOUS*

SHARK 1 (*hammerhead shark*) shevel-mout shaak, shevel-nose shaak   2 (*caribbean reef shark*) grung shaak, white shaak

SHAVED 1 clean   2 Also see *BALD*

SHE 1 shi, (and in rural areas only): him   2 Also see *IS; ISN'T; WAS; WASN'T*

SHEEP see *FOLLOWER*

SHELTERED (*naïve; innocent*) goody goody, grow wid yu granny

SHINY (*glossy*) shine

SHIRT 1 (n) shut   2 (*long-sleeved t-shirt*) gyanzi   3 (*sleeveless t-shirt or undershirt*) marina

SHIT 1 (n) see *POOP* 2 (*shit your pants; shit yourself*) shit up yuself 3 (*Shit!*) see *DAMN*

SHIT YOUR PANTS shit up yuself

SHITTY (*lacking ability; lacking quality*) no use, no wot, wukless, saaf (*soft*), too fenkeh, fenkeh fenkeh, dibby dibby, crebbeh, crebbeh crebbeh, kabba kabba, nyamps, pyaa pyaa, fluxy

SHOCK 1 (n) frightn, frightnation, fraid 2 (v. of electric current) lick, bun 3 (v. *astonish*) frightn, lick X fi ten (X=person)

SHOCKING frightenatious

SHOE 1 (n) boot, shoes, kickaz - *Where is the other shoe?* Weh di ada shuuz deh? - *I only have one shoe to wear*: A jos wan fut a shuuz mi av 2 Also see *SHOES*

SHOELACE shoes lace

SHOES 1 (n) boot, kickaz 2 (*canvas tennis shoes*) crep, puss boot 3 (*high-heeled shoes*) big heel boot, sketel boot, roach killa 4 (*sharp pointy shoes*) kick mi kill mi 5 (*a pair of* shoes) a shoes

SHOO (vt. as of an animal) shi shi, run

SHOOT 1 (of gun) fyah, buss, clap, blaze, rinse, knock 2 (of bullet or shot) fyah, buss, lick, beat, chump, send, press 3 (vt. at person) shot, tump, clap, knock, buss X inna, lick X inna (X=any word for *bullet*)

SHOPLIFT (v) crutch, scuffle

SHOPPING CART trolley

SHORT 1 (of person) shaat, tuku tuku, dugu dugu, (*stunted*) dungrow 2 (of thing) shaat, stumpy 3 (n. *very short or stunted person*) dungrow, duggy man, stumpy man, stumpy gyal, timini, punchin, kunchin, dufidaya 4 (n. *a short but stout person*) duggy man, tuku 5 Also see *LACKING*

SHORT ON (*lacking*) short a

SHORT TEMPERED ignarant, ig, cross, hot skull, warify, wassy, crabbit

SHORTCUT (v. *take a shortcut; find the easy way*) cut an go chu

SHORTS 1 (*a pair of shorts*) a shaats 2 (*tight skimpy shorts for female*) batty rider, bumpa rider, pum pum shaats, punaany printa, puny printa, printa

SHOT 1 (n. *injection*) jook 2 (*gunshot*) shot, clap 3 (v. *get shot*) get shoot, shoot, get tump, collect shells, pick up grains, pick up corn - *He got shot by police*: Him shuut bai poliis 4 Also see *GUNSHOTS*

SHOTGUN pumpie

SHOULD 1 (as modal verb of obligation) fi, shuda, betta   2 (*You should see* X; *You should hear about* X) Yu waan si X - *You should see what happened yesterday*: Yu waan si wa did gwaan yesadeh   3 Also see *LIKELY*

SHOULD HAVE (*should have* + v) did fi, shuda en, shudan, shuda did - *You should have come with us*: Yu did fi kom wid wi, Yu shuda en kom wid wi, etc.

SHOULDN'T no fi - *You shouldn't do that*: Yu no fi du dat

SHOULDN'T HAVE (*shouldn't have* + v) neva did fi, shouldn a en, shouldn en, shouldn did - *You shouldn't have come*: Yu neva did fi kom, Yu shudn a en kom, Yu shudn en kom, Yu shudn did kom

SHOUT 1 (v) bawl, bawl out, reel   2 (*shout at*) see *BERATE*

SHOVE 1 (v) chuck, shoob   2 (v. *jostle thru a crowd*) bump an bore, shoob chu, brace chu   3 (vt. *shove around*) bad up, hackle up, ruff up, manangle

SHOW ME WHAT YOU GOT! Mek mi see it!, Run it!, Sen on!, Up wid it!, Bring ih come!, Sen ih come!

SHOW OFF 1 (v. of one's appearance or clothes) moggle, pose off, palaav, hype, profile, cut figure, primps off, shock out, trash out   2 (of ones status or wealth) flass, palaav, braff   3 (of one's dancing ability) brok out   4 (n. *show-off*) double six

SHOW UP (*pay an unexpected visit*) come in wid di breeze

SHOWER 1 (n) fresh, washoff, (*quick shower*) chooks   2 (v. *take a shower*) bade, hol a X, tek a X (X=any word for shower)

SHREDDED 1 (adj) tear up tear up, shred up shred up, nyaka nyaka   2 Also see *MUTILATED*

SHRIMP swimz, swimps, janga, jumpisarie

SHRIVEL (v) quinge up, quinch up

SHRUNKEN shrink, swink, winji

SHUN see *REJECT*

SHUT 1 (v) shet, lock   2 (adj) lock   3 Also see *SHUT DOWN; SHUT OFF*

SHUT DOWN 1 (of supply or electric current) lock off, cut   2 (of a business) lock dung fi good, lock dung   3 (of motor or machine: *break down*) pop dung, seize up

SHUT OFF 1 (v. of machinery or device) lock off   2 (of supply) lock off, cut

SHUT UP! Shet yu mout!, Shet yu X! (X=expletive), Lock yu mout!, Kibba yu mout!, Kibba yu tongue!

SICK 1 (*ill*) sick out, poorly, mash up 2 (*nauseated*) sick stomach, sowa stomach, high stomach, sick belly, sowa belly 3 (*mentally ill*) touch, no righted, no balance, head no good, head lick, mad 4 Also see *MESSED UP; SICKEN*

SICK! see *AWESOME!*

SICKEN 1 (v) sickn, sick - *Too much rum will sicken you*: Tumoch rom wi sik yu 2 (*sicken due to too much sugar*) clide

SICKLY see *FEEBLE* or *SICK*

SIDE BY SIDE foot an foot

SIDE MAN Joe Grind

SIDE WOMAN /SIDE CHICK matey, deputy, conki

SIDEWAYS sideway

SIGNIFICANT (adj) real, seerous, big, crucial, critical

SILENCE 1 (n. *pure silence*) kananapo 2 (n. *cold silence; no reply*) kananapo

SIMILAR 1 (adj) same 2 (*similar to*) same like 3 Also see *RESEMBLE*

SIMPLE AST TENSE 1 (For affirmartive past tense, the following past tense markers can be used before any verb other than the Jamaican forms of the English verb *Be* and the modal verbs such as *kyan; maita; mosi; shuda; wi; etc*): did, di, id, en, ben, den, min - *I saw you*: Mi did si yu, Mi di si yu, Mi id si yu, etc. 2 (For negative past tense, the following past tense markers can be used in the same way) neva, nehn

SIMPLETON claffy, prekeh, dunce bat, kunumunu, menkeh, iddyboo, yam head, sample, salad, goose, cuffy, kwashi, kwaco, kwao, kwamin, bongo

SIMULTANEOUSLY one time

SINCE 1 (*from the time when*) fram 2 (*given that*) chu, afta, as, since as how, to how 3 (*especially since*) wuss laka how

SINCE I WAS A KID fram mi likl an a grow, fram mi yeye deh a mi knee (meaning *when my eyes were at the level of my knees*)

SINCE THE BEGINNING fram mawnin, fram di fuss

SINCERE 1 (of person) real, heartful, heartical, bonafide, goodup 2 (of action or intention) real, heartful, bonafide

SINCERELY (pred adv only) strait - *I'm telling you sincerely*: Mi a tel yu schriet

SINGLE (n. *a single male; a man without a woman*) Tarzan

SINK 1 (n. *wash basin*) basin, face basin, cestaan, sestant, zink, zenk 2 (n. *faucet; tap*) pipe

SINKHOLE sinket, bung

SIR sah, baba - *Yes sir!*: Yes sah!

SISTER 1 (n) sista 2 (title) Sista, Tita, Sta

SIT 1 (v) siddung, tek a sat 2 (*sit with legs crossed*) cut ten

SIT BACK 1 (vi. *sit back and watch; keep out of the action*) watch an pree, hol yu corner, tan so back, mass out, mass 2 Also see *RELAX*

SIT UP (v) ease up

SITUATION (n) setup, sityation

SIZE UP study, eyes

SKETCHY 1 (of person) shakey, switchy, sipple 2 Also see *DANGEROUS*

SKILLED 1 (*proficient*) skill, well skill 2 Also see *SKILLFUL* or *CLEVER*

SKILLFUL skill, well skill, bad, mad, wikid, terrible, superble, craab up, crabbit, no easy

SKILLFULLY 1 (adj) well skill 2 (adv. *with skillful swift motions*) swips swips 3 (v. *work skillfully*) drop han

SKIN see *COMPLEXION*

SKINK (*Celestus*) galliwass

SKINNY 1 (of person) mawga, slim, winji 2 (*tall and skinny; lanky*) lenga lenga, langalala 3 (n. *tall and skinny person*) langalala, tallis, pawpaw tree, wiss, cucucum stick 4 (*skinny woman; skinny girl*) slimmaz, mawga gyal, wiss, cucucum stick, winji gyal 5 Also see *FRAIL*

SKIRT (n) frock

SKULK 1 (*sneak about*) screechy, jim screechy, skull, go rung 2 (*avoid being seen*) mas out, mas (from *mask*), screechy, jim screechy 3 (*ditch work or school*) skull

SKULL head skull

SLACK (adj) luu, dutty, freaky, funky, nassy

SLACKER iglahs, waste man, cruff

SLANDER 1 (n) su su, carry go bring come, talk, re re, come come seh 2 (v) carry X name, wash yu mout pan X (X=person being slandered)

SLANG 1 (n) slangs 2 (*slang word*) slang 3 also see *LINGO*

SLANTED lean, cyaas, skeelt, offish

SLAP 1 (n) baks 2 (n. *a powerful slap; a bitch slap*) bitch lick, beast lick, ayzaz, gaza baks, gully baks 3 (vt) baks, shot X a baks (X=person)

SLAP DASH palla palla, kaba kaba, wid a lick an a promise

SLASH 1 (v. *slash at; slash up*) nyaka nyaka, saaka saaka 2 (*clear vegetation with a machete*) bill 3 (*slash at; slash up*) lass up, chop up chop up, nyaka nyaka, saaka saaka, malahack

SLEAZY (adj. *immoral; corrupt*) dutty, mud up, luu, low run, slacka slacka, chaka chaka, skrebbeh, krebbeh krebbeh

SLEEP 1 (n) sleep 2 (v) wax sleep, bunks yu res 3 (*go to sleep*) bunks yu res 4 (*fall asleep*) jrap asleep 5 (*sleep at a place temporarily; lodge*) cotch, stop 6 (as a baby: *put to sleep; rock to sleep*) baya 7 Also see *NAP* and *SNORE*

SLICE AT sawka sawka, nyaka nyaka, malahack

SLIM see *THIN* or *LANKY* or *SKINNY*

SLIMY 1 (adj. *having a slimy texture*) sipple, glammy 2 (adj. *corrupt; immoral*) dutty, mud up, luu, low run, slacka slacka, chaka chaka, skrebbeh, krebbeh krebbeh

SLINGSHOT cyatapul, bingy

SLIPKNOT choke knot

SLIPPERS (*flip flops*) juta, clappy, sampata, samplata, shampata

SLIPPERY sipple

SLOPPY see *MESSY; UNKEMPT*

SLOW 1 (*sluggish*) lowzy, lagga lagga, leggeh leggeh 2 (*mentally slow*) lagga head, dunce 3 (v. *slow down*) ease up, draw brakes 4 Also see *SLOWLY*

SLOW DOWN ease up, draw brakes

SLOWLY 1 (*sluggishly*) lowzy, legeh legeh 2 (*gradually; cautiously*) one one, likkle likkle, bit bit 3 (v. *move slowly and cautiously*) pinch an bite, tek time 4 (*slowly but surely*) likkle likkle, one one, bit bit 5 Also see *CAUTIOUSLY* and *LAG*

SLUGGISH lowzy, lagga lagga, leggeh leggeh

SLUM 1 (n) slump, shanty town   2 Also see *GHETTO*

SLUT dutty gyal, slack gyal, loose gyal, sketel, streggeh, batchry dolly, batta ears gyal, batta foot gyal, battabout, jezebel, credell, village mattress, village bike, Miss Cooba   2 (*old slut*) ole bike, ole mattress, battabout

SLUTTY dutty, slack, sketel, streggeh, manny manny

SLY see *CUNNING*

SMACK see *SLAP* or *HIT* or *COLLIDE WITH*

SMALL 1 (adj) likkle, lilly, winji   2 (*very small; tiny*) likkle bit, lilly bit, beenie, beenie bit, uku bit   3 Also see *SMALL AMOUNT; SMALL CHANGE*

SMALL AMOUNT smalls, skimps, kimps, toops, choops, chenks, kench, quips - *Give me a small amount*: Gi mi a kimps, Gi mi a smalz, etc.

SMALL CHANGE duss, coppa, dregz

SMALLER licklah

SMALLEST likklest, beeniest

SMART see *CLEVER* or *INTELLIGENT*

SMASH mash, buss

SMASH UP mash up, buss up

SMELL 1 (n) scent   2 (vt) simell   3 Also see *SMELL BAD; SMELLY*

SMELL BAD 1 (vi. *to smell bad in general*) simell frowzy, simell frownzy, simell rude, simell nassy   2 (~ *like body odour*) simell green, simell ripe   3 (*reek of urine*) simell renk   4 (~ *like stinky feet*) simell cheesey   5 (~ *like raw meat or fish or eggs*) simell raw   7 Also see *SMELLY*

SMELLY 1 (adj. *stinky; dirty smelling; musty*) frowzy, frownzy   2 (~ *like body odour*) green, ripe   3 (~ *like dirty socks*) cheesey   4 (~ *like urine*) renk   5 (~ *like fish or eggs or raw meat*) raw   6 (n. *stinky smelling person*) shit house

SMILE 1 (n) skinteet   2 (v) skin teet, kin teet, skin yu teet, kin yu teet, liff up yu mout, tun up yu mout caana

SMOKE 1 (n) smoke   2 (v. *smoke tobacco*) bun a cigarette, blaze a cigarette   3 see *SMOKE CANNABIS*

SMOKE CANNABIS black up, blaze di X, bun di X, bun X, lick di X, bless di X, blaze it, blaze up, bun it, bless it, lick it   (X=any word for *pipe* or *joint* or *cannabis*)

SMOKE WEED black up, blaze di X, bun di X, bun X, lick di X, bless di X, blaze it, blaze up, bun it, bless it, lick it (X=any word for *pipe* or *joint* or *weed*)

SMOOTH pr: si<u>muud</u>

SNACK 1 (n) ketch-up 2 (*packaged snacks*) dry food

SNAKE 1 (n) sinake 2 (*Jamaican boa constrictor; yellow bo*a) nanka

SNAP 1 (v. *lose your temper*) flip up, rail up, wild up, get ignarant, get ig, get raatid, gwaan a way 2 (*snap at*) flip up pan, rail up pan, trace

SNEAK screechy, jim screechy, skull (from *skulk*)

SNEAK IN /SNEAK OUT screechy, jim screechy, skull, (by scaling the fence or wall): boom fence

SNICKER (v) keke

SNITCH 1 (n) informa, culprit 2 (v) cry 3 (v. *snitch on; rat on*) cry pan, buss pan

SNOBBISH hitey titey, risto, stush, chest high, stucky, cockaty

SNOOP 1 (v) prips, screechy, peep, fass

SNORE draw snore, draw bungy

SNOT nose nat

SO BE IT If a so a so

SO IT GOES A so it go, A so it set, A so di ting set, A paat a life, Mek so

SO LONG AS long as, solanks, from, while

SO MUCH (*a lot; really badly; to the max*) cyaan done, so till, gaan tu bed, tu X, yu X (X=expletive), tu di fullness, full stop, yu feneh

SO SO 1 (of thing: *mediocre*) migglin, poko poko, pang pang 2 (*so so in talent or skill*) migglin, poko poko, pang pang

SOAK UP tek een

SOAKED wet up, sop up sop up

SOAP (*bar soap*) cake soap (other kinds of soap are just 'soap')

SOBER 1 (*not drunk; not high*) righted 2 (of personality: *sensible*) righted, reason, av sense, ha sense 3 (of topic: *serious*) crucial, seerous

SOCIALIZE 1 (*get out and mingle*) du road, mek links, fraa fraa, buttafly 2 (*socialize with*) paar wid, move wid, flex wid 3 Also see *HANG OUT WITH*

SOCKS 1 (*a pair of socks*) a socks 2 (*argyle socks*) diamond socks

SODA POP (n) drinks, jinks, cool jinks, juice

SODOMY bugarism, batty-ism, funny man ting, fishy bizniz

SOFA setty

SOFT 1 (*plush; pliant*) saaf, fluffilous 2 (*wimpy*) saaf, fenkeh fenkeh, pyaa pyaa, saps, sopsy, fluxy, nyamps 3 (v. *be soft on*) see *PAMPER*

SOFT DRINK (n) jinks, cool jinks, juice

SOGGY 1 (adj) sop up sop up, wetty wetty, sopsy 2 (*mucky*) mekeh mekeh, puttuh puttuh, pyaka pyaka, plaka plaka, plekeh plekeh

SOIL (n) dutty, dut 2 (v) dutty up, mud up, nassy up 3 (v. *soil yourself*) doodoo up yuself, shit up yuself

SOILED (adj) dutty up, mud up, pyaka pyaka, pyoko poko, potto potto

SOLD OUT (of food or products) sell off

SOLE 1 (*underside of foot*) foot bottom 2 (*only*) ongle, so so 3 (*the sole X, the last remaining X*) di one deggeh X (X=noun)

SOLID 1 (adj) tuff 2 Also see *SECURE*

SOLIDIFY cake up, sleep up

SOLVE (as in a riddle) clear

SOME (adj) a, a piece a - *I just got some money*: Mi jos get a moni; Mi jos get a piis a moni

SOMEBODY 1 smaddy, sumaddy, a one 2 (*somebody else*) a nex smaddy, one nex smaddy, a nex one

SOMEONE 1 smaddy, sumaddy, a one 2 (*someone else*) a nex smaddy, one nex smaddy, a nex one

SOMEONE ELSE a nex smaddy, a nex one

SOMERSAULT 1 (n) pupalick, bum flick, flick, kincat, cuffin 2 (n. *back flip*) bum flick 3 (*do somersaults*) kin pupalick, flick

SOMETHING 1 supm, sittn, sinting 2 (*something else*) a nex sittn, one nex sittn, wanedda sittn

SOMETIMES (adv) sometime, more time 2 (*once in a while*) every now an agen, once a while, once an now an agen

SOMEWHERE 1 someweh 2 (*somewhere else*) someweh different, a nex place, one nex place

SONG (n) chune, music, (*gospel song; hymn*) sankey - *I love this song!*: Lov da myuuzik ya!

SOON 1 likkle fram dis, likkle more, soon time 2 (*very soon*) soon soon

SORCERER obeah man, scientist, guzu man, zuzu man, booguman, (female sorcerer) madda ooman

SORCERY 1 (n) obeah, science, buzu, guzum, zuzu 2 (vi. *work sorcery*) bun bad cyangle, wok obeah 3 (v. *work sorcery on*) bun bad cyangle fi, wok obeah pan, put obeah pan, set obeah pan, set goat mout pan, mark, fix

SORE 1 (adj) hot 2 (n. *a sore body part such as a sore toe*) george

SORRY 1 (v. *feel sorry*) feel a way 2 (*feel sorry about*) feel a way bout 3 (*feel pity for*) sorry fi, cry fi 4 (*I'm so sorry to hear that!*) Hush! 5 (*Sorry!; Forgive me!*) Sorry sah!, Sorry mam!, Hush!

SORT OUT (*resolve*) saat out, maths out

SOUL (*person's spirit*) sunsum, duppy, shadow

SOUNDCHECK stringup

SOUR 1 (adj) sowa 2 (*tart*) sibble

SPANK /SPANKING pam pam

SPARE CHANGE duss, a smalls, loosaz, coppa

SPARKLER (*handheld firework*) starlight

SPARKLES mini mini

SPEAK 1 (*converse*) chat, hol a reason, reason 2 (*be able to speak a language*) chat - *He speaks French*: Him chat french 3 (*speak a language fluently or impressively*) cut 4 (*speak in tongues*) symbol, cut unknown tongue

SPECIES (n) speesh

SPECIFIC suttn (from *certain*), direck (pr: dairek)

SPECK (*tiny spot or mark; tiny amount*) toops, choops

SPELL 1 (n. *magic spell*) guzu, guzum 2 (v. *put a spell on*) set guzum pan 3 Also see *HEX* or *CURSE* for more

SPEND leggo, let off, lek off

SPEND TIME WITH see *CHILL OUT WITH*

SPERM (*semen*) man juice

SPIDER 1 (n) anancy, nancy 2 (*spider web*) anancy rope, nancy rope, nancy nest

SPIN (v. *twirl*) wheel, wheel an tun, tun tun

SPINE (*backbone*) back

SPINNING TOP gig

SPIRIT 1 (*soul*) sunsum, duppy, shadow 2 (*ghost*) duppy, shadow 3 (*vibe; energy; feel*) vibes

SPIRITISM kumina, myal, poco

SPIRITIST myal man, myalist

SPIRITUAL 1 (*divine*) hyah 2 (n. *spiritual mediumship*) myal

SPITE 1 (n) bad mind, grudgeful, violation 2 (v) badmind, grudge, violate, dis, harbourshark

SPITEFUL (adj) bad mind, misareble, pagan, low, cramoojin

SPLASH (v) plash, flash

SPLENDID (adj) splendacious, splendifarous

SPOIL 1 (vi. of food) pwile, gaan bad, tun frowzy 2 (vt. *botch*) mash up, sheg up, mud up, nassy up, kaba kaba, sawka sawka, soak 3 (vt. of child: *overly pamper*) powda, pet an pampa, spwile

SPOILED 1 (of food) pwile, gaan bad, fluxy, ruinate 2 (*slightly rotten; starting to go bad*) touch 3 (of child: *overly pampered*) brok-bad, getty getty 4 (of male adult: *pampered and lazy*) mama man

SPOT 1 (*meetup spot or hangout*) endz, chill spot, buckup 2 (v. *see; locate*) sight

SPOTLESS (adj) criss, clean clean

SPOTTED checky checky

SPRAWL palaaf

SPREAD THE WORD mad up di ting, loud up di ting, hype up di ting, spread out

SPREAD LEGS (v) skin out

SPROUT (v) spring, buss out, buss

SPY 1 (n) see *TRAITOR* 2 (v) prips, eyes, peep 3 (v. *spy on*) fass pan, prips pan, eyes, peep pan

SQUABBLE 1 (n) cass cass, cuss cuss, confusion, preke, puru, mix up, blenda, parangles, fandangles, bag a argument 2 (v) fuss an fight, cuss cuss, trow wud, fling wud

SQUABBLING see *DRAMA*

SQUASH 1 (n) see *PUMPKIN; CHAYOTE*; etc 2 (v) mash

SQUAT (v. *settle on land without having title*) captcha

SQUATTER (*illegal settler*) captchara

SQUEAK 1 (n) cry, kwee kwee 2 (v) cry - *The bed is squeaking*: Di bed a krai

SQUEAKY kwee kwee, cry cry

SQUEEZE queeze, quinge, squinch, quinch, scroonch, crunge

SQUIRREL scroowel

SQUISHY mashy mashy, sawfy sawfy, plaka plaka, fluxy

STAB 1 (n) jook 2 (v) jook

STABLE 1 (*physically stable*) tuddy 2 (*emotionally or financially stable*) sort out, solid, tight, concreet

STALK 1 (n. of a plant) staff, stick 2 (v. *obsessively pursue*) pree, tek set pan

STAMINA 1 (*physical fitness*) long bret, donkey bret 2 (v. *to have sexual stamina*) tan pan ih long 3 (*man with good sexual stamina*) stamina daddy, long distance stulla, cocks man

STAMMER 1 (n) tie-tongue, stamma 2 (v) stamma 3 (adj. *given to stuttering; having a stutter*) tie-tongue, stamma stamma 4 (*equivocate; hesitate*) hitch, hol back yu chat, block a soun, buckshuffle

STAMMERER (n) tie-tongue, stammara

STAND 1 (v) tan up, plant, plawnt 2 Also see *TOLERATE* or *ENDURE*

STAND BACK (vi. *keep out of the action*) watch an pree, hol yu corner, tan so back, mass out, mass

STAND UP TO tan up tu, shape up tu

STAR FRUIT chiney jimblin

STARCH 1 (*starchy food*) food kine 2 (*starchy root crops*) grong food

STARE 1 (v. *stare at*) eyes, study, stare pan 2 (v. *stare at with curiosity or interest*) pree, penny 3 (*lock eyes*) mek four yeye

STARS (*little imaginary twinkling stars seen due to dizziness*) mini mini

START OVER wheel and come again, haul an pull up, start back

START SHIT 1 (*provoke a fight*) flip up, rail up, look fight, lick out, chuck it 2 (*cause a commotion*) mek alarm, hype up, rail up, wild up, bring dong excitement, call crowd, draw dong scandal 3 (*start shit with*) see *PROVOKE*

STARTLE (v) giv fraid, giv heart attack, lick dung flat

STATEMENT soundz

STATUS pr: stietos 1 (*reputation*) name, knowinz 2 (*move up in status*) step up inna life, step up, rank up, notch up 3 (adj. *high in status; highly respected*) rankin, notchilous 4 (*man of high status*) notch, rankin, bantan, general 5 (*woman of high social status*) goodaz

STAY 1 (*lodge temporarily*) cotch, stop, black, hitch 2 (*remain in position*) tan, hitch, plant, klutch, quat, bats 3 Also see *REMAIN*

STAY AWAY keep weh, stay wide

STEAL (v) tief, tief weh, scuffle, screechy, jim screechy, (as a humorous euphemism): borrow

STEM (n. of a plant) staff, stick

STEP BACK dress back, back back

STEP BY STEP likkle likkle, one one, bit bit

STETHOSCOPE 1 (n) trumpet 2 (v. *listen with a stethoscope*) soun

STICK INSECT duppy riding-horse, devil riding-horse, devil horse

STICK OUT 1 (vt. *thrust out*) cock out, push out, tretch out, shub out, (of tongue) long out 2 (vi. *protrude*) cock out out

STICK UP cock up, jook out

STICKINESS gumption

STICKING OUT (adj) a cock out

STICKING UP (*jutting up*) cock up, jook out

STICKY 1 (adj) glammy, clammy, clammish, stiffy, tarry, gummy 2 (v. *make sticky*) clammy up, gummy up

STING 1 (vt. as an insect) bite, jook 2 (vi. *to sting with pain*) bite, bun, hot - *My arm stings*: Mi han a bait mi

STINGRAY (n) tingry, whipry, numb fish

STINGY (*miserly*) mean, cubbitch, geechy, tight-han, chinky, pinchy cubby

STINK see *SMELL BAD; SUCK*

STINKY see *SMELLY*

STOCKED (*fully stocked*) chock an belay, chock

STOCKY see *SHORT; MUSCULAR*

STOKED see *HAPPY* or *REPLENISHED*

STOMACH pr: stomok, tomok 1 (*belly*) belly, gut, bem bem 2 (*pot belly; paunch*) bang belly, wanga gut, ten penny 3 Also see *STOMACH ACHE*

STOMACH ACHE 1 (n) bad belly, colic, gripe, low stomach, belly hot 2 (v) gripe - *My stomach is aching*: Mi beli a graip mi

STONE (n or adj) rockstone

STONED (adj. *high on weed*) frass, head crab up, black up, red, unda yu sensi, unda yu medz

STOOL pira - *sit on a stool*: kach pan pira, sidung pan stuul

STOP BY pass chu, touch X gate, touch (X=person or place being visited)

STORY 1 (*personal anecdote*) live story 2 (*second-hand account*) ded story 3 (*funny story; joke*) rhyme 4 (*story of a building*) floor 5 (*second story; second floor*) upstaiz, uptaiz 6 (*tell X a story*) pop story gi X

STOVE (*black cast-iron stove*) coal pot

STRABISMUS 1 (n) cyaas eye 2 (adj. *having amblyopia*) cyaas eye, look a bush

STRAIGHT AWAY 1 same time, sed time, juss so, slam bam 2 (pred adv only) same time, quick time, quick stick, quick quick, swips, braps, slam bam - *Tidy up your room at once!*: Pran op yu ruum kwik stik!

STRAIGHT HAIR 1 (*naturally straight or wavy hair*) good hair, tall hair, coolie hair 2 (*chemically straightened hair*) cream hair 3 (*hair straightened with an iron*) bun head

STRAIGHT UP (*without reservations; unabashadly*) straight, plain up - *He straight up told me to shut up*: Him chriet tel mi fi lak mi mout; Him plien op tel mi fi lak mi mout

STRAIGHTEN 1 (v) traitn 2 (v. of hair) cream, bun - *Why do you straighten your hair?* Wa mek yu a bon yu hed?

STRAIGHTEN OUT 1 (vt. *straighten person X out; pull X into line*) sort X out, draw X up, liff X up, raise X up 2 Also see *STRAIGHTEN UP*

STRAIGHTEN UP 1 (*pull oneself together*) fix up, balance, sort out yuself, de-chakalise yuself, liff up yuself, raise up yuself, draw up yuself, set up yuself 2 Also see *STRAIGHTEN OUT*

STRAIGHTENED 1 (v) traitn 2 (adj) cream 3 (*hair straightened with an iron*) bun head 3 (*chemically straightened hair*) cream hair

STRAIGHTFORWARD 1 (adj) strait, no easy, coas, dry yeye, widout folly 2 (v. *be straightforward*) talk di tingz, no skin teet, no skin up, no lotion

STRANGE 1 (of object) diffrant, funny 2 (of person: *odd*) diffrant, funny

STRANGER (n. of the unwelcome variety) falla-line, blue foot

STREET SMART (adj) skill, no easy, cunny, know bout, soonah

STREET VENDOR higgla

STREETWISE (adj) skill, no easy, cunny, know bout, soonah

STRENGTH chrent, trong, gumption

STRESS presha, bodderation, hacklinz, fretration

STRESS OUT 1 (vi. *get all worked up*) fret up yuself, kill up yuself, hackle yuself, hot up yu head, hot up yu skull, wok yu head 2 (vt. *stress out person X*) run up X blood presha, hot up X brain

STRESSED OUT frazzle out, all sheg up, fret up, belly bottom a bun yu - *I'm stressed out*: Mi beli batam a bon mi

STRETCH (v) long out, tretch out

STRICT see *MEAN*

STRICTLY (*nothing but*) peer, bare, bey, pure, so so, lone

STRIKE see *HIT; RUN INTO; SLAP; PUNCH*

STRIVE 1 (*struggle to achieve something*) kill up yuself, hackle yuself, buss yu shut (from *bust your shirt*), buss yu skin 2 Also see *STRUGGLE* or *HUSTLE*

STROKE (n. *stroke from lack of bloodflow to brain*) strokes

STROLLER (*baby stroller*) pram

STRONG 1 (*physically strong*) trong, tuff, samba 2 (of person: *resilient*) talawah, haad back 3 (*durable*) tuff, tuddy, goodup, trong 4 Also see *MUSCULAR*

STRUCTURE structa

STRUGGLE 1 (n. *the struggle; the effort to survive*) chuggle, chyalz, judgement 2 (v. *to strive; struggle to achieve something*) chuggle, suffah, kill up yuself, hackle yuself, try a way, buss yu shut (from *bust your shirt*), buss yu skin, suck salt chu wooden spoon, ban yu belly, ban yu belly an bawl 3 Also see *HUSTLE* or *IMPROVISE*

STRUGGLES (n. *difficulties; hardship*) chugglz, crosses, chyalz, judgement

STRUT 1 (*walk with a dip in the stride*) bop 2 (*walk pretentiously*) moggle, pose off, hype, profile, shock out, trash out, nyanga

STUBBORN 1 (adj) hard ears, purpose, no easy 2 (n. *stubborn person*) board head 3 (*You're too stubborn*) Yu iez tuu haad; Stik brok ina yu iez; Yu tuu purpos

STUBBORNNESS hard ears

STUCK 1 (adj) faasn, kotch, kotch up 2 (v. *get stuck*) faasn, kotch, kotch up 3 (adj. of machine or device) seize up

STUCK UP chest high, boasy, risto, stush, stucky, hitey titey, cockaty

STUD 1 (*man who excels at sex*) grindsman, stulla, cocks man, slappa, champion lovah, stamina daddy, bedroom bazooka, marathon man, jocky, ridah 2 Also see *PLAYER*

STUDENT (child or teenager only) skoolaz

STUDY see *OBSERVE*

STUDYING (n) studderation

STUFF 1 (*personal possessions*) bag an pan, ray ray, bangarang, curroaches, carowzin, corojungo, cruchment, jing bang, jeng jeng 2 (*useless things lying around*) kuru kuru, koro koro, ray ray, ruggage, nyaka nyaka, boogooyaga, bangarang, riff raff, jing bang, jeng jeng, curroaches, carowzin, corojungo, cruchment 3 (*gunk*) plekeh plekeh

STUMBLE (*trip*) slip up, tumble, pitch

STUMP (n) tumpa

STUNNED (*dazed*) stonted, tonted

STUNTED (of person or tree: *short; unable to grow*) dungrow, stumpy

STUPID 1 (adj) chupid, dunce, fool fool, claffy 2 (n. *stupid person*) claffy, prekeh, menkeh, dunce bat, kunumunu, coco head, yam head, lagga head, iddyboo, eedyboo, poppy show, sample, goose, salad, cuffy, kwashi, bongo

STUPIDITY 1 (*lack of intelligence*) chupidness, choopity 2 (*foolishness*) folly grong, eedyat ting, foolinish, foolooloos, fuckry, sheggry

STURDY (adj) tuddy

STUTTER 1 (n) tie tongue 2 (v) stamma 3 (adj. *given to stuttering; having a stutter*) tie-tongue, stamma stamma

STUTTERER (n) tie-tongue, stammara, stamma stamma

STYLE 1 (*type; pattern*) pattan, fashion, stylee 2 (*personal attitude and style*) style, ting, kenteh 3 (*the current style or vogue*) di lick, di shot, di hype, di ray, di ray an di tay 4 Also see *IN STYLE; OUT OF STYLE*

STYLISH 1 (of apparel or person) hype, mad, shot, a happn, a lead, a run road, tun up, buck, name brand, sell off, craab up, slap weh, slap, clap, swaggerific, bashy, criss 2 (*dressed stylishly*) shot, hype, craab up, tun up, tun ova, buck, fabilocious, trash an ready, trash, criss up, criss, inna yu crissaz, dress tu puss foot 3 (n. *stylish male*) star bwoy, kwengaquenga, dappa 4 (n. *stylish female*) star gyal, hot gyal, glamma gyal

SUBSIST 1 (vi) nyam a food, eat a food, get on, try a way, tun yu han mek fashion, fadge 2 (*subsist on*) liv pan 3 Also see *HUSTLE*

SUBTRACT reduck, tek weh

SUCCEED 1 (v) reach pan a level, get chu, go chu, pass, gaan clear

SUCCESS *Person X is having success*: Big tingz a gwaan fi X, Tingz a gwaan gud fi X, X reach pan a level

SUCCESSFUL 1 (of person) pan a level, reach pan a level, big an large, hype, a happn 2 (v. of person: *be successful*) reach pan a level, step up inna life, gwaan good, gaan a road 3 (v. of product or event: *be successful*) sell off, sell up, slap weh, gaan a road, shell dung, pop off

SUCCUMB (vi. *surrender*) bow

SUCK 1 (*be bad at something*) flop, cyaa manage, no pass, no mek it 2 (*That sucks*) Dat damp, Dat salt, Dat dark, Dat dusty, Dat bleak, Dat sheg up 3 Also see *FELLATIO; CUNNILINGUS*

SUCTION CUP (n) sucture

SUDDENLY all pan a suddn, suddn, juss so, same time, baps, foops, bragadaps

SUFFER 1 (vi. *experience life's hardship*) suffah, cry, bawl, feel it, belly bottom bun - *They're suffering*: Fidem beli batam a bon dem 2 (*suffer pain*) feneh, faleetee 3 (vt. *bear*) suffah, go chu, deal wid, pass chu, liv out, cross ova 4 (*suffer the consequences*) falleety, feneh, tata

SUFFERING (n) sufferation, crosses, trials, tribulation

SUGAR APPLE (*Annona squamosa*) sweetsop

SUGARDADDY boops, brinks

SUGGEST sojes, sujess

SUIT 1 (*three-piece suit*) three-piece 2 (v) fit - *The job suits me*: Di jab fit mi

SUITABLE fit

SUITCASE Dulcimina grip, grip

SULLY mud up, dutty up, nassy up

SUMMON 1 (*invoke*) call dung 2 (*summon person X*) sen fi X, sen X come, sen call X, sen come call X - *Did you summon me?* Yu sen fi mi?, Yu sen mi kom?, Yu sen kaal mi?, Yu sen kom kaal mi?

SUNGLASSES daakaz

SUNRISE fuss light, day light, day cut, gunfyah

SUPERB 1 superble 2 Also see *EXCELLENT*

SUPERFICIAL 1 (of person: *fake; insincere*) poppy show, kinteet, so so mout, fulla gyow, so so gyow, tingz fren 2 (of thing or injury: *at the surface*) pan di skin 3 (of effort: *incomplete*) palla palla, kaba kaba

SUPPORT 1 (n. *backing*) backative 2 (*encouragement*) upliffment, ratings 3 (*support of bad behavior*) upholance 4 (*a prop or wedge*) cotch 5 (*to physically prop up*) cotch up 6 (*provide for*) carry, uphol 7 (*endorse; root for*) back, carry, defend, X mi seh! - *I'm supporting Brazil!* Brazil mi seh!

SUPPOSE 1 spoze, poze 2 see *ASSUME*

SUPPOSED 1 (*supposed to*) spoze fi, poze fi 2 (*supposed to be able to*) spoze fi cyan, poze fi cyan - *It's supposed to be able to run Windows*: It spuoz fi kyan ron Windows

SURE 1 (of plan: *confirmed*) set, lock, suttn 2 (of person, regarding information) suttn, shuor 3 (*X sure is Y!*) Wat a X Y! - *That dog sure is crazy!*: Wat a dag mad! 4 (*X sure can Y!*) Wat a X cyan Y! - *That guy sure can sing!*: Wat a man kyan sing! - *Those kids sure can dance!*: Wat a pikni-dem kyan dans! 5 Also see *OF COURSE; SURE CAN*

SURE CAN (*sure can* + v) Wat a X cyan Y - *That boy sure can sing!*: Wat a bwai kyan sing!

SURELY 1 (adv) mussi, mussa, no muss, muss - *Surely you think I'm crazy*: Yu no mos tink seh mi mad - *That's surely a firefly*: A mosi peeni-wali dat

SURFACE (n) skin

SURGEON FISH (n) docta fish

SURPRISE 1 (v) frightn - *You'd be surprised to know*: Yu uda fraitn fi nuo   2 Also see *STARTLE*

SURRENDER 1 (vi. *admit defeat*) bow, lap yu tail   2 (vt. *hand over*) leggo

SURVIVE 1 (vi. *persist; live*) get chu, liv it out, mek it, clear it, pass, get ova, come ova, cross ova, cross it, push on chu, gaan clear, tun han mek fashion   2 (vi. *subsist*) nyam a food, eat a food, get on, get chu, tun yu han mek fashion, try a way, run wid it   3 (v. *subsist on*) liv pan   4 (vt. *confront and overcome*) go chu, pass chu, get chu, liv out, get ova, come ova, cross ova, clear   5 Also see *HUSTLE*

SUSTAINABLE LIVING natural livity, naturality

SWAGGER 1 (n) swag, nyanga   2 (v) moggle, pose off, hype, profile, shock out, trash out, nyanga

SWALLOW 1 swalla   2 (v. *gulp*) gwap dung, gwap

SWAMP 1 (n) morass, bog   2 (v) flood out

SWAP MEET bendung market bendung plaza

SWARM 1 (vi) rush   2 (vt) rush, fly dung pan, run een pan

SWEAR 1 (*cuss*) cuss badwud, fling badwud, chip badwud, (vulgar): cuss rass, cuss claat, buss two claat, chip two claat, fling two claat   2 (*make an oath*) nyam bible leaf, tek God off a di cross   3 (*I swear!*) Kill mi ded!, As a god!   4 Also see list of expeletives in Appendix

SWEATY (adj) sweat up

SWEET TALK 1 (n) lyrics, sweet mout   2 (v) sweet mout, drap lyrics

SWEETHEART 1 (*lover*) spoogy, spoogz, spree, bibi   2 (some terms of endearment) putus, dudus, sweetie puss, boolooloops, boonoo<u>noo</u>noos, tutu, lulu, bibi, boso   3 Also see *BOYFRIEND; GIRLFRIEND*

SWELL 1 (v) buff out, bang   2 (v. of stream or river) come dung

SWIFTLY (pred adv only) swips, foops, floops - *He swiftly stole the purse*: Him skofl di purs so, swips!

SWIM 1 (n. *a short swim; a dip*) baat, washoff 2 (n. *a dip in the ocean*) sea baat 3 (n. *a dip in the river*) riva baat 4 (v. *take a short swim or dip*) hol a baat 5 (v. *swim a distance or competitively*) swim

SWIM TRUNKS baat chrunk

SWIMSUIT baat suit

SWINDLE 1 (n) bandulu business 2 (v) jinnal, bait up, fool up, cyaad, bandulu, lamps, craff, samfai, maringle, pop

SWING (n. *swing for children*) zing zang

SWOLLEN 1 (of belly) bang, swell 2 (of other body part or of object) swell, buff out, buff up, puff up puff up, buffo buffo, bufu bufu, bufutu, pulp, pum pum

SYMPATHIZE 1 (vi. *relate*) ovastan, ovaz, penetrate, groundz 2 (*sympathize with*) cry fi

SYRUP sorop

SYRUPY cliding, glammy, clammy, clammish, stiffy, tarry

SYSTEM pr: sistim (n. *the system; the general way things work*) di runninz, babylon

TACKLE 1 (v. *detain by force*) buckle-hol, collar, grabble, rassle 2 Also see *DEAL WITH*

TAINTED touch, mud up

TAKE 1 (v) tek 2 (*take along; take with you*) tangalang 3 (*take X to Y*) kyari X go a Y - *Take Lisa home*: kyari Lisa go a yaad - *Take the food to the park*: Kyari di fuud go a paak

TAKE A BREAK 1 (*take a break from X*) put X pan pause 2 Also see *RELAX*

TAKE A NAP hol a five, hol a shut yeye, hol a puss nap

TAKE A WALK du road, mek a walk, crush di road, mek a trod, go pan a flex, mek a yadd, mek a tracks

TAKE ADVANTAGE 1 (of situation) advantage 2 (of person) advantage, tax, tek step a, live pan, nyam a food off a, boops out, nyam out

TAKE ASIDE draw one side

TAKE AWAY tek weh

TAKE CARE see *GOODBYE* or *BE CAREFUL!*

TAKE CARE OF 1 (*of household or children: care for*) mine, look afta, wife up, govern, control 2 (*resolve; sort out*) look about, look bou, lok afta, clear, maths out 3 (*manage*) canchol, govern, look afta, run, angle, hol dung

TAKE IT EASY see *RELAX; CALM DOWN; EASE UP; SETTLE DOWN!*

TAKE IT EASY ON 1 (v) low, tek time wid 2 (*be too forgiving*) pet

TAKE NOTE mark how, memba mi tell yu

TAKE OFF 1 (*take to the air*) liff up 2 (*of clothing: remove*) back off 3 (*of shoes: remove*) kick off 3 Also see *LEAVE; RUN OFF*

TAKE OUT 1 (vt) draw, draw out, back out - *He took out his pocket knife*: Him bak out him rachit 2 (*omit*) tek weh, lef out 3 Also see *DESTROY; KILL*

TAKE OVER tek ova, capture

TAKE PART 1 (v) tek paat, penetrate, full-ticipate, run een, chune een, rope een, fall een 2 (*take part in*) tek paat inna, penetrate, rope een pan, run een pan

TAKE SHIT (v. *take shit from someone; tolerate bullshit*) tek check, caytah, skin teet, skin up

TAKE UP SPACE nyam up - *The bed takes up the whole room*: Di bed a nyam op di wol a di ruum

TALENTED (adj) bad, mad, wikid, terrible, superble, well skill, craab up, crabbit, no easy

TALK 1 (v) chat, reason, hol a reason, hol a vibes 2 Also see *CHATTER*

TALK BACK TO back ansa

TALK SHIT 1 (*say negative things*) chat fuckry, badmout, dis, hype 2 (*talk shit about*) chat fuckry bout, hype pan, badmout, dis, violate, tek liberty wid, walk up an dong pan X name (X=person) 3 Also see *GOSSIP*

TALKATIVE chatty chatty, labba labba

TALL 1 (adj) long, gara gara 2 (*of person: tall and skinny*) lenga lenga, langalala 3 (*tall and skinny person*) langalala, tallis, pawpaw tree, wiss

TAM (*knitted tam to cover dreadlocks*) crown, tam

TAMARIND tambrin

TANGELO ugly fruit, ugly

TANGERINE (rural Jamaica only) mangerine

TANGLED UP (adj) ketch up

TANK TOP marina

TART (adj. as of fruit) stainy, stain, sibble, sowa laka baaj

TASTELESS see *BLAND* or *TACTLESS* or *VULGAR*

TASTY nice, sweet, eat nice

TATTERED tear up tear up, nyaka nyaka, chaka chaka, ragga ragga, reggeh reggeh, raggy raggy, yagga yagga, boogooyaga, streggeh

TAUNT 1 (n) violation, dis, bulla, boof 2 (v. *ridicule; jeer*) style, violate, class, bait, hype pan, draw cyaad pan, pop style pan, bluff, dress dung, low count, laaf afta, jeri, reduce, tek X mek pappy show, tek X mek preke (X=person) 3 Also see *PROVOKE*

TAXI 1 (n) cyab, red plate 2 (*unlicensed taxi operating illegally*) robot

TEACH teach, laan - *My father taught me how to fish*: Mi pupa laan mi ow fi kech fish

TEAR DOWN see *DEMOLISH*

TEAR UP (*begin to cry*) waata come a yu yeye - *I began to tear up when I heard the news*: Waata kom a mi yai az mi a ier di nyuuz

TEAR(S) 1 (*teardrop*) yeye waata drop 2 (*tears*) yeye waata 3 Also see *TEAR UP*

TEASE 1 (vt. *playfully tease*) ramp wid, draw cyaad pan, pop style pan, cyaad, style 2 (*mean-spiritedly tease*) laaf afta, style, jeri, tek X mek papi show, tek X mek prekeh (X=person) 3 Also see *SEDUCE*

TECHNIQUE style, flex

TEENAGER jubie, (male only): youtman, yout, (female only): dawta, fresh vegetable, filly, prison bait

TEETH 1 (n) teet, choppaz 2 (*buck teeth*) buff teet

TEMPER 1 (n. *hot temper*) hot skull, ignorancy 2 (v. *lose your temper*) flip up, rail up, lick out, get ignarant, get ig 3 Also see *HOT TEMPERED*

TEMPERAMENTAL waasi, ignarant, ig, warrified, flighty

TERMINATE 1 (*finish*) done 2 (*dismiss from employment*) leggo, run

TERMITES (n) duck ants, wood ants, chi chi

TERRIBLE pr: turbl (adj) bad bad

TERRIBLY 1 (pred adv. only after negative-connotation adjectives such as *angry; difficult; damaged; disfigured*) bad 2 (pred adv. only after verbs such as *suffer*) bad bad

TERRIFIC see *EXCELLENT* or *WONDERFUL*

TERROR (n. *dread*) frightenation, frightration, col' sweat

TERRORIZE see *INTIMIDATE; BULLY; ROUGH UP*

TEST 1 (n) tess 2 (v. *size up*) tess, study

TESTICLES 1 (n) seed, stone, tone 2 (*scrotum*) seed bag

TETANUS mirasmy

TEXT 1 (n) tex 2 (v) tex, knock

THAN dan, an

THANK YOU Tanks, Tenky, Gi tanks, Respeck, Nuff respeck, Blessid Love, Raspeck, Ites, Blessid Love, Love Rasta, Giv tanks an praise

THANKS 1 (*gratitude*) tanx, appricialove 2 (*Thanks!*) see *THANK YOU*

THAT 1 (n) dat, desso 2 (*That X*) dat X deh, da X deh, dat deh X deh (X=noun) 3 (relative pronoun, as in: *the toy that you want*) weh 4 (when following a verb to give more specific information as in: *I didn't know that you were sorry*) seh

THAT'S HOW a so - *That's how I got famous*: A so mi bos

THAT'S HOW IT GOES A so it go, A so it set, A so di ting set, A paat a life, Mek so

THAT'S IT 1 (*That's the one*) Same one 2 (*That's all there is*) A it dat

THAT'S LIFE A so it go, A paat a life, Mek so

THAT'S NOT TRUE Nuttn no go so, A no so

THAT'S POSSIBLE Coulda so ih go

THAT'S RIGHT! see *YES*

THAT'S WHAT I MEAN 1 A dat mi a tell yu seh 2 Also see *EXACTLY!*

THAT'S WHEN 1 a dat time 2 a desso

THAT'S WHERE a desso - *That's where it is*: A deh so i deh

THAT'S WHY a dat mek, a it mek, a so comes, a sukkums

THE OTHER DAY 1 (*Just the other day...*) Wah day, Fuss nite, Di adda day, Tadda day, Tedda day, Tidda day 2 (pred adv) weh day, fuss nite, di adda day, tadda day, tarra day, tedda day, tidda day - *The other day I saw Lisa at the market*: Wa die mi si Lisa a di maakit - *We saw Lisa the other day*: Wi si Lisa weh die

THE WHOLE TIME all di while, fram mawnin

THEFT tiefry

THEIR dem, fi dem

THEIRS fidem

THEM dem

THEMSELVES 1 (n) demself 2 (adv for emphasis) same one - *Didn't they themselves let it happen?* No dem siem wan mek it apm?

THEN 1 (conj) den 2 (*subsequently*) likkle afta dat, afta dat

THERE 1 (n. *that place*) desso 2 (adv) deh 3 (*in there*) in deh, een deh 4 (*right there*) right deh so, deh so 5 (*There X is; There X are*) Si X deh, Desso X deh - *There it is*: Si it deh, Deso it deh 6 Also see THERE IS; THERE ARE; THERE IS NO; THERE ARE NO

THERE ARE 1 yu av, yu ha 2 (*There are some X*) yu av some X, couple chree X deh - *There are some nice hotels in Miami*: Yu av som kris otel a Miami, Kopl chrii kris otel deh a Miami 3 Also see THERE ARE NO

THERE ARE NO (*There are no X*) No X no deh - *There are no boxes behind the house*: No bax no deh rounabak

THERE IS 1 yu av, yu ha 2 (*There is a X*) yu av one X, one X deh - *There's a church on the hilltop*: Yu av wan choch pan di hiltap, Wan choch deh pan di hiltap 3 Also see THERE IS NO or THERE IS NOTHING

THERE IS NO (*There is no X*) No X no deh - *There is no food in the kitchen*: No fuud no deh ina di kichin

THERE IS NOTHING Nuttn no deh - *There is nothing on the table*: Notn no deh pan di tiebl

THERE IT IS See it deh, Desso it deh

THERE YOU GO See it deh

THESE 1 (n) demya - *Look at these*: Ku pan demya 2 (adj) dem X ya - *These mangoes are delicious*: Dem manggo ya swiit

THESE DAYS (*nowadays*) dem time ya, tideh day ya

THEY 1 dem 2 Also see ARE; AREN'T; WERE; WEREN'T

THICK 1 (adj) tick, broad 3 (*of liquid: viscous; syrupy*) glammy, clammy, clammish, stiffy 4 Also see *MUSCULAR* or *FAT*

THIEF 1 (n) tief, tekka, puss 2 (*armed robber*) steppa, gunman tief 3 (*petty thief*) come rung

THIEVING (adj) tief tief, fingafarin

THIGH leg

THIN 1 (of person) mawga, slim, winji 2 (*tall and skinny; lanky*) lenga lenga, langalala 3 (n. *tall and skinny person*) langalala, tallis, pawpaw tree, wiss, cucucum stick 4 (*skinny woman*) slimmaz, mawga gyal, wiss, cucucum stick 5 Also see *FRAIL*

THING 1 supm, sittin, sinting, ting - *That's a good thing*: A gud ting dat 2 (*thingy; gizmo; doohickey*) badang

THINK 1 (v) tink, medz 2 (*think about*) tink bou, pree, tink pan, medz, penny, penetrate 3 Also see *THINK OVER; THINK IT OVER;* etc

THINK ABOUT tink bou, pree, tink pan, medz, penny, penetrate, ponda

THINK IT OVER tink pan ih, medz pan ih, medz it ova, medz ih, check again, penny it, penetrate it, wok yu head, study yu head, tuddy yu head, consida yu head, tun it ovah inna yu head

THINK OVER tink ova, tink pan, pree, medz, penny, penetrate

THINK TOO MUCH buss yu brain, pree too deep, worry yu head, ovatink, hot up yu head, hot up yuh skull, fret up yuself

THINKING (n. *higher thinking and pondering*) studderation

THIS 1 (n) dis, yasso - *This is good*: Dis gud, Yaso gud 2 (adj) da X ya - *This mango is delicious*: Da manggo ya swiit

THIS AND THAT ray an tay, ray tay

THORN macca, macka

THORNY (*prickly*) macka macka, jooky jooky, picky picky

THOROUGHLY 1 (adv) well, full - *It's thoroughly wet*: It ful wet 2 (*utterly*) strait, bline, ded, full - *You're thoroughly insane*: Yu schriet mad; Yu blain mad; etc. 3 (pred adv) done, full, full stop, full hundred, til ih buck, clear, clean clean

THOSE 1 (n) demdeh - *Look at those*: Ku pan demdeh 2 (adj) dem X deh - *Those mangoes look ripe*: Dem manggo deh luk fit

THOSE DAYS dem time deh

THOUGH 1 (*nevertheless; anyway*) still   2 (*even though*) all doah

THREAT 1 (n) chret   2 (*empty threat; bluff*) olo, olo gyow, gyow

THREATEN (*make threats to*) bad up, wild up, coarse up, chuck it pan, chuck pan

THRIFTY 1 (adj) cave-headed, cavey (*cheap*) chinky

THRIVE (v) strive, get chu

THROUGH chu

THROW 1 (v. *toss*) chrow, fling   2 (*discard*) dash   3 (as a party or event) keep - *They're having a conference*: Dem a kip a kanfrens   4 (*throw dice*) nick dice

THROW AWAY dash weh, chrow weh

THROW OFF (v. *shake off*) fling weh

THRUSH 1 (type of bird) fish eye, glass eye   2 (disease) trash

THRUST 1 (v) jook, jam   2 (v. in sex: *thrust relentlessly*) sawka sawka

THUG tuggz, hot skull, rudebwoy, starbwoy, guineagog, tegereg, screwface, ruffneck, ruffian, russian, shotta, gyangsta, knockist, kwenga, bandolero, gundolero, war monga, sluggard, tuff, scufflah, baddaz, chucky, radge, bullbucka, badlaw, baddy boo

THUMB big finga, tumpy

TIC TAC TOE tee taa toe

TICK (n. the biting insect specifically) tix

TIDY 1 (adj) criss, primps   2 Also see *TIDY UP*

TIDY UP 1 (v) dechakalize, primps up pran up spruce up   3 (*clean hastily*) gi a lick an a promise, gyow out

TIGHT 1 (adj. *taut; clenched*) toonch up, toonk up   2 (adj. *close, as friends*) tick   3 (adj. vagina only) ukubit, likkle an cute, glue

TIGHT FISTED mean, cubbitch, geechy, tight han, chinky, pinchy cubby

TILED FLOOR taris

TILTED lean, cyaas, skeelt, offish

TIMID fraidy fraidy, puss boot

TIMIDLY krah krah

TINKER (v) panka panka

TINT (n) tilt

TINY likkle bit, lilly bit, beenie bit, uku bit, jinji, mini mini

TIP (*helpful piece of information*) prips

TIP OFF 1 (*give a helpful hint*) prips off 2 (*inform someone about a cheating spouse or partner*) pinch, buzz, page

TIP OVER kin ova, pitch ova

TIPPING POINT 1 (n) bump 2 (v. *reach the tipping point*) come up to bump

TIRE (vt) tyad X out (X=person or thing) - *This job tires me*: Dis jab ya a tayad mi out

TIRED 1 (adj) tyad 2 (*tired of* + noun) tyad a 3 (*tired of* + verb) tyad fi - *I'm tired of it*: Mi tayad a it - *I'm tired of watching*: Mi tayad fi wach 4 Also see *EXHAUSTED*

TISSUE tissyu, tushu

TIT FOR TAT du fi du

TITLE tykle

TO 1 (when followed by verb) fi 2 (when followed by noun or pronoun) tu

TO THE MAX til it buck, full hundred, tu di fullness, full stop

TOBACCO shag, jackass rope

TODAY tideh

TOGETHER 1 tugedda 2 (adv. *side-by-side*) foot an foot 3 (adj. *joined in a romantic relationship*) deh, inna dealinz

TOGETHERNESS oneness, tugeddaness, (Rasta) I-nity

TOLERATE 1 (*allow for; accept*) low 2 (*not tolerate; not accept*) no caytah tu, no low, no defend, bun, bun out 3 Also see *PUT UP WITH; TAKE SHIT*

TOM CAT ram puss

TOMATO 1 (n) tumatis 2 (*large variety of tomato*) salad

TOMORROW 1 tumarRo, inna di marrows 2 (*Early tomorrow morning*) Fuss light, Day light

TONGUE-IN-CHEEK (adj) play play

TOO 1 (*also*) as well, same way, tu 2 (*excessively*) too, chree - *They're not too bad*: Dem no chrii bad

TOOTH 1 (n) teet, choppa 2 (*buck tooth*) buff teet

TOOTHPASTE Colgate

TOOTHPICK chew stick, chaw stick

TOP 1 (*highest point*) toppa top 2 (toy: *spinning top*) gig 3 (*bottle top that screws off*) cork, cova, screwcork, bokkle cork 4 (*bottle top that needs to be pulled with an opener*) bokkle stoppa 5 (*on top of*) tappa

TOP QUALITY (adj) name brand, quality, top shelf, top a di top, toppity top, toppa top, original

TOP RATE (adj) name brand, top shelf, top a di top, toppity top, toppa top, preps

TOPPLE (v) lick dung

TORMENT (v) tek set pan

TORN (adj) tear - Also see *SHREDDED; TATTERED; AMBIVALENT*

TORN UP see *SHREDDED; CUT UP; TATTERED; UPSET*

TOSS fling

TOTAL 1 (*sum*) lumsum 2 (*the total charge*) di tax 3 (*entire*) full

TOTALLY 1 (*fully*) well, full - *It's totally wet*: It ful wet; It wel wet 2 (*utterly*) strait, bline, dead, full - *You're totally insane*: Yu schriet mad; Yu blain mad; etc.

TOTALLY! (*Absolutely! I totally agree!*) Strait!, Fi real!, Tank yu very much!, Yu done know!, Chat bout!, A mi fi tell yu!, Every time!, Mmm Hmm!, Rrrr!, A it dat!, A it mi a seh!, A dat mi a seh!, No dat mi a seh?, Desso mi a seh!, Sed speed!, To di worl!, No chu?, No so?, Yu tink a joke?

TOUCH 1 (*a small amount*) a kimps, a kemps, a tups, a chenks, a kemch 2 (v) fingle, brush 3 (*Don't touch it*) Mek ih stay, Mek ih tan 4 Also see *FEEL* or *GROPE*

TOUCHY 1 (*persnickity*) stush, itey titey, meckam peckam 2 (*sensitive*) cry cry, bawly bawly

TOUGH 1 (*solid; strong*) tight, trong 2 (of person: *resilient*) talawah, haad back, no easy, tuffa 3 (of situation: *difficult; tricky*) sticky, technical 4 Also see *ROUGH; HARSH*

TRACE (n. *small amount*) toops, choops - Also see *BERATE*

TRACK 1 (n. *horse track; walking path*) chail, chack, paat, pass 2 (n. *train track*) line, chack 3 (v. *pursue*) falla backa, run dung

TRAGEDY shame, joke, alms-house

TRAIL 1 (n. *path*) chail, chack, paat 2 (v. *walk behind*) falla backa

TRAITOR frenemy, switcha, culprit, Judas, tuncoat, twincoat, back bitah, bag-o-wyah, back-an-belly, back-an-belly rat, white belly rat, snake inna di grass, two-face cutlass

TRAITOROUS switchy, back an belly, two mout, twin mout, twin coat, Judas

TRANSLATE twiss - *She can translate it into Spanish for you*: Shi kyan twis i ina spanish fi yu

TRAPPED (adj) ketch up

TRASH (n) gyabbage, rubbish, ruggage

TRASH CAN gyabbage pan, rubbish pan, ruggage pan

TRAUMA 1 (*emotional trauma*) drama, frightenation, frightration, bodderation 2 (*physical trauma; impact*) lick, baff, boof, bam bam, palam pam

TRAUMATIZE(D) cut up, sheg up, all sheg up, dramatize

TREACHEROUS ceitful, pagan, deceptious, shakey, switchy, sipple, sipple an lie, too lie, jinal, samfai, bandulu, back and belly, two mout, twin mout, twin coat

TREAT 1 (n. *something given free of charge*) freeness 2 (n. *a little something extra*) brawta, mek up 3 (v. *behave towards*) du, angle (from *handle*) - *Why do you treat me that way?*: Wa mek yu a du mi so?

TRENDY /TRENDING 1 (of fashion or product) hype, shot, shot a road, a du road, a run road, a lead, a happn, sell off, slap weh, a slap, a clap, a tek, a lick, big, craab up, tun up, buck, bashy - *Skinny jeans are trendy right now*: Chriet jiinz a slap ya now 2 Also see *POPULAR*

TRESPASS (v. *break in to a proptery by scaling the fence*) boom fence, boom di fence

TRIANGLE terrengle

TRICK 1 (n. *a magic trick*) guzum 2 (*ploy; scheme*) rake, scyam, bandulu skeem, chicaney, ligues, rungles, gimmicks 3 (*practical joke*) rungles, rungus, gungus, cyaad, gimmicks 4 (v. *play a joke on*) fool up, run joke pan, cyaad, play cyaad pan, gimmicks 5 (*deceive*) jinnal, bait up, cyaad, draw cyaad pan, bandulu, samfai, lamps, craff, maringle, rungles 6 Also see: *MISCHIEF*

TRICKERY jinnalship, samfai bizniz, bandulu bizniz, rungles, maringles

TRICKY 1 (*complicated*) technical 2 (*touchy; thorny*) technical, sticky 3 (*crafty; cunning*) trickify, sipple, trick, cunny

TRINKETS (n. *gaudy ornaments; trinkets*) fandangles, fandangus, parangles, bangarang

TRIP 1 (n. *excursion*) tracks, trod, flex 2 (v. *stumble*) slip up, tumble, pitch, trip up yuself 3 (v. *lose one's sense of reason*) luu, liv inna luu, liv luu (from *illusion?*) 4 (v. *get angry*) flip up, rail up, lick out, get ignarant, get ig 5 (v. *take a trip*) mek a tracks, mek a trod, mek a flex

TRIP OUT 1 (v. *lose one's sense of reason*) luu, liv inna luu, liv luu (from *illusion?*) 2 (v. *get angry*) flip up, rail up, lick out, wile up, get ignarant, get ig

TRIVIAL dibby dibby, pwoko pwoko

TROUBLE 1 (n. *difficulty*) chubble, chubbles, trials, crosses, hacklinz, bodderation 2 (*You're in trouble; You're gonna be in trouble*) Dog nyam yu suppa, Yu corner dark, Yes now Spanish Town! 3 Also see *HASSLE*

TROUBLEMAKER (*ruffian; hooligan*) tuggz, hot skull, rudebwoy, starbwoy, guineagog, tegereg, screwface, ruffneck, ruffian, russian, war monga, sluggard, scufflah, baddaz, chucky, radge, tuff, bullbucka, badlaw, baddy boo, (female only): bad gyal, war boat, ratchet, champong nanny

TROUBLES see *HASSLES; PROBLEMS; HARDSHIP*

TRUCK 1 (n) chuck, kruck 2 (*single-box non-diesel truck*) van 3 (*dump truck*) dumpa 4 (*pickup truck*) open back van 5 (*truck bed*) van back, truck back

TRUE 1 (adj. *factually correct*) chu 2 (*That's true; It's true*) A chu 3 (*That's not true*) Nuttn no go so, A no chu, Dat no chu 4 Also see *LOYAL*

TRUMPET FISH chumpitah, fifah, flute fish, piper, long-jaw

TRUNCHEON (n) baton stick, junka

TRUNK 1 (n. of car) boot 2 (*storage trunk*) tin case

TRUNK FISH sheep head

TRUSTED (of friend) heartical, goodup, cool

TRUSTWORTHY (of person) goodup, artical, heartical, bonafide, deestant, ites, conscious, cool

TRUTH chute

TRY 1 (v) chry 2 (v. *sample*) chry, gi chry, gi tase 3 Also see *TRY AGAIN*

TRY AGAIN wheel and come again, try back, try once more again

TRY TO FIGURE OUT study, maths out

TUBERS grung provision, grung food, food

TUMERIC tambric

TURN 1 (v) tun 2 (v. *become*) kom, tun, X up - *It's turning yellow*: It a yelo op 3 (v. *turn* + age in years) reach, ketch, touch 4 (*rotate*) wine 5 (v. *spin*) wheel, reel

TURN AWAY (vt. of person: *to reject*) tun out

TURN OFF 1 (of lamp or light) out 2 (of electrical appliance) lock off 3 (of power supply or water supply) lock off, cut 4 (v. *sexually turn off*) kill di vibes, chill di vibes, brok di spell, brok X spell, kill X nature, cut X nature (X=person)

TURN ON /TURNED ON see *AROUSE*

TURN OVER kin ova

TURN TO see *RESORT TO*

TURNCOAT frenemy, culprit, informa, back bitah, back-an-belly rat, white belly rat, twincoat, snake inna di grass, bag-o-wyah

TURTLE turkle

TWERK 1 (n. *twerking*) dutty wine 2 (v. *to twerk*) cock it up, dash it out, wine dutty

TWIG 1 (*sharp pointed twig*) sprong 2 (*twigs*) ticky ticky

TWIRL (vi) wheel, wheel an tun, tun yu roll 2 (vt) tun tun

TWISTED 1 (*physically twisted*) twiss up, cyaas 2 (*perturbed*) offish, freaky, underin 3 (*depraved*) evilous, wikid, ugly

TWO-FACED back and belly, pagan, deceptious, twin mout, twin coat, samfai

TYPE 1 (n. *kind*) sort, manna 2 (*all types of*) all manna

UDDER bres (breast)

UGLINESS ugly

UGLY 1 (adj) zugly, fugly, crawny, zutupeck, zutupeng, bush, baboon face, baboon, patu, pancoot, muckumdash, bongo, face fayva X (X=any ugly thing) 2 (n. *ugly person*) accident, zutupeck, zutupeng, pancoot, baboon, monkey Jesus, patu doudou, pancoot, muckumdash, bongo 3 (*At least I'm not ugly*) Afta tree nah grow inna mi face!

UHEALTHY 1 (*sickly*) para para 2 Also see *FRAIL*

UMBILLICAL CORD belly string, nabel string, nabel tring

UNATTRACTIVE crawny, wormy, tyad body, lazy body, no mek it

UNAWARE 1 (*generally clueless*) dark, simple, born back a cow, born when yu big, grow wid yu granny, juss fall out a di truck   2 (v. *to be unaware of things and happenings*) no know bout, no know di time, no know wah clock a strike, no know what o'clock, no know di Schweppes

UNCARING donkya, dry yeye, ded yeye

UNCENSORED 1 (adj) naked up, raw chaw   2 Also see *EXPLICIT*

UNCIVILIZED see *BACKWATER* or *UNREFINED* or *VULGAR*

UNCLEAR mud up

UNCOMFORTABLE (adj. of situation: *awkward*) cute, funny, teknikal

UNCOMPROMISING 1 (adj. *uncompromisingly committed*) trong eye, crabbit   2 (*stubborn and contrarian*) purpose, trong eye

UNCOOPERATIVE (v. *be uncooperative*) Diss di program

UNCOUTH 1 (of behavior) renk, dutty, slack, slacka, luu, butu, sketel, raw chaw, brawlin, streggeh, screbbeh, crebbeh, hoggish, zutupeck, zutupeng, jingbang, boogooyaga, boogoo boogoo, chamba chamba   2 (of person) butu, brawlin, raw chaw, cruff, screbbeh, crebbeh, streggeh, hoggish, nassy, renk, slack, slacka, outa aada, zutupeck, zutupeng, boogooyaga, boogoo boogoo, (female only): sketel   3 (n. *uncouth person*) butu, cruff, streggeh, screbbeh, screbz, crebbeh, zutupeng, zutupek, dutty bungle, boogooyaga, boogoo boogoo, pancoot, (female only): sketel, dutty stinkin gyal, nassy gyal, credell

UNCOVER see *EXPOSE* or *DISCOVER*

UNCULTIVATED see *UNCULTURED* or *WILD*

UNCULTURED 1 (of behavior or speech) butu, sketel, batta foot, raw chaw, brawlin, hoggish, common, dark, streggeh, screbbeh, crebbeh, boogooyaga, boogoo boogoo, zutupek, zutupeng, chamba chamba, bongo, backawall, backabush, backamoko   2 (of person) butu, batta foot, brawlin, raw chaw, dark, cruff, crebbeh, screbbeh, streggeh, hoggish, zutupeck, zutupeng, jingbang, boogooyaga, boogoo boogoo, backawall, backabush, (female only): sketel   3 (n. *an uncultured person*) butu, crebbeh, cruff, streggeh, screbbeh, screbz, dutty bungle, batta foot, boogooyaga, boogoo boogoo, zutupeng, zutupek, jingbang, (male only): cuffy, kwashi, kwamin, kwaco, kwao, bongo, (female only): sketel, pancoot, credell

UNDER CONTROL 1 (*secure*) lock, set, strap up, deh pan ice, chock an belay, fit an frock, cook an curry   2 (*to keep under control*) hol dung, canchol, mantrol, manchol, angle

UNDERGO 1 go chu, pass chu 2 Also see *SUFFER* or *SURVIVE*

UNDERNOURISHED see *EMACIATED*

UNDERQUALIFIED no ready, rooks

UNDERSTAND unnastan, ovastan, ovahs, penetrate, sight, ear

UNDERSTANDING 1 (*ability to comprehend*) ovastandin 2 (*specific interpretation*) ovastandin, medz 3 (*sympathy*) lov, respeck 4 (n. *wisdom*) sense, sabi-so

UNDERVALUE (vt) low count, no mention, no respek, no preeshalove

UNDERWEAR 1 (*underpants*) drawz, undapants 2 (*panties*) panty, draws, baggy, (*large panties*) bingo

UNDO tek weh

UNDONE tek weh

UNEASY kra kra

UNEDUCATED see *IGNORANT* or *UNREFINED*

UNEMPLOYED (often pr): anemplai

UNETHICAL luu, mud up, ugly, sheg up

UNEXPECTEDLY suddn, juss so, baps, foops, widout waanin, bragadaps

UNFAIR mud up, sheg up

UNFAIRNESS (n) iniquity, parshality

UNFAITHFUL 1 (adj) switchy 2 (adj. of male: *promiscuous*) dutty, girly girly 3 (adj. of female: *promiscuous*) dutty, manny manny, mud up, leggo, outlaw, sketel 3 (n. *unfaithful woman*) cridell, jezibel 4 (adj. *without religious faith*) worlian, eeden (from *heathen*)

UNFASHIONABLE butu, boogoo boogoo

UNFASTEN fly, pull

UNFIT 1 (*unqualified*) nyamps 2 (*out of shape*) tyad body, pop dung, crenky, no mek it 3 Also see *UNDERQUALIED*

UNFORTUNATE 1 (of situation) damp, daak, dusty, bleaky 2 (of person) badlucky, bad luckid, bleaky, corner dark, des, dry, mafeena 3 (n. *an unfortunate person*) suffara, bogga, mafeena

UNFRIENDLY misareble, crampify, cramoojin

UNHEALTHY 1 (of person: *unwell*) poorly 2 (of food or activity) no good 3 Also see FEEBLE

UNIMPORTANT dibby dibby, pwoko pwoko, pyaa pyaa

UNINHIBITED dashout

UNITED STATES (*The United States of America*) Foreign, Big Foreign

UNITY oneness, tugeddaness, (Rasta) I-nity

UNIVERSAL pr: yuunivurshal

UNKEMPT 1 (of person) streggeh, slacka, slacka slacka, chaka chaka, nyaka nyaka, raggy raggy, ragga ragga, reggeh reggeh, frazzle out, frazzle, boogooyaga, boogoo boogoo 2 (of place) chaka chaka, nyaka nyaka 3 (n. *unkempt person*) cruff, streggeh, raggamuffin, dutty bungle, boogooyaga, boogoo booogoo, chapunko

UNLOCK pull

UNLUCKY 1 (*unlucky by nature*) badlucky, bad luckid 2 (*out of luck*) salt, dog nyam yu suppa, corner dark 3 (n. *unlucky person*) bogga, mafeena

UNPLUG /UNPLUGGED plug out

UNPREDICTABLE 1 (of person: *moody and unreliable*) switchy, head craab up, flighty 2 (n. *an unreliable person*) bad bargain

UNPRODUCTIVE 1 (of person) wukless, lowzy 2 (or policy or method) no wut, wutless, floopsy

UNREFINED 1 (of behavior or speech) butu, sketel, batta foot, raw chaw, brawlin, hoggish, common, dark, streggeh, screbbeh, crebbeh, boogoo boogoo, boogooyaga, zutupek, zutupeng, chamba chamba, bongo, backawall, backabush, backamoko 2 (of person) butu, batta foot, brawlin, raw chaw, dark, cruff, crebbeh, screbbeh, streggeh, hoggish, zutupeck, zutupeng, jingbang, boogooyaga, boogoo boogoo, backawall, backabush, (female only): sketel 3 (n. *an unrefined person*) butu, crebbeh, cruff, streggeh, screbbeh, screbz, dutty bungle, batta foot, boogooyaga, boogoo boogoo, zutupeng, zutupek, jingbang, (male only): cuffy, kwashi, kwamin, kwaco, kwao, bongo, (female only): sketel, pancoot, credell

UNRELIABLE 1 (of car or device) fenkeh fenkeh, crebbeh crebbeh, cabba cabba, fluxy, pyaa pyaa 2 (of person) shakey, fenkeh, fenkeh fenkeh, crebbeh, cruff 3 (n. *an unreliable person*) bad bargain 4 Also see WEAK; LAZY

UNRIPE green, no reddy

UNRULY 1 (of behavior) brokwile, luu, leggo, outta aada, jingbang 2 (v. *get unruly*) gwaan buckwile, go luu, run up and dung 3 (n. *unruly and vulgar person*) leggo beast, hog inna menty, teggereg, virago, kinarky

UNSALTED (especially of nuts or peanuts) Ital

UNSIGHTLY crawny, zutupek, hoodias

UNSOPHISTICATED see *BACKWATER* or *CRUDE* or *UNREFINED*

UNSTABLE (of a structure) ruku ruku, frekeh frekeh, palla palla

UNSTEADY 1 (*trembling*) chimble chimble 2 (*wobbly; unstable*) ruku ruku, frekeh frekeh

UNSUCCESSFUL 1 (of person) flop 2 (or policy or method) flop 3 (n. *unsuccessful person*) zero, waste man, waste gyal, double blank

UNTANGLE pull, free up

UNTIDY 1 (of personality) slacka, slacky tidy 2 Also see *DISORGANIZED; MESSY; UNKEMPT*

UNKEMPT 1 (of person) streggeh, slacka, slacky tidy, slacka slacka, chaka chaka, nyaka, nyaka nyaka, raggy, ragga ragga, frazzle out, frazzle 2 (of place) chaka chaka, nyaka nyaka 3 (n. *unkempt person*) cruff, streggeh, raggamuffin, dutty bungle, boogooyaga, chapunko

UNTIE 1 (*untie an animal or object*) loose, free up, fly 2 (of knot) pull

UNTIL so till, so tel

UNTRUSTWORTHY (of person) shakey, switchy, sipple, deceptious

UNWIELDY wagga wagga, lagga lagga, lugga lugga, bufutu

UP THERE 1 (adv) up deh, up deh so 2 (if location can be seen by both parties and is not far) up so

UPBEAT upful

UPBRINGING 1 (n) broughtupsy 2 (n. *lousy upbringing*) dragupsy

UPDATE 1 (n. *an update*) ketch-up 2 (v. *to update*) ketch up

UPPER CLASS 1 (n. *the upper class; the bourgeosie*) society, di bigga heads dem, di risto dem, di top rankin dem, di saaf han dem, di tapanaris dem 2 (n. *an upper-class person*) topanaris, top rankin, society, ristocrat, risto, money man, saaf han 3 (adj. *of upper class quality and attitude*) stoosh, uptong, hitey titey, chest high, risto, top rankin

UPPITY boasy, hitey titey, chest high, stucky, stush

UPRIGHT 1 (pred adj. *in a standing position*) pan foot 2 (adj. *protruding upwards*) cock up 3 (adj. *respectable*) artical, heartical, bonafide, deestant, God-bless, goodup goodup, irie, upstandin

UPRIGHTNESS characta

UPROAR 1 (n) kanfusion, piece a noise, bag a noise, galangin, bangarang, palangarang, palam pam, bam bam, jingbang, hell an powda house, ruption, ruption, rig jig   2 (v. *cause commotion*) mek alarm, hype up, rail up, wild up, bring dong excitement, call crowd, draw dong scandal

UPSET 1 (adj. *emotionally upset*) ben, ben up, cut up, bun up, sheg up   2 (v. *to hurt the feelings of person X*) mash X sore toe   3 (*feel upset*) feel a way   4 (*get upset*) ben   5 (of person and their behavior: *be upset with*) lose off a - *I'm upset with you*: Mi luuz aaf a yu   6 Also see *ANGRY*

UPSETTING 1 (*hurtful*) hotful, utful   2 (*distressing*) bexashous, bodderashous   3 (*shocking*) frightenatious

US wi - *They don't worry us*: Dem no wori wi

USE 1 (*use regularly*) beat   2 (*take advantage of*) tax, advantage, tek step a, live pan, nyam a food off a, boops out, nyam out

USE UP nyam up, beat, done out

USED 1 (esp of clothing: *secondhand*) wear an leff, poop eena, (of any item) ole brok   2 (*various used items in good condition for purchase*) ray ray

USED UP (*consumed*) done out, nyam off

USELESS 1 (*worthless; low quality*) crebbeh crebbeh, tufenkeh, fenkeh fenkeh, fluxy, dibby dibby, wutlis, wuklis, batta foot, batta ears, sketel, streggeh, screbbeh screbbeh, kaba kaba, chamba chamba, boogooyaga, butu, common, half inch, half staff, knockoff, riff raff, casco, tikki tikki, jingbang, pyaa pyaa, no wut, no use, pop dung, ol bruck, nyamps   2 (n. *useless stuff*) see *JUNK*   3 (n. *useless ineffectual person*) see *WORTHLESS*

USUALLY more time, more while

UTTERLY see *COMPLETELY*

VAGINA 1 (innocent terms) front, miggle, ting, sinting, whatsitnot, tarra warra, coco bread, pokie, property, crotches; (more sexualized) kitty, kyatty, nookie, buff, good good, eva bless, heaven gates, entrance, zum zum, Benz, glamity, glimity-glamity, cherry pie, panti pie, bammy-an-pear, pum pum, pumselle, cherry, cho cho, tomato, salad, veggie, salt ting, salt fish, fattaz, buffaz, clump; (vulgar terms) punani, nani, di nana, puni, punash, nash, nush nush, katash, kitash, fishy, tuni, tun-tuni, tun tun, chune chune, beef, renkin meat, fur burger, hairy bank, bumbo   3 (n. *very tight vagina*) neegle eye, glue, tight gift, tightness, ukubit, uku

VAGINAL LUBRICANT (*natural secretions*) juice, pum pum juice, punanny juice, glimmity

VAGRANT dutty bungle, boogooyaga

VAIN see *CONCEITED; SELFISH*

VALUABLE value, wut, dear

VALUE 1 (n) wut   2 (v. *regard highly*) count, rate   3 (vt. *boost the value of something*) value up

VARIED different different

VARIOUS (adj) different different - *There were various kinds of fish for sale*: Difren difren fish did deh deh a sel

VACILLATE block a sound, buckshuffle, bob an weave

VEHICLE chansport

VENDOR 1 sella   2 (*street vendor*) higgla

VERSUS gainst

VERY well   2 (pred adv. *very much*) cyaa done, so till   3 (*the very X*) di said X - *That's the very car I was talking about*: A di sed cyaar mi did a taak

VINDICTIVE (adj) bad mind, misareble, pagan, cramoojin

VINE wiss

VIOLENCE pr: voilens (n) badness

VIOLENT 1 (of personality) brawlin, rhygin, ignarant, ig, warify, ruffa, teggeregish   2 (of place) voylent, danjarous, sticky, hot, red hot   3 (v. *get violent*) lick outchuck it

VIRGINITY 1 (n) maiden   2 (for girl: *lose virginity*) brok out

VIRILITY naycha, back

VISIT 1 (v) touch, pass chu   2 (*pay a visit to*) check, check fi, look, look fi

VITILIGO (n. skin condition) leopard skin, peel skin, chicolarchy

VOLATILE 1 (of situation or material) hot, red, sipple   2 (of chemical) hot   3 (of person) crabbit, ignarant, ig, warify, wassy, jumpy

VOLUNTEER (v. *work without pay*) mek allibutton

VOLUPTUOUS 1 (*fat yet sexy; curvacious*) fluffy, flufflilous, fluffalishous, buffy, bufflilous, bufflilicious, tick, tickarous, trang, roun, fat, boonoonoos, Boonoonoonoos

VOLUPTUOUS WOMAN 2 (n. or term or address: *voluptuous woman*) Fluffy, Flufflilous, Fluffalishous, Buffy, Bufflilous, Bufflilicious, Fatty, Fat girl, Trong girl, Roun girl, Tick girl, Tickarous, Boonoo<u>noo</u>noos

VOODOO see *SORCERY; SPIRITISM*

VOODOO PRIEST obeah man, scientis, guzu man, zuzu man, booguman, (priestess) madda ooman

VULGAR 1 (of behavior) renk, dutty, slack, slacka, luu, butu, sketel, raw chaw, brawlin, streggeh, screbbeh, crebbeh, hoggish, zutupeck, zutupeng, jingbang, boogooyaga, boogoo boogoo, chamba chamba 2 (of person) butu, brawlin, raw chaw, cruff, screbbeh, crebbeh, streggeh, hoggish, nassy, renk, slack, slacka, outa aada, zutupeck, zutupeng, boogooyaga, boogoo boogoo, (female only): sketel 3 (n. *vulgar person*) butu, cruff, streggeh, screbbeh, screbz, crebbeh, zutupeng, zutupek, dutty bungle, boogooyaga, boogoo boogoo, pancoot, (female only): sketel, dutty stinkin gyal, nassy gyal, credell, jezibel

VULNERABLE (*exposed to danger*) headback expose, expose

VULTURE john crow, crow, cyan crow (from *carrion crow*), jamaica turkey

WAG (v. as a dog's tail) fan

WAIT 1 (*stay put for now*) tan, hitch, klutch, lay, bats, quat, satta 2 (*wait for*) wait pan

WAIT A MINUTE see *HOLD ON*

WAIT FOR wait pan

WAKE (*funeral wake*) setup, ded yaad, nine nite, gerreh

WALK 1 (v) trod, yadd, crush road, beat road, tek di ankle express, tek di ten toe turbo, tek di legz-us 2 Also see *TAKE A WALK; WALK AWAY; WALK OUT ON; WALK THE STREETS*

WALK AWAY walk weh galang, walk galang, trod weh, walk gwaan

WALK OUT ON gwaan leff, run leff, cut leff, splurt pan

WALK THE STREETS crush di road, beat di road

WALLET billy

WALLOW walla walla

WANDER 1 (*wander aimlessly*) box bout, walk up an dung, walk an tun, tun-rung tun-rung, spin-rung spin-rung 2 (*travel and explore*) trampooze, trod di lan, trod di eart

WANDERER falla-line

WANNABE 1 (n. *one who aspires to be something other than what they are*) wagonist, moutwata (from *mouthwater*) - *wannabe rasta*: moutwaata rasta - *wannabe gangster*: moutwaata shata   2 also see *FAKE; IMITATION; KISS ASS*

WANT 1 waan   2 (*really want; sincerely want*) well waan   3 (*want something badly*) waan X bad, waan X bad bad

WAS 1 (when followed by a noun) a did, a en - *I was the champion*: Mi a did di champyan; Mi a en di champyan   2 (+ adj) did, en - *She was glad*: Shi did glad; Shi en glad   3 (+ verb) did a, en a - *She was jumping*: Shi did a jomp; Shi en a jomp   4 (+ location) did deh, en deh - *I was here*: Mi did deh ya; Mi en deh ya   5 (*was to* + v) did fi - *He was to finish his work*: Him did fi don him wok   6 (*It was* + adj) a did, a en - *It was crucial*: A did kruushal; A en kruushal

WASHED UP (adj. *old and worn out*) pop dung, rev out

WASN'T 1 (when followed by a noun) a neva - *She wasn't the one*: Shi a neva di wan   2 (+ adj) neva, neh - *I wasn't upset*: Mi neva bex; Mi neh bex   3 (+ verb) neva did a, neh a - *Rain wasn't falling*: Rien neva did a faal; Rien neh a faal   4 (+ location) neva deh, neh deh - *It wasn't on the desk*: It neva deh pan di deks; It neh deh pan di deks

WASP 1 (n) wass wass   2 (*mud-dauber wasp*) free mason   3 (*paper wasp*) house wass

WASTE TIME see *LOAF*

WATCH 1 (v. *guard; watch over*) mine, look afta, govern   2 (*observe*) pree, study, eyes, tek een, tek a stock a, clock, program, penny, penetrate   3 (v. of movie or show or event) pree, tek een, penetrate

WATCH OUT! 1 (*Heads up!*) Eh-eh!, Yow!, Stay wide!   2 (*Be careful!*) Mind sharp!, Mine sharp!, Tek time!, Have Caution!, Tekyah!, Tek sleep mark death!

WATER waata, earth wine

WATERFALL waatafall, fallin

WATERY (of drink or soup) long, mekeh mekeh

WAY 1 (*path*) trod   2 (*means*) way (pr: wie)

WE 1 wi   2 Also see *ARE; AREN'T; WERE; WEREN'T*

WEAK 1 (of person: *physically weak*) saaf, pyaa pyaa, crenky, fenkeh   2 (of thing: *structurally weak*) fenkeh, fluxy, ruku ruku   4 (*weak of character; unmanly*) saaf, saps, fenkeh, pyaa pyaa, nyamps

WEAKLING 1 (n) saps, saafaz, nyamps, fenkeh   2 Also see *COWARD*

WEALTHY 1 (adj) set up, pocket long   2 (n. *wealthy person*) money man, long pocket, risto, Missa T   3 Also see *UPPER CLASS*

WEAPON tool, supm

WEAR 1 (v) av on, dress up inna 2 (*wear frequently*) beat 3 (*wear flashy clothes*) shock out, flash out, trash out

WEATHER time - *The weather is hot!*: Di taim hat!

WEDGE /WEDGED 1 (n. *a wedge*) a kotch 2 (v. *to wedge*) kotch 3 (adj. *wedged*) kotch up, kotch

WEE HOURS howaz

WEED see *CANNABIS*

WEEK trong

WEIRD funny, diffrant, offish

WELL DRESSED shot, hype, craab up, tun up, tun ova, buck, fabilocious, trash an ready, trash, kris up, dress tu puss foot

WELL KNOWN see *POPULAR* or *ESTABLISHED*

WELL MANNERED balance, mannersable, come out a good house

WENT gone, go, did go, en go

WERE 1 (when followed by a noun) a did, a en - *We were friends*: Wi a did fren, Wi a en fren 2 (when followed by an adj) did, en - *They were glad*: Dem did glad, Dem en glad 3 (+ verb) did a, en a - *They were singing*: Dem did a sing, Dem en a sing 4 (+ location) did deh, en deh - *We were there*: Wi did deh deh, Wi en deh deh 5 (*were to* + v) did fi - *They were to wait here*: Dem did fi wiet ya 6 Also see *WEREN'T*

WEREN'T 1 (when followed by a noun) a neva - *We weren't friends*: Wi a neva fren 2 (when followed by an adj) neva, neh - *They weren't ready*: Dem neva redi, Dem neh redi 3 (+ verb) neva did a, neh a - *They weren't looking*: Dem neva did a luk, Dem neh a luk 4 (+ location) neva deh, neh deh - *You weren't here*: Yu neva deh ya

WEST INDIES (*the rest of the West Indies not including Jamaica*) Likkle Foreign

WHAT 1 wa, weh 2 (*What a mess!*) Wat a piis a mes! 3 (*What a pretty girl!*) Wat a gyal priti! 4 (*What delicious food!*) Wat a fuud swiit! 5 (*What hyperactive* kids) Wat a pikni-dem mad! 6 Also see *WHAT?; WHAT DO YOU MEAN; WHAT ARE YOU DOING?* etc

WHAT? A wah?, Seh wah?, Come again?, Weh yu juss seh likl while?, Weh yu juss seh? - Also see *WHAT ARE YOU TALKING ABOUT?*

WHAT A HOT DAY! Wat a day hot!, Di sun a talk!, Di sun no ramp fi hot!, Di sun a seh one!

WHAT ARE YOU DOING? 1 Weh yu a du?, Weh yu a deal wid?, Weh yu deh pan? 2 (*What are you trying to do?*) Weh yu fa?, A who yu?

WHAT ARE YOU TALKING ABOUT? see *WHAT ARE YOU TRYING TO SAY?* or *ARE YOU CRAZY?* or *ARE YOU KIDDING?*

WHAT ARE YOU TRYING TO DO? Weh yu fa?, A who yu?

WHAT ARE YOU TRYING TO SAY? Weh yu a deal wid?, Weh yu a defend?, Weh yu really waan fi seh?, Weh yu a chat seh?, Weh yu fah?

WHAT DO YOU MEAN? Weh yu mean?

WHAT DOES THAT MEAN? A wa name so?, A wa dat mean?

WHAT DOES X MEAN? A wa name X?

WHAT ELSE? Wah again?

WHAT IF…? spose, pose - *What if it rains?* Puoz it rien?

WHAT IS IT? A wa?

WHAT IS THAT? A wa dat?

WHAT IS THIS? A wa dis?

WHAT IS X DOING? Weh X a du?, Weh X a deal wid?, Weh X deh pan?

WHAT TIME IS IT? A weh di time?, Wah di time?

WHAT'S HAPPENING? Wah a gwaan? - Also see *HELLO*

WHAT'S THE MATTER? Wah wrong? - Also see *ARE YOU CRAZY?*

WHAT'S UP? Wah a gwaan?, Wah di pree?, Wah ih pree?, Weh yu deh pan?, Weh yu ah deal wid?, Weh yu ah seh?

WHAT'S YOUR NAME? A weh yu name?, A weh di I name?

WHEN 1 (interrogative) A wen   2 (*at the time that*) same time, az, so X soY - *When the thunder rolled she woke up*: Siem taim di tonda ruol shi wiek op, So di tonda ruol so shi wiek op

WHEN I WAS A KID 1 wen mi did pikni, wen mi yeye deh a mi knee (meaning *when my eyes were at the level of my knees*)   2 Also see *IN THE OLD DAYS*

WHENEVER when time, wheneva time

WHERE 1 (interrogative) A weh, A which paat, A weh paat   2 (*at the place that*) which paat, weh, weh part

WHERE ARE YOU? A weh yu deh?, A which paat yu deh?, A weh paat yu deh?

WHERE IS X ? A weh X deh?, A which paat X deh?, A weh paat X deh? - *Where is the sugar?*: A weh di shuga deh?, A wich paat di shuga deh?, A weh paat di shuga deh?

WHEREVER whicheva paat, every which paat, any which paat, which paat

WHILE 1 (*during the time that*) az, meantime, meanwhile, during di while 2 (*a while ago*) some time aback 3 (*a little while ago*) no too lang, likkle while 4 (in a little while) likkle fram dis, likkle more, soon time

WHINE (v) ningy ningy, nengeh nengeh, run up your mouth

WHINGE (v) run up yu mout, nyingi nyingi, nengeh nengeh

WHINY ningy ningy

WHISPER 1 (n) su su 2 (v) su su

WHISTLE 1 (n) fee fee 2 (v) wissle, fee fee 3 (*whistle at*) wissle afta

WHITE see *WHITE PERSON*

WHITE PERSON 1 (n) white, whitey, Jake 2 (*white slavemaster or oppressor*) bakra - *There's a lot of white people in MoBay*: Nof wait a MoBay

WHO 1 (interrogative) A who 2 (relative) weh

WHO ARE YOU? A who yu?, Weh yu fah?

WHO IS IT? A who?

WHO IS THIS (THAT)? A who dis?, A who dat?

WHOLE pr: wol 1 (*the whole thing*) di wol ting 2 (*the whole time*) all di while, fram maanin 3 (*this whole time*) dis long time, dis long while

WHOLESOME 1 roots, nachral 2 (*wholesome according to Rasta standards*) Ital

WHORE see *SLUT* or *PROSTITUTE*

WHORING see *SLUTTY*

WHOSE 1 (interrogative), A foo, A whofah, A foofah - *Whose gum is this?* Afuu gom dis?, A uufa gom dis? 2 (relative) weh, whofah - *The man whose car they broke into is a doctor*: Di man weh kyaar dem brok a dakta, Di man uufa kyaar dem brok a dakta

WHY 1 (interrogative) Wa mek, Mek, How 2 (adv) wa mek - *I don't know why they're laughing*: Mi no nuo wa mek dem a laaf

WIKID low, low run, evilous, renk, funky, funkify, cussid, custed

WIKIDNESS (n) badness, fuckry, sheggry, muckry, neckry, ugliness, ugly, buzu

WIDE broad

WIELD (as a gun) pop off, rise

WIFE princess, empress, lioness, queen, superintendant, wifey

WILD 1 (of flora or fauna: *undomesticated*) wile, bush 2 (of personality or nature: *hyperactive; rambunctious*) brokwile, leggo, jingbang 3 (of current mood: *hyped up*) rail up 4 (of behavior: *excessively wild and unruly*) luu, buckwile, outta aada, leggo 4 see *GO WILD*

WILDERNESS bush

WILT /WILTED quinge up, quail

WIMP soffaz, saps, press-button, remote, salad, guy, mantu, mama man, mampala, saaf-han bwoy

WIMPY saaf, sapsy, pyaa pyaa, fenkeh fenkeh, saaf-han, mampala

WINCE 1 (v. *recoil*) quinge 2 (v. *make a facial expression of disgust*) kin up yu face, mek up yu face 3 (v. *cause someone to wince*) nedge X teet - *That sound makes me cringe*: Da soun deh a nej mi tiit

WIND breeze

WINDMILL (n) breezemill

WINDOW pr: winda (n. *windshield of a car*) glass

WINDSHIELD glass

WIPE OUT (v. *eliminate*) radicate, bun out, x out, kill out, done out

WISDOM sense, sabi-so

WITCH DOCTOR 1 bush docta, bushman, scientist, shepherd 2 Also see *SORCERER*

WITH REGARD TO far as, wen it come on tu, bou

WITHDRAW 1 (*extract*) draw out 2 (*retreat*) tun back, ease off 3 (*withdraw from an agreement; renege*) tun back, sheriff 4 (*withdraw from*) back out fram, leggo, tek weh yuself fram

WITTY (adj. of person) no easy, jokify

WOBBLY ruku ruku, frekeh frekeh

WOMAN 1 (n) ooman, empress, lioness, queen 2 (*young woman*) princess, dawta 3 (*attractive woman*) goodaz, hottaz, hot gyal, criss ting, hottie hottie, glama gyal, goody goody, filly, fatty, block-traffic, boonoonoonoos 4 (*skinny woman*) slimmaz, mawga gyal, winji gyal, maskita 5 (*loyal and respectable woman*) goodaz, goody goody, empress, lioness 6 (*female stud; bedroom performer*) champion, stulliesha, buddy brucka, ridah 7 (*tough woman; rebel woman*) big ooman, champong nanny, bad gyal, ratchet 8 (*woman who feeds off men*) kinarky, parasite, pazart 9 Also see *UNFAITHFUL WOMAN; SLUT; UGLY WOMAN; SEXY WOMAN; ELDERLY WOMAN; VULGAR WOMAN; GIRLFRIEND; WIFE; MISTRESS*

WOMANIZER 1 (n) gyalis, (lady's man): girls man, slappa, cha cha bwoy, strikah 2 (adj. *having many mistresses*) girlie girlie

WONDERFUL 1 boonoonoonoos, splendacious, splendifarous, fabilocious, terrible, superble, wow, tun up, tun ova, turnt, mad, wicked, a seh one 2 Also see *EXCELLENT*

WOOD (often pr): hud - (n. *lumber*) boad

WORD /WORDS 1 wud 2 (*in words; with words*) wordical

WORK 1 (n) wok 2 (v. *work hard; toil*) kill up yuself, buss a swet, buss yu shut (from *bust your shirt*) 3 (*work skillfully on*) drap han pan 4 (*function*) run, wok 5 (*That's not gonna work*) Dat naa kip, Dat naa go wok

WORK IT! 1 Buss it!, Angle it!, Flex it!, Flick it!, Flash it!, Gi dem! 2 Also see *GO FOR IT!*

WORK OUT 1 (*resolve*) saat out, mats out 2 (*lift weights; pump iron*) push ayan 3 (*come to fruition; come to a resolution*) saat out 4 (*That's not gonna work out*) Dat naa kip

WORK WITHOUT PAY mek allibutton

WORM bugaboo

WORN OUT 1 (*overused*) rev out, done out 2 (*old and tattered*) tear up tear up, nyaka nyaka, ragga ragga, streggeh, reg jeg 3 (*exhausted*) mash up, done out, frazzle out

WORRIED 1 (n) fretful 2 (v. *feel worried*) fret, belly bottom a bun yu - *I'm feeling worried*: Mi beli batam a bon mi

WORRIES 1 (*mental anxiety*) fretration 2 Also see *ANXIETY; HASSLE; HARDSHIP*

WORRY 1 (n) fretration 2 (v) fret, cry, fret up yuself, hot up yu head, hot up yu brain 3 (*worry about*) fret pan, watch, cry fi 4 (*Don't worry about it; Don't take it personally*) No fret up yuself, No worry yuself, No watch no face, No feel no way, No cry fi no guy

WORSE wuss, wussa

WORST wussara, wussest

WORTH 1 (n) wut 2 (v. *be worth*) value

WORTHLESS 1 (of thing) crebbeh crebbeh, tufenkeh, fenkeh fenkeh, fluxy, dibby dibby, wutlis, wuklis, batta foot, batta ears, sketel, streggeh, screbbeh screbbeh, kaba kaba, chamba chamba, boogooyaga, butu, common, half inch, half staff, knockoff, riff raff, casco, tikki tikki, jingbang, pyaa pyaa, no wut, no use, pop dung, ol bruck 2 (of person: *lacking ambition or value to society*) wutless, wukless, pissy tail, dibby dibby, donkya, crebbeh, screbbeh, crebbeh crebbeh, screbbeh screbbeh, fenkeh fenkeh, tufenkeh, cruff, boogooyaga, boogoo boogoo, batta iez, long seed, pyaa pyaa, nyamps 3 (n. *worthless stuff*) kuru kuru, koro koro, ruggage, nyaka nyaka, boogooyaga, brokinz, riff raff, jingbang, bangarang 4 (n. *worthless person; somebody without ambition*) dutty bungle, cruff, streggeh, waste man, waste gyal, zutupeck, zutupeng, pancoot, long seed bwoy, donkya man, donkya, floppaz, eedyat, eedyat bwoy, eedyat gyal, pissy tail bwoy, pissy tail gyal, long seed man, long seed bwoy, grey tone man, batta foot bwoy, batta foot gyal, batta iez bwoy, batta iez gyal, crebbeh, screbbeh, creb, screbz, crebbeh crebbeh, screbbeh screbbeh, dibby dibby, fenkeh fenkeh, boogooyaga, mafeena (male only), nyamps 5 Also see *LAME; LOSER*

WOULD woulda, wuda, oulda, uda

WOULD HAVE (*would have* + ppl) wuda en, wudan, wuda did - *I would have told you if you had wanted to listen*: Mi wuda en tel yu ef yu did waan fi lisn

WOULDN'T wouldn, wuddn, ouldn, uddn

WOULDN'T HAVE (*wouldn't have* + ppl) wudn did, wudn a en, wudn en, wuda nen - *I wouldn't have known*: Mi udn did nuo, etc.

WOW! See Appendix for list of Exclamations of surprise

WRAP (v. as an octopus tentacles) lap, lash

WRENCH (n) spanna

WRESTLE rassle, grabble, ketch up

WRIST (n) wris, wrisk

WRITHE wiggle wiggle, winji winji

WRITHING wiggle wiggle, winji winji

WRITTEN 1 (ppl) write 2 (adj) wordical - *written by*: write by - *written for*: write fi, write fa - *written down*: write dong - *a written message*: one wordical message - *written instructions*: wordical instruckshan

Y'KNOW 1 (always placed at end of statement) ino, yu see, yaa sah, yaa ma (from *you hear ma'am*) - *He's crazy you know*: Him mad ino, Him mad yu si, Him mad yaa sa, Him mad yaa ma 2 Also see *YOU KNOW?* for more

YAM (n) renta yam, renta, afu

YAWN (v) draw bungy

YEAH yeh, Ee hee

YEARN FOR (v) henka fi, fret pan, cry fi

YELL AT see *BERATE*

YELLOW FEVER Bilyas Feevah

YES 1 (simple confirmation) Ee-hee, Yah man 2 (*Yes, that is correct*) Strait, Yu done know, Like yu juss seh, Hol dat, A so, Sed way so, Sed speed, Prezactly 3 Also see *OF COURSE!*

YESTERDAY yesadeh, fuss day (from *first day*)

YET (adv) yet, aready - *You haven't sold them yet?*: Yu no sel dem aredi?

YIELD 1 (vi. *surrender*) bow 2 (v. *offer up*) faawud up, leggo, let off

YOLK (*egg yolk*) red

YOU 1 (singular) yu, di man, di I 2 (plural) unu, di I dem 3 Also see *ARE; AREN'T; WERE; WEREN'T*

YOU KNOW? 1 (checking for comprehension) yannastan?, yu see weh mi a seh?, yovahs?, yu si mi?, yu seet?, yu no seet?, zeen?, seen?, sight?, yu see weh mi deh?, yu see weh mi a deal wid?, yu ites weh mi a seh? 2 Also see *Y'KNOW*

YOU'RE WELCOME Ya man, No seh a wud, Yu good, Yu cool, Yu arite, Yu criss, How yu mean, Cool breeze, Irie

YOUNG MAN yute, youtman

YOUNG PEOPLE 1 (*young people in general*) di yute dem, di younga heads dem, yout an yout 2 (*a group of young guys*) wan set a yout, some yout

YOUR 1 (singular) yu, fiyu, di I 2 (plural) unu, fi unu, di I-dem

YOURS 1 (singular) fi yu, fi di I 2 (plural) fi unu, funu, fi di I dem

YOURSELF 1 (n) yuself 2 (adv for emphasis) same one - *Didn't you yourself tell me to go?* No yu siem wan tel mi fi go?

YOURSELVES 1 (n) unuself 2 (adv. for emphasis) same one - *Didn't you yourselves tell him?* No unu siem wan tel him?

Z pr: zed

ZERO nil, ducks

ZIGZAG (v) cross an pile

ZINC zungu

EXPLETIVES & EXCLAMATIONS*

MILD EXPLETIVES

backfoot
box covah
blouse an skirt
blouse an frock
blouse knot
blow wow
blurt neet
blurt seed
puss foot
puss jook
raatid
rat not
Raaf Claak (*Ralph Clark*)
Rasta Jaaj (*Rasta George*)
rockstone
tarra warra
warra warra

SEMI-VULGAR EXPLETIVES

backside
batty fish (*butt fish*)
batty fawt (*butt fart*)
blood baat (*blood bath*)
blood cleet
blood knot
blood seed
bombaat
bongo
bongo kyaat
bongo graas kyaat (*bongo grass cart*)
bongo push di graas kyaat
blurtcleet
caca fawt
graas kyaat
raas (*ass*)

VULGAR EXPLETIVES

batty claat (*butt cloth*)
blood claat
blood fawt (*blood fart*)
bombo (*vagina*)
bombo claat (*vagina cloth*)
bombo foot
bombo raas
bombo raas claat
bombo raas pussy claat
bombo raas pussy blood claat
bombo blood pussy raas claat
muma claat (*momma cloth*)
pussy fawt
pussy claat
raas claat (*ass cloth*)
raas bombo claat
raas bombo blood claat
raas bombo pussy blood claat
raas pussy blood claat
raas pussy bombo claat

* Expletives are not to be confused with exclamations. An <u>exclamation</u> is a brief statement of emotion that stands on its own, such as *Crap!* or *Damn it!* An <u>expletive</u> is a gratuitous word or phrase inserted into a sentence to add emphasis (for example, the word *hell* in the sentence *He doesn't know what the hell he's doing*).

MILD EXCLAMATIONS

Babamscram!
Babwah!
Backfoot!
Bambayeh!
Budcage! (from *birdcage*)
Blouse an skirt!
Blouse an frock!
Blouse cup!
Blouse knot!
Blow wow!
Blurdseed!
Blurtneet!
Box cova!
Brown dog!
Caranapuff!
Cho!
Foot bottom!
God bline mi!
Jeezam!
Jeezam peem!
Jeezam peas!
Jeezam peezam!
Karamba!
Kiss mi brown dog!
Kiss mi granny!
Kiss mi neck!
Kiss mi neckback!
Kiss mi neckstring!
Kiss mi granny neckback!
Kiss mi whatsitnot!
Laad!/ Lawd!
Ladamassi! (from *Lord have mercy*)
Laaks!/ Lawks!
Mi granny!
Po!
Puff!
Puss foot!
Raatid!
Ralph clark!
Rock of ages!
Rockstone!
Raaf Claak! (*Ralph Clark*)
Rasta Jaaj! (*Rasta George*)
Royal cyaad! (*royal card*)
Wat a liv an bambayeh!
Wat a X! (X=any mild expletive)
Woy! (to express amazement, not anger)

SEMI-VULGAR EXCLAMATIONS

Backside!
Batty fawt! (*butt fart*)
Batty crease!
Blood baat! (*blood bath*)
Blood cleet!
Blood knot!
Blood seed!
Blurd cleet!
Bombaat!
Bongo cyaat! (*Bongo cart*)
Bongo graas cyaat!
Bongo push di graas cyaat!
Caca fawt!
Caca raas!
Graas cyaat! (*grass cart*)
Kiss mi backside!
Kiss mi batty!
Mi backside!
Mi raas! (*my ass*)
Nanny raas!
Puss jook!
Puss nawt!
Wat a X! (X=any expletive)

VULGAR EXCLAMATIONS

Batty claat! (*butt cloth*)
Batty hole!
Blood claat!
Bombo! (*vagina*)
Bombo claat!
Bombo foot!
Bombo hole!
Bombo raas!
Bombo red!
Bombo raas claat!
Bombo raas pussy claat!
Bombo raas pussy blood claat!
Bombo blood pussy raas claat!
Caca claat!
Caca raas!
Kiss mi bloodclaat!
Kiss mi bombo!
Kiss mi raas!
Mi bombo!
Pussy fawt!
Pussy claat!
Raas claat!
Raas bombo claat!
Raas bombo blood claat!
Raas bombo pussy blood claat!
Raas pussy claat!
Raas pussy blood claat!
Raas pussy bombo claat!
Raas pussy bombo blood claat!
Wat a X! (X=any vulgar expletive)

METATHESES & HYPERCORRECTION

The following words were born when people took English words and switched the positions of letters or inserted unnecessary letters in an attempt to make up for erroneously perceived shortcomings. (The intended meaning is in parentheses.)

aks (ask)
atatarise (authorise)
bextatious (vexatious)
brebrage (beverage)
cramoojin (curmudgeon)
cursted (cursed)
deks (desk)
deestant (decent)
drownded (drowned)
fambly (family)
fishnin (fishing)
flim (film)
foolinish (foolishness)
hucks (husk)
hateridge (hatred)
huntnin (hunting)
infilence (influence)
laskit (elastic)
loaftah (loafer)
morgrage (mortgage)
mechiz (message)
nombaddy (nobody)
parssl (parsley)
pomptious (pompous)
poscrishan (prescription)
prockupine (porcupine)
preform (perform)
preformance (performance)
promishan (permission)
riks (risk)
salamon (salmon)
sachiz (sausage)
serfitikit (certificate)
shortridge (shortage)
skrimps (shrimp)
swimps (shrimp)
swims (shrimp)
skruwel (squirrel)
slandaz (sandals)
stonted (stunned)
voylence (violence)

MALAPROPISMS & MONDEGREENS

The following terms came about when people confused two different English words that sounded similar. The intended meaning is in parentheses.

accident (accent)
aggravate (activate)
boom (bomb)
common assault (common as salt)
devil up (develop)
disgust (discuss)
dramatise (traumatise)
excape goat, escaped goat (scapegoat)
extinguish (distinguished)
fertilise (fraternise)
information (inflammation)
main tenants (maintenance)
new Mona (pneumonia)
ol' timers (Alzheimers)
ol' tomatoes (ultimatums)
ostrich (hostage)
pacific (specific)
paddlepuss (platypus)
wrench (rinse)

PORTMANTEAU & CREATIVE ALTERATION:

(Jamaican term on left, English source words on right)

ageable = age + eligible
apprecialove = appreciate + love
bashco = casco (imitation) + bashi (stylish)
bodderation = bother + frustration
braff = brag + show off
braggadoshous = brag + atrocious
dungpressa = down + oppressor
dungstroy = down + destroy
Earliyah! = Later!
fluffalicious = fluffy + delicious
full-ticipate = fully + participate
grabbalicious = grab + avaricious
Gyalchesta = Manchester (*gyal* instead of *man*)
likklemos = almost (*little* instead of *all*)
livicate = dedicate (*live* instead of *dead*)
nearlymos = nearly + almost
nigretful = neglectful + regretful
nex strong = next week (*strong* instead of *weak*)
ovastan = understand (*over* instead of *under*)
prezackly = precisely + exactly
smaddification = somebody + qualification
studdaration = study + -ation (the act of studying)
superble = super + terrible
three much = (instead of *too* much)

JAMAICAN PLACE NAMES

The spellings of these places in Jamaica offer little service in helping an outsider to guess how they are actually pronounced by locals, or which syllables are stressed. For this reason, stressed syllables are underlined where needed. Cassidy (Jamiekan) spellings are used here to clarify pronunciation (see section 7 of the introduction).

ACCOMPONG – A<u>kam</u>pong
BOSCOBEL – <u>Bas</u>kabel
CLARENDON – <u>Kla</u>rindan
GORDON TOWN – Gaadn Tong
LIGUANEA – <u>Li</u>gani
LITTLE LONDON – Likl Landan
LUCEA – <u>Luu</u>si
MAVIS BANK – Mievis Bank
MONTEGO BAY – Mantiga Bie, <u>Mo</u> Bie
MORANT BAY – Marant Bie
OLD HARBOUR – Uol Aaba
ORACABESSA – A<u>ra</u>ka<u>be</u>sa
ORANGE BAY – Arinj Bie
NEGRIL – <u>Ni</u>gril
PORT MORANT – Puot Marant
PORT ROYAL – Puot Rayal
RIVERSDALE – Rivazdiel
SAVANNA LA MAR – Sav La Mar, Sav
SEAFORD TOWN – Siifod Tong
SEAFORTH – Siifuot
ST. ANN – <u>Sen</u>taan
ST. ANN'S BAY – <u>Sen</u>taanz Bie
ST. ELIZABETH – Sintilizibet, Sint Bes
TIVOLI GARDENS – <u>Ti</u>vali Gyaadn
TRENCHTOWN – Chrenchtong
WESTMORELAND – <u>Wes</u>molan

PLANTS & TREES OF USE IN JAMAICA*

*Caution: There may be mistakes in this list. This information does not ensure medicinal or culinary authority

ABRUS PRECATORIUS – john crow beads
ACALYPHA WILKESIANA – headache bush
ACHYRANTHES INDICA – colic weed
ACROCOMIA SLEROCARPA – (macaw palm) makafat
ALBIZZIA LEBBEK – woman tongue
ALCHORNEA LATIFOLIA – lob lob; jimmy wood
ALLIUM SATIVUM – (garlic) gyaalix
ALOE VULGARIS – sinkle bible; bitters; bittaz
AMARANTUS SPINOSUS – prickly calaloo
AMARANTUS TRISTIS – Spanish calaloo
AMARANTUS VIRIDIS – green calaloo
AMOMIS CARYOPHYLLATA – pimento
ANACARDIUM OCCIDENTALE – (cashew) kushu
ANANAS COMOSUS – (*pineapple*) sweet pine; pine
ANDIRA INERMIS – cabbage tree
ANDROGRAPHIS PANICULATA – rice bitters
ANNONA MURICATA – sowasop; soursop
ANNONA RETICULATA – custard apple
ANNONA SQUAMOSA – sweetsop
ARALIA GUILFOYLEI – aralia
ARGEMONE MEXICANA – mexican poppy; tissle
ARISTOLOCHIA ELEGANS – duppy fly trap; duppy basket
ARTEMISIA – garden bitters; gyaadn bittaz
ARTOCARPUS INCISA – breadfruit; breshi
ASCLEPIAS CURASSA VICA – red head; blood flower
ASCLEPIAS NIVEA – white head
AVERRHOA BILIMBI – blim blim
AVERRHOA CARAMBOLA – Chiney jimbilin; star fruit
BAMBUSA – bamboo
BAUHINIA JIVARICATA – bull hoof; bull foot; cow foot
BIDENS PILOSA – Spanish neegle
BLECHUM BROWNEI – john bush
BLIGHIA SAPIDA – ackee
BOERHAVIA SCANDENS – easy-to-bruck
BORRE VERTICILLATA, LAEVIS – button weed
BROMELIA PINGUIN – pinguin; pingwing
BRYA EBENUS – ebony; coccus wood
BRYOPHYLLUM PINNATUM – leaf a life
BUMELIA SALICIFOLIA – white bullet
BURSERA SIMARUBA – red birch; gumbo limbo
CAESALPINIA BONDUC – yellow nicker
CAESALPINIA BONDUCELLA – grey nicker
CAESALPINIA CORIARIA – dibi dibi
CAJANUS CAJAN – gungo pea
CALEA JAMAICENSIS – bee bee; camphor bush

CANELLA WINTERANA – wild cinnamon; whitewood
CANNABIS SATIVA – ganja; kali weed
CAPSICUM FRUTESCENS – (*bird pepper*) bud peppa
CASSIA FISTULA – cassia stick tree; purging cassia
CASSIA LIGUSTRINA – piss-a-bed
CASSIA OBOVATA – Jamaica senna
CASSIA OCCIDENTALIS – stinkin weed; johncrow pea
CASUARINA EQUISETIFOLIA – willow; casuarina
CEDRELA ODORATA – jamaican cedar
CEIBA PENTANDRA – cotton tree
CENCHRUS – burr grass
CHAMISSOA ALTISSIMA – basket wiss
CHAPTALIA NUTANS – kema weed; heal-it-an-draw
CHENOPODIUM AMBROSIOIDES – worm weed; bitta weed
CHRYSANTHELLUM AMERICANUM – trong back
CINNAMOMUM CAMPHORA – camphor tree
CINNAMOMUM ZEYLANICUM – cinnamon
CISSAMPELOS PAREIRA – velvet bush
CISSUS SICYOIDES – puddin wiss; snake wiss; yaws bush
CISSUS TRIFOLIATA – sorrel vine; puddin wiss
CITRUS MAXIMA – shaddock
CITRUS RETICULATA x PARADISI – ugly fruit; ugly
CITRUS VULGARIS – sibble orange
CLIBADIUM SURINAMENSE – jackass breadnut
CLIDEMIA HIRTA – soap bush
COCCOTHRINAX JAMAICENSIS – tatch palm; silva tatch
COLA ACUMINATA – cola nut; bissy nut
COLEUS AROMATICUS – Spanish thyme; country borage
COLOCASIA ESCULENTA – coco yam; coco; dasheen
COMMELINA ELEGANS – waata grass
CORCHORUS SILIQUOSUS – broom weed
CORDIA CYLINDRISTACHY – black sage
CORDIA GLOBOSA – black sage; john charles; gout tea
CORDIA SEBESTERA – scarlet cordia
CRESCENTIA CUJETE – kalabash; paki; gordy
CROTON HUIS – peppa rod
CROTON LINEARIS – Spanish rosemary
CROTON WILSONI – peppa rod; docta john; john charles
CUCURBITA PEPO – punkin
CUPHEA PARSONIA – K weed; trong back
CURCUMA LONGA – (*tumeric*) tambric
CUSCUTA – love bush
CYMBOPOGON CITRATUS – feva grass; lemon grass
CYNODON DACTYLON – dog teeth grass
CYPERUS ARTICULATUS – aadroo
CARICA PAPAYA – (*papaya*) pawpaw
DATURA STRAMONIUM – jimson weed
DELONIX REGIA – poinciana
DESMODIUM – wild pinda; puss gut
DIANTHERA PECTORALIS – fresh cut; gyaadn balsam
DRYOPTERIS – white stick

ECHITES UMBELLATA – maroon weed
EIA SAGITTATA – consumption weed
ELEPHANTOPUS MOLLIS – elephant foot; iyan weed
ERIGERON BONARIENSIS – azma weed
ERIGERON CANADENSIS – ded weed
ERIGERON KARVINSKYANUS – daisy
ERYNGIUM FOETIDUM – fit weed; fit bush; spirit weed
EUCALYPTUS – gum tree
EUGENIA MALACCENSIS – see *SYZYGIUM M.*
EUGENIA UNIFLORA – (*suriname cherry*) cherry
EUPATORIUM MACROPHYLLUM – hemp agrimony
EUPATORIUM ODORATUM – jack-inna-di-bush; bitta bush
EUPATORIUM TRISTE – old woman bitta bush
EUPATORIUM VILLOSUM – old woman bitta bush
EUPHORBIA – spurge; wart weed
EUPHORBIA BRASILIENSIS – spurge; wart weed
EUPHORBIA THYMIFOLIA – wart weed; yeye bright
EVOLVULUS ARBUSCULA – seaside thyme
FEVILLEA CORDIFOLIA – antidote cocoon
FICUS PUMILA – ivy
FLEMINGIA STROBILIFERA – wild opps
FOENICULUM VULGARE – fennel
FUNASTRUM CLAUSUM – K wiss
GESNERIA – rock bush
GLIRICIDIA SEPIUM – quick stick; grow stick
GOSSYPIUM – cotton bush
GOUANIA LUPULOIDES – chew stick; chaw stick
GRACILARIA – irish moss
GUAIACUM OFFICINALE – lignum vitae
GUAZUMA ULMIFOLIA – elm
HAEMATOXYLUM CAMPECHIANUM – logwood
HELICTERES JAMAICENSIS – screw tree
HELIOTROPIUM INDICUM – scorpion weed
HIBISCUS ELATUS – blue mahoe
HIBISCUS SABDARIFFA – red sorrel
HIBISCUS TILIACEUS – seaside mahoe
HIPPEASTRUM PUNICEUM – red lily; maroon lily
HIPPOMANE MANCINELLA – (*manchineel*) swell hand
HYMENAEA COURBARIL – stinkin' toe
HYPTIS CAPITATA – cesar obeah; iyan wort
HYPTIS PECTINATA – piabba
HYPTIS SUAVEOLENS – pig nut
HYPTIS VERTICILLATA – john charles
IBLECHUM BROWNEI – mada lookup
IPOMOEA DISSECTA – pursh; know-yuh
IRESINE PANICULATA – juba's bush; bitta weed
ISOTOMA LONGIFLORA – star flower; horse poison
JATROPHA CURCAS – fizik nut
JATROPHIA GOSSYPIFOLIA – cassada; belly ache bush
LANTANA CAMARA – white sage
LANTANA CROCEA – black sage

LANTANA INVOLUCRATA – wild mint
LANTANA TRIFOLIA – goat weed
LEONOTIS NEPETAEFOLIA – pick nut; bald head
LIPPLA GEMINATA – colic mint; guinea mint
LITCHI CHINENSIS – (*lychee*) chiney guinep
LUFFA CYLINDRICA – (*loofah*) poril
MALACHRA ALCEAEFOLIA – wild broom; wild okro
MALPHIGHIA GLABRA – Barbados cherry; cherry
MALVASTRUM COROMANDELIANUM – broom weed
MAMMEA AMERICANA – mammee apple
MANIHOT UTILISSIMA – cassada; cassava
MELICOCCUS BIJUGATUS – guinep
MELOCHIA TOMENTOSA – tea bush; raychee
MENTHA VIRIDIS – gyaadn mint; black mint
MICONIA LAEVIGATA – chicken net; johnny berry
MICROMERIA BROWNEI – pennyryal
MICROMERIA VIMINEA – peppamint
MIKANIA – guaco bush
MIMOSA PUDICA – shame bush; shame a lady
MIRABILIS JALAPA – four o'clock
MOMORDICA CHARANTIA/BALSAMINA – cerasee
MORINDA CITRIFOLIA – (*noni*) duppy soursop; hog apple
MORINGA OLEIFERA – moringa; maranga
MORINDA ROYOC – duppy poison; trong back
MUCUNA PRURIENS – cow itch; curr itch
MUSA PARADISIACA – (*plantain*) plantin
MYRISTICA FRAGRANS – (*nutmeg*) nuttn-egg
NASTURTIUM FONTANUM – (*water cress*) waata crishiz
NEUROLAENA LOBATA – albert weed; bitta bush
OCHROMA PYRAMIDALE – (*balsa*) baasa tree; kaakwood
OCIMUM MICRANTHUM – wild baasy; maskita bush
OPUNTIA TUNA – indian fig
ORYCTANTHUS OCCIDENTALIS – God bush; missle toe
OXALIS CORNICULATA – sowa grass
PANICUM MAXIMUM – guinea grass
PASSIFLORA FOETIDA – love-in-a-mist; granadilla
PASSIFLORA MALIFORMIS – (*passion fruit*) sweet cup
PASSIFLORA RUBRA – goat foot
PASSIFLORA SEXFLORA – duppy punkin; bat wing
PECTIS – stink weed
PECTIS CILIARIS – consumption weed
PEPEROMIA PELLUCITDA – peppa helda
PERSEA AMERICANA – (*avocado*) avocado pear; pear
PETIVERIA ALLICAEA – guinea hen weed; trong man weed
PHTHIRUSA PAUCIFLORA – missle toe; skaan-di-urt
PHYLLANTHUS ACIDUS – baj; jimbilin; cherrymeena
PHYLLANTHUS NIRURI – carry-me seed; chamber bittaz
PHYSALIS ANGULATA – wild tomato; hog weed
PICRAENA EXCELSA – bitta wood; bitta hash
PICRAMNIA ANTIDESMA – ol woman bitta; bitta wood
PILEA MICROPHYLLA – wild thyme; baby puzzle

PIMENTA DIOICA – (*allspice*) pimento
PIMENTA OFFICINALIS – (*allspice*) pimento
PIPER AMALGO /NIGRINODUM – jointa bush; black peppa
PIPER UMBELLATUM – cow foot
PISCIDIA PISCIPULA – jamaica dogwood
PLANTAGO MAJOR – English plantain
POLYPODIUM EXIGUUM – hug-me-tight
POLYPODIUM PHYLLITIDIS – cow tongue
PORTULACA OLERACEAE – pussly
PRIVA LAPPULACEA – clammy burr; rakkle weed
PSEUDELEPHANTOPUS SPICATUS – iyan weed; packy weed; dog tongue
PUNICA GRANATUM – (*pomegranate*) pranganat
RICINUS COMMUNIS – (*castor oil plant*) oil nut
RIVINA HUIS – dog blood; blood berry
RUELLIA TUBEROSA – duppy gun; minnie root
RYTIDOPHYLLUM TOMENTOSUM – search-mi-heart
SABAL JAMAICENSIS – bull tatch
SALVIA OCCIDENTALIS – wild mint
SALVIA SEROTINA – chicken weed; likkle woman
SAMANEA SAMAN – guango tree
SAMBUCUS SIMPSONII – elda
SANSEVIERIA TRIFASCIATA – (*snake plant*) monkey figgle; duppy fee fee
SAPOTA ACHRAS – neesberry
SAUVAGESIA BROWNEI – trong back
SAX BALBISIANA – china root
SECHIUM EDULE – cho cho
SENECIO DISCOLOR – white back
SIDA ACUTA – broom weed
SIDA URENS – wind bush
SMILAX REGELII – sasparilla; blood wiss
SOLANUM ACULEATISSIMUM – cockroach poison
SOLANUM MAMMOSUM /TORVUM – susumba
SOLANUM NIGRUM – guma
SPATHODEA CAMPANULATA – flame tree; rain man
SPIGELIA ANTHELMIA – pink root; pink weed
SPONDIAS DULCIS – (*ambarella*) june plum; jew plum
SPONDIAS MOMBIN – hog plum
SPONDIAS PURPUREA – red coat plum
STACHYTARPHETA JAMAICENSIS – verveen
STYLOSANTHES HAMATA – donkey weed; cheesy toes
STYLOSANTHES VISCO – poor man's friend
SYZYGIUM JAMBOLANUM – (*java plum*) jamblin
SYZYGIUM MALACCENSIS – oti-iti apple; iti-oti apple; apple
TAMARINDUS INDICA – (*tamarind*) tambrin
TERMINALIA CATAPPA – almond tree
THRINAX PALVIFLORA – tatch palm; brown tatch
TOURNEFORTIA HIRSUTISSIMA – cold wiss; crocus bush
TRIBULUS CISTOIDES – police macca; kill backra
TRIUMFETTA – bur weed; bur bush
TURNERA ULMIFOLIA – ramgoat dash along
UANDROGRAPHIS PANICULATA – rice bitters

UMICONIA LAEVIGATA – fowl bone; white wakkle
URENA LOBATA – ballard bush
URTICA DIOICA – (*nettle*) scratch bush
VERNONIA DIVARICATA – ole man bitta bush
VINCA ROSEA – (*periwinkle*) ramgoat rose; brown man fancy
WALTHERIA AMERICANA – waata weed
WEDELIA GRACILIS – marigold; consumption weed
WEDELIA TRILOBATA – running marigold; gold cup
ZANTHOXYLLUM MARTINICENSE – prickly yellows
ZEBRINA PENDULA – red waata grass; rolling calf bed
ZIZYPHUS MAURITIANA – coolie plum

*Caution: There may be mistakes in this list. This information does not ensure medicinal or culinary authority

*Much of this information was acquired from:
Asprey, G. F. and Phyllis Thornton. Medicinal Plants Of Jamaica. West Indian Medical Journal. Vol. 2 No. 4. Vol. 3 No. 1 (Also available online in PDF format)

Printed in Great Britain
by Amazon